The Prepared Family Cookbook

Enola Gay

Editors

Grace Tome
Eileen Rowlands

Any recipe contained in this book dealing with the canning of dairy products is not recommended. These recipes are antidotal only and not intended for use. The home canning of dairy products is not recommended by the USDA.

First Edition June 2013

Printed in USA

ISBN: 978-1490544373

Enola Gay
www.paratusfamiliablog.com

Other Books by Enola Gay

The Prepared Family Guide to Uncommon Diseases

From the author

This cookbook has truly been a labor of love. It has taken much, much longer than I ever anticipated, but has been far and away more rewarding than I could have imagined. And an added benefit? I will finally have all of my recipes in one place! My daughters will be thrilled.

As I came close to finishing this endeavor, I was pretty sure that I was missing a huge amount of information. I was positive that there where not nearly enough soup recipes and that the canning section wasn't complete, but finally, I decided that I either had to say that enough was enough or I would never see this through to completion.

My desire, with this cookbook, was to share our favorite recipes along with a few of the things I have learned over our many years of living off the grid. It was my intention to help those wanting to live a more prepared, self-sufficient lifestyle in their journey.

This book is not intended to be a preparedness, self-sufficiency or off-grid bible. Rather, it is just a compilation of a few good recipes and a thing or two that we have learned and wanted to pass along to you.

Every household should have a solid selection of indispensible reference books and it is my hope that this little book is worthy of being added to your collection.

Enola Gay
Providence Farms
American Redoubt
March 21, 2013

Table of Contents

Chapter I

Food Storage/Preparedness

Y ears ago, a friend of mine asked if we bought food in bulk. I smiled and innocently replied, "of course – we shop at Costco!" Little did I know that "bulk" to her meant 50# bags of wheat and 5 gallon buckets of honey.

My husband and I began our food storage journey as a practical, money saving venture. I had recently left the world of working women to become a homeschooling, cow milking, stay-at-home mother, and we were looking for any way to cut our grocery bill.

We started small. A pound of pepper here and 20 pounds of oatmeal there. Pretty soon we were experimenting with bags of chives the size of pillowcases and three gallon buckets of peanut butter. As our pantry filled up with gallon jars of spices, beans and dehydrated potatoes, we found ourselves frequenting bakeries and deli's hoping to acquire four and five gallon buckets to stow our supplies of flour, sugar and wheat berries.

The Y2K scare prompted us to ramp up our food storage efforts. What once had been a hobby had become a full-fledged obsession. Now, rather than buying 50#'s of wheat at a time, we were buying tons – literally! We no longer stored flour, sugar and wheat in five gallon buckets, but in 55 gallon barrels.

Y2K came and went, and the world still spun on its axis. Although we felt foolish for buying into the biggest non-event in history, we loved the wisdom and experience we had gained while preparing for disaster.

In 2000, we experienced our own, personal Y2K. We moved to 30 acres in the country with no electricity, no running water, no flushing toilets and no house – only a 30' x 30' shop in the middle of a windy prairie. And then we ran out of money.

Our Y2K preparations were our only lifeline to a "normal life". We heated our "shouse" (shop/house), cooked our food, did our laundry and heated our water on our wood cook stove (a Y2K purchase). We lit our cave-like shop with Aladdin lamps (kerosene) and a Petromax (multi-fuel) lantern (also Y2K purchases) and we fed our family with our stored foods (you guessed it, purchased for Y2K).

And we learned that it doesn't take a major national catastrophe or even a natural disaster to reduce your circumstances. "A prudent man sees the signs of the times and takes refuge". It is prudent to have a food storage system in place as a hedge against major national/international upheaval or minor personal inconveniences.

Our experience has led us to believe that the best food list is unique to each family. If you love black-eyed peas and hate black beans, it only makes sense to stock up on black-eyed peas. If you can't stand oatmeal, it seems to reason that buying a ton of it would be a bad investment. The first thing that we did when we began storing food in earnest was make menus. We chose 30 days worth of breakfasts and dinners and crafted our food storage plan from those basic menus.

Here is what our basic stored foods list looks like:

Grains (Store for 30+ years)
- Hard red wheat
- Hard white wheat
- Spelt
- Kamut
- Golden wheat
- Barley
- Rice (white only – brown has a very short storage life)
- White flour (wheat flour goes rancid very quickly)
- Oat groats (can be ground into cereal)

Cereals (Store for 5 years)
- Thick cut oats (oatmeal)
- Farina (cream of wheat)
- 10 grain cereal mix

Beans (store for 10 years –they become to hard to cook after 10 years – beans can also be ground as used as thickener in soups and as bean flour)

- Black eyed peas
- Split peas
- Red beans
- Pinto beans
- Navy beans
- Black beans

Fats (store in cool, dark place)

- Olive oil (3-4 year shelf life, may go rancid but will still be edible)
- Vegetable oil (1 year shelf life)
- Shortening (5 years unless develops off color or taste)
- Lard (same as shortening)
- Tallow (make and use fresh or can for later use)

Sugars/Sweeteners (Store for 30+ years)

- White sugar
- Brown sugar
- Confectioners sugar
- Turbinado (raw sugar)
- Honey (indefinite shelf life)
- Corn syrup
- Maple syrup (must be refrigerated if real syrup)

Vegetables (Store for 30+ years)

- Dehydrated corn
- Dehydrated onions
- Dehydrated potatoes
- Dehydrated green peppers
- Dehydrated broccoli
- Dehydrated celery
- Canned vegetables of every variety

Miscellaneous

- Powdered milk
- Powdered sour cream

- Butter/margarine powder
- Powdered eggs
- Vinegar (for cooking and cleaning uses)
- Pectin
- Gelatin
- Soy sauce
- Worcestershire sauce

Spices (indefinite – will lose flavor over time)
- Pepper
- Salt
- Cajun Seasoning
- Tabasco
- Oregano
- Basil
- Thyme
- Mustard Powder
- Chives
- Parsely
- Garlic Powder
- Garlic Salt
- Poppy seeds
- Poultry seasoning
- Cinnamon
- Nutmeg
- Cloves
- Bouillon
- Allspice
- Lemon peel
- Orange peel
- Seasoning salt
- Sausage spices
- Pickling spices
- Dill
- Taco seasoning
- Chili powder
- Paprika
- Ginger

Baking Needs
- Baking powder (2 years + if cool)
- Baking soda (indefinite)
- Cream of Tarter (indefinite)
- Baking cocoa (indefinite)
- Yeast (10 years if cold)
- Corn starch (indefinite)
- Chocolate chips (indefinite)
- Nuts (1 year if cool 2 – 3 years if frozen)

Fruits (5 years)
- Raisins
- Craisins
- Coconut
- Dried apple chips
- Dried banana chips
- Canned fruits (all manner)

Beverages (indefinite)
- Coffee
- Tea
- Lemon juice
- Kool-aid
- Tang
- Nesquick
- Creamer
- Instant tea

Extracts (indefinite)
- Vanilla
- Maple
- Peppermint
- Orange
- Almond

Condiments
- Ketchup
- Mustard
- Mayonnaise (very limited shelf life)

- Salad dressing

Non-food related kitchen items
- Bread bags
- Meat wrapping paper
- Plastic wrap
- Tin foil
- Waxed paper
- Parchment paper (for canning bacon)
- Canning lids
- Plastic baggies
- Garbage bags
- Cheese wax
- Cheese cloth

Our storage systems have evolved over the years. When we first started out, we stored most things in 1 gallon glass jars and occasionally stored our "bulk" items in five gallon food grade buckets. As our knowledge and stored food supplies grew, we graduated to mostly 5 gallon buckets and 55 gallon drums. Now we store most of our grains, some of our sweeteners (white and turbinado sugars) and powdered milk in 55 gallon drums lined with food grade plastic bags. The bags provide another layer of protection and make it much easier to get to the contents at the bottom of the barrel. As a general rule, we have at least two or three barrels for any given storage item. This enables us to properly rotate our food supplies. If you only have one barrel for powdered milk, you have to use all of it before you can replenish your stock. However, if you have two barrels you can be using your milk from one barrel while you are adding to or replenishing your supplies in the other barrel.

We deal similarly with our buckets. When we fill one bucket, we label it with the contents and fill date. That way, we use the foods stored earliest so that our food stores are always fresh. We also write the date of purchase on everything we plan on putting into long term storage, whether it is tins of coffee, buckets of peanut butter or containers of olive oil. Fresh is always best!

All bulk foods that are put into long-term storage require some method of treatment to ensure that the insect larva (present in all harvested grains) don't mature and consume your carefully stored supplies. There are numerous ways to achieve this goal, while also maintaining freshness in your stored foods. Our preferred method of grain preservation is freezing. When we fill new buckets with grains, we tote them to a protected area outside during the first long, hard freeze of the fall. We allow the buckets (or barrels) to freeze hard for a full three days. This effectively kills any larva that are present in the grains. If you are not inclined to move your grains into the great outdoors, you can put your bags of grain into your freezer before putting them into buckets or barrels, or you can use an alternative treatment method. Other tried and true methods are oxygen absorptions packets (these deprive larva of oxygen, thus rendering them harmless), washing your grains with nitrogen (an inert gas), using dried ice to neutralize the oxygen present in your bucket or mixing diatomaceous earth (in proportions of 1 cup diatomaceous earth to 50 pounds of grain) with your grains before putting them into long-term storage. It is essential to choose one method or another and religiously treat all your newly stored grains, or you will open a bucket with the expectation of great bounty and instead will be greeted with wriggling masses of greedy grubs.

Although food storage is absolutely essential, it is equally important to store non-food items. Cleaning agents, bedding, health and beauty supplies and personal hygiene items are critical to your health and well being. Consider stocking up on and regularly rotating essential non-food items. Things we keep in our preparedness rotation are:

Cleaning
- Dish soap (antibacterial)
- Laundry detergent
- Bleach (not just for cleaning, but for sterilizing and treating water)
- Pine sol
- Bon ami

Health and Beauty
- Shampoo
- Bar soap (we like Kirk's castile)
- Deodorant
- Foot powder
- Bag balm (for chafing, rashes, cuts, etc.)
- Body lotion
- Toothpaste
- Tooth brushes
- Plackers or dental floss
- Razors/blades

Bathroom/Hygiene
- Toilet paper (we also have a supply of wash clothes to be used if our toilet paper supply runs out)
- Feminine hygiene (we use washable pads)
- Hot water bottles (use for comfort, enemas and douches)
- Cloth diapers
- Incontinence pads (sick, young or elderly)
- Bedpans
- Extra towels

Bedding
- Sheets (can be used as bulk fabric)
- Blankets
- Sleeping bags
- Wool blankets
- Pillows
- Baby receiving/regular blankets

Clothing
- Underwear
- Socks
- Bras
- Cold weather gear
- Boots

Miscellaneous
- Reading glasses
- Glasses repair kits
- Extra prescription glasses/contacts
- Sun glasses
- Gloves

Remember that every family's preparedness stores are going to be unique. Each family has a different set of needs and requirements. It is essential that you tailor your food and non-food storage items to suit your family's specific needs.

There is no way to prepare for every eventuality or to stock up for infinity, but by having a well rounded storehouse of provisions, you will comfortably see your family through uncertain times and have the capacity to meet the challenges of whatever the future may hold.

Preparedness Apologetics

I have had a lot of people ask me if Preparedness/Survival was a "Christian Tenet", or rather, if Christians weren't supposed to be relying on God to take care of them in all situations, even emergencies. After much conversation with my husband I have come up with what I consider "Preparedness Apologetics". We do believe that being prepared is a biblical principle. Here are our reasons.

We absolutely believe that God is the author of life and sustains us from even before our very first breath. It is His providence that sees us through each day and provides hope for the future. However, He did give us biblical principles to live by and preparedness is one of many.

When God spoke to Noah, he told him to prepare for judgment. He gave him very specific instructions about building an ark, loading it with life sustaining food and preparing his family for the trials of the days ahead. Now, if anybody had a reason to doubt, it was Noah. For over 100 years, Noah worked on the ark. I have no doubt there were many naysayers and hecklers, but Noah persevered. Noah built a boat in a world that had never seen rain, never seen a flood, never even seen an "act of God". What faith! God could have saved Noah and his family by "Divine Intervention", but instead, he chose to have Noah "prepare".

The story of Joseph may be an overused example of preparedness, but it is without a doubt a perfect picture of God's faithfulness through preparedness. Once more, God could have chosen not to allow the famine, but instead, he readied His servant Joseph to care for his people. What would have happened to the people of Egypt and the surrounding areas had Joseph not headed God's voice? The face of God's people would be entirely different.

The example of the ten virgins in Mathew, although directly relating to the returning of the bridegroom, is instructive in discerning the wise from the foolish. The wise virgins brought with them their lamps and their oil, conversely, the foolish virgins brought their lamps, but lacked the foresight to bring oil. My desire is to be known as wise rather than foolish.

Another thought is that God always starts with something. When He made man, he started with dirt. When He made woman, he started with man. God instructed Elijah to have the widow feed him. She explained that she had only enough flour and oil for one loaf for she and her son, and then they would die. He instructed her to feed him first and their supplies would last. THEY DID! She had something, and God multiplied it. Even Jesus, with His very first miracle, started with something. He didn't just conjure up wine for the wedding, he started with water. Later, at the Sermon on the Mount, he started with a few loaves and fishes, and fed 5000 men, not counting women and children. He used what was available and multiplied it. Those examples, at the very least, should spur us to have SOMETHING. God, in His sovereignty, will use what we have - but we need to start with something. We don't have to panic about not having everything we think we need, but we do need to make an effort to acquire SOMETHING.

And then we get into the Proverbs. They are a goldmine of preparedness advice:

Proverbs 6:6-8
Go to the ant, you sluggard; consider its ways and be wise! It has no commander, no overseer or ruler, yet it stores its provisions in summer and gathers its food at harvest.

Proverbs 21:20
In the house of the wise are stores of choice food and oil, but a foolish man devours all he has.

Proverbs 22:3
A prudent man sees danger and takes refuge, but the simple keep going and suffer for it.

Proverbs 27:12 (this one is even mentioned twice!)
The prudent see danger and take refuge, but the simple keep going and suffer for it.

Proverbs 30:25
Ants are creatures of little strength, yet they store up their food in the summer.

Proverbs 31 is one of my favorite chapters. It is like a job description for a Godly wife. A couple of verses really speak to me when it comes to preparedness. 31:15 "She gets up while it is still dark; she provides food for her family and portions for her servant girls". 31:21 "When it snows, she has no fear for her household; for all of them are clothed in scarlet". 31:25 "She is clothed with strength and dignity; she can laugh at the days to come". The Proverbs 31 woman provided food for her household. She did not wait for someone else to provide for her. She was not afraid of the cold, because she had already made sure that her household was well clothed. She laughed at the days to come. I think this is my favorite verse. For a woman, the only way that you can laugh at the days to come is if you feel that you have taken care what needs to be taken care of. When you have laid in supplies, a part of you says "bring it on!". Then you truly can laugh at the days to come.

As Christians, it is our responsibility to be wise stewards. How can we be a beacon of hope in a dark world, if we, ourselves are dependent on the charity of others? How can we bring glory to God if we are stealing to survive? We must be like the prudent man who sees danger and takes refuge rather than the simple man who keeps going and suffers for it.

Chapter II

Hospitality

Have you ever noticed that the root word of hospitality is hospital? Can you think of any better place to minister to the needs of your family, friends and others, than the welcoming embrace of your family home? I can't either!

The truth of the matter is that our homes provide the perfect environment to minister to the physical and spiritual needs of our family and those that enter our home's sheltering embrace. And as women, we are the administrators of this institution – the home - mankind's first "hospital".

In this modern age, true hospitality is quickly becoming a lost art. We have given up the throne of our home for the lure of a corner office, and in the process, we have forgotten how to serve our family and everyone else within our sphere of influence.

When I was a little girl, I loved getting coffee for my daddy. I couldn't wait until I was old enough to learn to make it and once old enough, I took great pleasure in making sure he had fresh coffee before he even knew he wanted it. A number of times, ladies that were visiting our family would say cutting things like "your dad can get his own coffee – his legs aren't broken!", and for a moment, just a moment, I would wonder if somehow I was breaking some cardinal rule, serving my father. And then, I would take a breath and remember – serving was my calling. I was just being hospitable. I was ministering to those within my reach.

Over the years I have learned that hospitality truly begins at home. My husband is the king of his castle and I do everything I can to make him feel welcome and honored in his own home. I have found that I have many opportunities throughout the day to minister to him. I rise first in the morning, kick the wood cookstove in the guts and put water on for tea. I light candles on the tea table (a trunk in the middle of our kitchen), set teacups and creamer and sugar out and fill the teapot with hot water to heat it before setting the tea to steep. I mill around a bit, picking up little things that the children left out the night before, put the dog outside and generally get the house ready to greet the day. As soon as tea is done steeping, my husband settles himself in the big rocking chair opposite the love seat and warmed by the heat of the cookstove, we enjoy a few cups of tea before he braves the elements of a new day. We discuss our plans for the day, funny little things the kids have said and problems we are not looking forward to having to handle. Essentially, we arm each other for the day ahead. We pray together. This is practical hospitality.

During the day, as my children and I hurry from one task to the other, I make sure to set aside some time to read to the littles or play a game. I spend much of my day talking to the older children – about everything from their favorite animals to the character qualities they want in a future mate. This is practical hospitality.

When a car drives up our driveway, I immediately have one of our older daughters put on the tea kettle or fill glasses with ice in anticipation of lemonade or iced tea. The younger children scurry around putting toys away or clearing school books from the table. Our entire focus becomes welcoming our guests. We do our best to minister to their needs, whatever they may be. We laugh with them, cry with them, rejoice with them and mourn with them – whatever the occasion calls for. We keep confidences and bandage wounds. We speak words of encouragement and words of truth. This is practical hospitality.

More often than not, hospitality is all about binding wounds. It's about building marriages and strengthening relationships. It's about smoothing over hurt feelings and drying tears with words of comfort. It's about hugging someone who needs a hug and gently speaking the truth to someone who is in the wrong. Hospitality is much more than nourishing the body. Hospitality is ministering to the soul.

When my husband returns from work, I have tea waiting for him. We reconnect. Talk about our day. We share our highs and lows. There are no children allowed. Just my husband and I. I minister to him. He ministers to me. This is practical hospitality.

I still love to get coffee for my daddy. I love to get coffee for my husband as well. But now, my daughters often beat me to it. They too, have learned to love serving the people in their lives. Any more, I don't even have to ask to have the kettle put on or the glasses filled with ice – my hospitable young daughters just do it. And it is not just my daughters. My sons will quietly whisper "aren't you going to invite them in for tea, mom?", when an unexpected visitor shows up at our door. Hospitality, it seems, is catching.

In a world filled with "entertaining", true hospitality is a life-giving breath of fresh air. True hospitality will build new relationships and strengthen old ones. True hospitality will bind wounds and strengthen bonds. True hospitality isn't fancy and doesn't put on airs – true hospitality is practical hospitality.

Hospitality Checklist

- Your home doesn't have to be perfect, just inviting
- Make sure that the main rooms are tidy (again, they don't have to be perfect!)
- Offer guests the best of what you have – even if that is a glass of water served in your best glass
- Turn off the television, computer and gadgets and concentrate your energies on your guest(s)
- Teach your children to address people respectfully (Mr. & Mrs., Uncle & Aunt, Sir & Ma'am)
- Teach children not to interrupt
- Listen more than you talk
- Speak kindly, gently and encouragingly
- Endeavor to delight your guests, not impress them
- Offer sympathy, empathy and joy in due season
- Never gossip or speak unkindly about others

- Make sure that your animals are trained not to jump on people or otherwise invade their space
- Keep seating areas free of pet hair
- Make sure side tables and coffee tables are conveniently located near seating areas so that your guests have a close-at-hand spot to put their teacup or glass

Remember, it is fine to set limits, even with hospitality. You may find that some people seem to overstay their welcome or continually show up when you are in the middle of school. You can politely tell them that now is not a good time and let them know what would work for you. It is o.k. to hustle people out of the house when you need to get little children ready for bed. Opening your home to others when you or your family are ill is not hospitable, it is just plain reckless.

When practiced with joy, hospitality can mend broken hearts, mend torn down fences and mend broken marriages. It can strengthen bonds and build relationships. Hospitality in the Christian home is the foundation on which our relationships blossom and flourish.

Chapter III

Wood Cook Stove Cookery

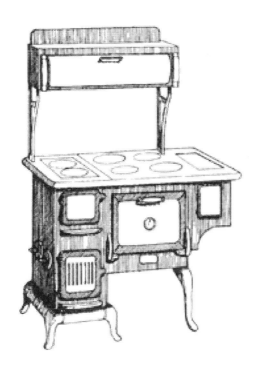

Everything I know about cooking and baking on a wood cook stove, I have learned by the seat of my pants. I didn't grow up using a wood cook stove and had never seen one in use (for anything other than boiling soup) until our brand new, shiny Pioneer Maid was delivered from Lehman's Hardware in Ohio.

I started my wood cook stove journey using the stovetop. Soup was first, followed by waffles, pancakes and bacon. Pretty soon, I was itching to open the oven door (and a huge oven it was!). I found that meatloaf and roasts and other forgiving dinner staples were really rather easy to cook in the wood cook stove oven. The inconsistent temperature didn't seem to bother them much and the only thing I had to be really careful of was burning our dinner on the side closest to the wood box. I quickly learned to regularly rotate our food, making sure it browned evenly.

One big difference I have noticed between gas/electric ranges versus wood ranges is the temperatures and times required for cooking and baking. Generally, I bake things at a lower temperature for slightly less time than in a conventional oven. I bake biscuits at about 325° (at least according to my temperature gauge) and bread at somewhere between 300° and 325°. I have learned that if I can only hold my hand in my wood cook stove oven for about 6 or 7 seconds, the temperature is just right for baking biscuits, but if I can keep my hand in the oven for about 10 to 11 seconds, it is just right for yeast breads. Roasts bake longer at a lower temperature and turn out wonderfully, turkeys brown up beautifully and the stovetop area farthest away from the firebox makes a fabulous crockpot setting.

The longer I have cooked on a wood cook stove, the more I have come to realize the importance of a few good cooking utensils. I find that I turn to the same pans and skillets over and over because of their superior performance both on the stove-top and in the oven. Using my stove has been an education, but the lessons I have learned have been invaluable. It has afforded me the opportunity to refine my technique while I gather appropriate tools. The following is a list of wood cook stove "tools" that I find indispensible.

Cast iron: The beauty of cast iron is that it is durable and perfect for use both on the stovetop and in the oven. It cooks evenly and holds heat well – and after it has been properly seasoned, withstands the high heat of a wood cook stove remarkably well. I have a variety of cast iron in many shapes and sizes. Skillets, by themselves are a workhorse, but coupled with a lid, they are indispensable. I use skillets for all manner of stovetop dishes, but I use them extensively in the oven as well. They are perfect for cooking a Frittata on the stovetop and finishing in the oven. When I make pizza in the wood cook stove, I always cook it on the stovetop first. Wood cook stoves are notorious for browning or even burning the tops of your baked goods while leaving the bottom white and gooey. The answer to this problem is cooking on the stovetop first and popping into the oven for the final cooking and browning. Cast iron is perfect for this. Not only does it perform well on the top of the stove, but equally well in the oven. In addition to numerous skillets, I have enamel coated, cast iron Dutch ovens. Bread bakes to golden perfection in these when covered with the lid.

Roasting Pans: The wonderful thing about roasting pans is that they have lids. One thing that I quickly learned was that things brown long before they are cooked through. You either have to buy truckloads of tin foil or have pans that you can cover to slow the browning process. I generally bake until the top is golden brown and then cover with a lid. This allows whatever I am baking to cook all of the way through but not become a charred mess.

Cake pans with slide on covers: Just like roasting pans, these cake pans have a cover. One of the biggest challenges in wood cook stove cookery is keeping the tops of your foods from burning. Covers also keep moisture in casseroles and other dishes. Wood heat is very dry. Covering your dishes while they cook keeps them from drying out.

Pie Shields: Just like cast iron lids, roasting pans and cake pans with covers, pie shields will keep your pies from becoming burnt offerings. It is amazing how a tiny, thin piece of metal protects your crusts from becoming inedible.

Tin (aluminum) foil: Some of your pans just don't come equipped with lids. As you can tell, my main concern while cooking on my cook stove is keeping the tops of all my cakes, pies, breads and everything else from becoming blackened soot. A few rolls of tin foil are worth their weight in gold.

Most wood cook stoves have non-standard oven sizes. My folks have a cook stove with a rather small oven. My mom has had to search high and low for skillets and pans and cookie sheets that will fit in her oven. Finding the proper cookware will be the difference between success and sheer frustration.

Wood cook stove cookery is an art and a science. It is a challenge that is well worth the effort.

A Guide to Cook Stove Temperatures

My wood cook stove comes equipped with an oven temperature gauge (although older models do not). That is not to say the temperature gauge works perfectly. Foods cooked in a wood cook stove cook and bake differently than in a conventional oven. Over the years, I have found that there are far more effective methods of determining proper cook stove temperatures than using a thermometer. My favorite method is the "hand" method:

Very hot oven: Hold had in oven for less than 5 seconds (some breads, some pastry)

Hot oven: Hold hand in oven for 6 – 7 seconds
(biscuits, scones, pizza)

Moderate oven: Hold hand in oven for 10 – 11 seconds
(yeast bread, casserole, cakes, muffins, cookies, pies)

Slow oven: Hold hand in oven for 20 seconds
(roasts, slow-cooker meals, some cakes, some breads)

And the equivalent temperatures;

Very Hot oven: 450° to 550°
Hot oven: 400° to 450°
Moderate oven: 350° to 400°
Slow oven: 250° to 300°

Another method:
Place a tablespoon of white flour into an oven proof bowl or crockery. If the flour turns brown in 1 minute the oven is a perfect temperature for baking – somewhere between 325° and 350°.

And another:
Put a piece of white paper into the oven for 5 minutes. If the paper turns a golden brown the oven heat is moderate (bake bread, cakes etc.). If the paper turns a dark brown, the oven is hot (biscuits, scones).

Baking Bread in a Wood Cook Stove

After baking in my wood cook stove for a number of years, I have learned that it is relatively easy once you understand a few simple truths.

First, your temperature gauge (if you have one) is a vague guide at best. Unlike gas and electric heat, wood heat is very penetrating. The temperatures you are used to baking and cooking at are drastically reduced when using a wood cook stove. If you normally bake your bread at 425° in your electric or gas oven you would slide your bread into your wood cook stove at roughly 325°.

Frustratingly, when I began baking in my cook stove, I filled the woodbox with small pieces of dry wood, cranked the drafts open and waited until my temperature gauge read 425°. Red in the face and dripping with perspiration, I carefully put my risen bread into the oven, set the timer for 10 minutes (I knew enough to know that I would have to turn the bread half-way through the baking time) and started cleaning up the kitchen. Approximately 8 minutes later, smoke started rolling out of my oven and the acidic smell of burnt dough filled the house. When I opened the oven, completely blackened loaves of bread met my eyes. Turning the ruined loaves out of the pans, I was surprised to see perfectly white bottom crusts. They had not even begun to brown. A quick tap to the bottom echoed with a heavy, thick thud, indicating a raw center. My bread was ruined. I had no idea where I had gone wrong. I had been baking bread for years. The dough was right. The temperature was right. All I had to show for my efforts were burned/raw lumps of unappetizing goo.

I persevered and soon discovered my problem. It was, of course, the temperature. Once I dropped the temperature by 100°, my bread began baking much more evenly. The next challenge was getting the bread to cook evenly on both sides and keeping the top from burning while making sure the bottom cooked through.

As I baked, I learned to rotate my bread about every 10 minutes (depending on the temperature of my oven). I would put a loaf of bread in the oven, let it bake for about 10 minutes and then rotate it completely, turning the other side to face the firebox. As that side browned, I would rotate the bread so that one of the ends was facing the firebox, and then the other. If the top of the bread began to darken too much, I would cover it with tin foil.

Wood cook stove ovens are hotter in the top of the oven than they are in the bottom of the oven. If you bake your bread on a rack (even in the middle of the oven), your loaf can look perfect, however, when you turn the loaf out of the pan, it will be completely white on the bottom (and underdone). It is important to bake your bread on the oven floor (I don't even use a rack) for at least half of your baking time. I generally like to begin my baking time with the loaves on the oven floor and finish baking them on a rack so that they brown nicely. When baking more than one rack of bread, I rotate on the rack and also from the rack to the oven floor.

Sometimes, depending on the wood I am using, the stove gets too hot, threatening to burn whatever I happen to be baking. When the temperature rises too high, the first thing I do is add wood (I know, seems backwards) and shut down the vents (drafts). This slows the rate of combustion, cooling the stove. If the temperature is still too hot, I manually adjust it by propping the oven door open with something non-combustible. This allows the heat to escape quickly without affecting the baked goods.

When the stove is too hot, I have to be very studious about turning and rotating the baked goods. Often I have to cover the tops of the loaves with tin foil so that they can continue to bake without burning.

Generally, because we heat our "shouse" with our cook stove, we don't have a problem with the oven not being hot enough to bake in, however, we do keep small wood cut for just that purpose. If the oven is not quite warm enough, I open the drafts, pile it full with small wood and cock the lid (or door, to allow more air into the firebox). Within minutes, the oven heats quite sufficiently to bake just about anything.

Our wood cook stove is one of our most vital survival resources. With it, we can heat our home, heat our water and cook our meals. We can warm towels, can food and dry clothes. It is the very heart of our little house. If you can only afford one preparedness tool, a wood cook stove should be at the very top of your list.

Wood Cook Stove Maintenance

Like any other tool, wood cook stoves require a certain amount of maintenance. Things to attend to are:

Firebricks must be replaced when they are broken or cracked. If they are not replaced promptly, you run the risk of burning out your firebox, rendering your cook stove useless. It is a simple thing to invest in a number of bricks for your stove and have them at the ready.

Ash needs to be cleaned from the stove regularly. After burning for an extended period of time, ash builds up and hampers the draft as well as the conductivity of the heat, making baking a challenge.

Water Reservoir (if you have one) must be maintained with a minimum of 2" of water. If you allow the water reservoir to dry out completely you run the risk of breaking the welds the next time you fill it with water. If you do let the water reservoir go completely dry, and your stove is hot, fill the water reservoir with hot water from the tap (or that you have heated up on the stovetop). This may keep the welds from breaking.

Stovepipes require regular cleaning to discourage chimney fires. There are products sold that are specifically designed to clean a chimney (you burn them in the firebox) that are very effective. Chimney sweeping is another way to keep the stovepipe clean. Regular burning of a hot fire helps keep the creosote at bay, however, if you shut your (airtight) wood cook stove down at night, you will get a certain amount of creosote buildup regardless of how hot of fire you have during the day. Creosote also builds up depending upon the types of wood you burn.

Wood Cook Stove Anatomy

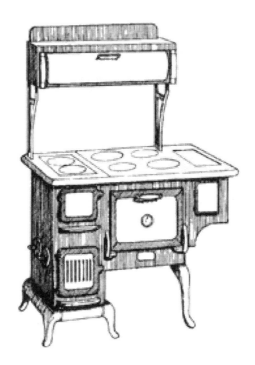

Warming shelf: The perfect place to keep butter soft and honey liquid.

Warming oven: Just right for keeping food warm and heating dinner plates.

Backsplash: Keeps heat where you want it and keeps grease from splattering.

Plates: These are for cleaning out ash and in some cases, loading firewood. They are not "burners".

Water Reservoir: A reservoir full of water – on tap. This water generally stays moderately warm, typically warm enough for doing dishes. The reservoir must maintain at least 2" of water in it at all times when the stove is in use.

Firebox: The firebox is where you build the fire. Firebox sizes vary according to the stove you have. Some are tiny (antiques) just large enough for kindling and small wood, others are quite large – enough to keep a fire going all night (stoked and shut down).

Oven: Wood cook stove ovens vary in size also. Some are petite while others are huge, capable of baking numerous loaves of bread at once. Every oven bakes differently. The more you use your wood cook stove, the more you will become acquainted with its peculiarities.

Drafts or Dampers: These are knobs or levers on the side, back or front of the firebox that control the amount of air that is allowed into the firebox. Opening the drafts allows more air and closing the drafts reduces the amount of air. When you want a hot fire you open the drafts. When you want to cool the firebox, you want to close the drafts down a bit.

Ash pan or Cleaning Grate: The ash from the firebox collects in the ash pan. If you are burning hardwood (oak, maple or fruit wood) this is where you would collect ash to make lye for soap-making purposes. The ash must be regularly cleaned from the stove so as not to build up. Ash is also a nice additive for the garden or compost pile.

Chapter IV

Recipes

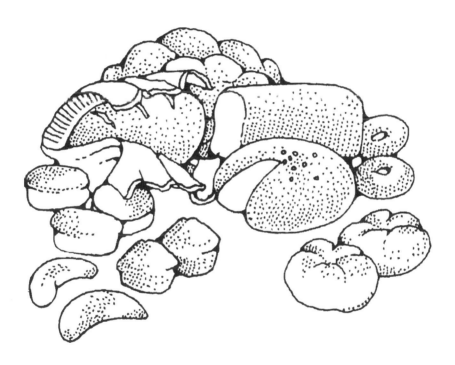

I grew up cooking and baking. My grandmother cooked lavish meals for all of our family get-togethers. My mom baked all of our bread, made all of our meals from scratch and planned menus with unerring accuracy.

When I was little, I would stand by my mother's elbow, watching her dice, slice and sauté. She talked while she worked, telling me what she was doing and why. Not only did I learn the purpose of meticulously whisking all of the lumps out of roux for gravy, I also learned our family history. I listened to stories of my mother learning to bake bread (after years of churning out inedible bricks). I learned that my grandpa thought all vegetables were supposed to taste burned, because my great-grandmother had always put the veggies on to cook and then went to play her piano (her great enjoyment). The result was inevitably the same – overdone vegetables with a slightly acidic flavor. To this day grandpa prefers his veggies VERY well done. I learned how my grandparents met and what my parents did on their first date.

When I was older, I was allowed to "help" with the bread. After mom had finished kneading the dough to perfection, I got to push the bread around on the table. As I pressed the dough with the heel of my hand, I learned to quickly fold it in half and press again. Over and over I would knead, loving the feel of the silky smooth dough beneath my fingers. I would proudly present my dough to my mother and she would proclaim it perfect. And the very best thing of all – when my mother served the bread, she never failed to say "Isn't this bread wonderful? Enola made it!".

When I was newly married and making meals on my own, I found that I wasn't the cook that I had thought I was. I learned that it is harder than it looks to get a meal to the table while everything is still hot. I came to know that my meals would be perfect, every time, until company came, and then they wouldn't be fit to feed to the dog. The more I cooked, the less I knew, and the more I came to realize that my mother and her mother before her had been miracle workers in the kitchen.

I built on what I learned in my mother's kitchen. I started with the things I had successfully made while growing up and then branched out into other areas, making the same thing over and over until I had perfected the recipe. The more I cooked, the more confident I became. As I gained skill, I began to tweak recipes here and there, molding them to the tastes of our family.

Over the years, I have accumulated many recipes that have become family favorites. I am drawn toward simple things, not requiring out-of-the-ordinary ingredients. These are most likely meals that you will remember from your childhood or at the very least, heard stories of Grandma making when the family got together for a celebration.

These are our heirlooms, we hope they become yours.

NOTE: *Most of the recipes in this book are presented in their original form, however, I have also included stored foods substitutions (in bold parenthesis, next to the original ingredient), along with wood cook stove directions where applicable.*

Substitutions
&
Equivalents

There comes a time in every cook's kitchen that she runs out of an ingredient and can't run to the store for more. That is where our substitution section comes in. Many things that are common pantry items can be easily substituted for other pantry staples with no noticeable difference in the finished product.

Another key kitchen helper is a list of equivalents. How many times have you wondered how many cups of powdered sugar were in a pound? I can't count the number of times I have been in the middle of a recipe that calls for "an 8 oz. package...", and because I buy everything in bulk, I have no idea how many cups corresponds with "an 8oz. package". These equivalents have been indispensable in my kitchen and I hope they will be in yours.

Dairy Products

	Weight	Yields
Nonfat Dry Milk Solids	1 lb.	4 C.
Cheese	1 lb.	4 C. grated
Cottage Cheese	1 lb.	2 C.
Cream Cheese	8 oz.	1 C.
Butter/Shortening/Lard	1 lb.	2 C.

Dried Beans

	Weight	Yields (Cooked)
Kidney	1 lb. (1 ½ C.)	6 C.
Lima	1 lb. (2 1/3 C.)	6 C.
Navy	1 lb. (2 1/3 C.)	6 C.
Soybeans	1 lb. (2 1/3 C.)	6 C.
Split Peas	1 lb. (2 C.)	5 C.
Lentils	1 lb. (2 1/3 C.)	6 C.
Black-eyed Peas	1 lb. (2 C.)	5 C.

Eggs

	Yields
7 small eggs	1 C.
6 medium eggs	1 C.
5 large eggs	1 C.

Flours & Grains

	Weight	Yields
White flour	1 lb.	4 C. sifted
Cake flour	1 lb.	4 ½ C. sifted
Whole wheat	1 lb.	3 ½ C.
Rye	1 lb.	4 C.
Soy	1 lb.	6 C.
Cornmeal	1 lb.	3 C.
Oatmeal	1 lb.	4 ¾ C.

Nuts

	Weight	Yields
Almonds	1 lb. in shell	1 ¾ C. shelled
	1 lb. shelled	3 ½ C.
Pecans	1 lb. in shell	2 ¼ C. shelled
	1 lb. shelled	4 C.
Peanuts	1 lb. in shell	2 ¼ C. shelled
	1 lb. shelled	3 C.
Walnuts	1 lb. in shell	1 2/3 C. shelled
	1 lb. shelled	4 C.
Coconut	1 whole	2 – 3 C. shredded
	1 lb. shredded	5 C.

Pasta & Rice

	Weight	Yields (cooked)
Rice	1 lb. (2 C.) dried	6 C.
Macaroni	1 lb. (4 C.) dried	8 C.
Spaghetti	1 lb. (5 C.) dried	9 – 10 C.
Noodles	1 lb. (6 C.) dried	10 ½ C.

Vegetables

Garlic	2 medium cloves	1 tsp. minced
Onions	1 medium	½ to ¾ C chopped
Bell Peppers	1 large	1 C chopped
Tomatoes	3 medium	1 ½ C chopped

Sugars

	Weight	Yields
Granulated	1 lb.	2 C.
Brown	1 lb.	2 ¼ C.
Confectioners	1 lb.	3 ½ C.
Honey	1 lb.	1 1/3 C.
Molasses	1 lb.	1 1/3 C.

Miscellaneous

1 pkg. dry yeast	1 T.
1 envelope unflavored gelatin	1 T.
1 lemon	2 – 3 T. juice
	2 tsp., rind, grated
1 orange	1/3-1/2 C., juice
	1-2 T. rind, grated
1 lb. bananas (3-4)	2 C. mashed
1 lb. dates	2 ½ C. pitted
1 lb. seedless raisins	2 ¾ C.
1 lb. raw potatoes	2 C. cooked, mashed

Substitutions

If you don't have....	*Use.....*
1 tsp. baking powder	¼ tsp. baking soda plus ½ tsp. cream of tartar
½ C brown sugar	½ C granulated sugar plus 2 T. molasses
1 oz. (square) baking choc.	3 T. baking cocoa plus 1 T. shortening or butter
1 C heavy cream (for baking not for whipping)	¾ C. whole milk plus ¼ C melted butter
1 C cake flour	1 C minus 2 T all purpose flour
1 C self-rising flour	1 C flour plus ½ tsp. salt plus 1 ½ tsp. baking powder
1 C honey	1 ¼ C granulated sugar plus ¼ C water

1 pkg. dry yeast	1 T bulk yeast or 1 cake compressed yeast
1 C sour cream	1 C plain yogurt
1 C buttermilk	1 C milk plus 1 T lemon juice or vinegar (let stand 5 minutes)
1 T cornstarch	2 T flour or 2 tsp arrowroot
1 clove garlic	1/8 tsp. garlic powder
1 C tomato sauce	½ C tomato paste plus ½ C cold water
1 tsp. vinegar	2 tsp. lemon juice
1 C whole milk	1 C skim milk plus 2 T melted butter
½ C light corn syrup	½ C granulated sugar plus 2 T liquid (honey, fruit juice, water etc.)
1 tsp. fresh grated orange or lemon peel	½ tsp. dried peel
1 tsp. pumpkin pie spice	½ tsp. cinnamon, ¼ tsp. nutmeg, 1/8 tsp. allspice, 1/8 tsp. cardamom

Appetizers, Beverages *and* Tea Time Indulgences

Although we don't eat a lot of what may be considered appetizers we do have afternoon tea everyday at 4 O'clock. I have included our tea treats, along with many beverage recipes that we have enjoyed over the years.

Some of the drinks are holdovers from my childhood. The Russian tea was a staple in our home that I anxiously awaited every fall. The hot cocoa we developed ourselves after trying numerous recipes and combining a few, coming up with what we consider the perfect brew.

During the summer months, we are never without a jar of or two of iced tea and a jar of lemonade. The moment my husband returns from work, I fill his hand with a huge glass of iced tea to cool him down. When company appears, the children immediately ask if they would like something to drink. More often than not, we solve the world's problems while we wet our whistles.

Sharing a cup of tea with a friend is truly the knitting of hearts. It nourishes your soul as it nourishes your body.

Cheese Pots

These are a wonderful tea time treat, especially served with toast made using homemade bread. Homemade crackers will also work in a pinch.

3 lbs. cheddar cheese *{may used canned cheese}*
½ lb. butter
¾ C sherry *{may use wine, water or milk}*
Salt
Pepper

Roughly grate cheese and place over moderate heat with butter, stirring continuously until cheddar and butter have melted. If mixture separates, remove from heat and beat well. Beat in sherry and salt and pepper to taste. Pour into small pots, allow to cool and set. Use to spread on savories (crackers) or bread.

Devonshire Cream (Mock)

This is a staple in our home. Scones are always welcome at the tea table and nothing is nicer with scones than Devonshire Cream and Lemon Curd. This is quick and simple and lasts quite a while in the refrigerator.

Beat until smooth:
1 package cream cheese (8 oz.) *{homemade is best}*
¼ C sour cream

Slowly add:
6 T powdered sugar *{more or less to taste}*

Serve on warm scones with a dollop of lemon curd or homemade jam.

Hot Chocolate Mix

When my children were little, I tried homemade hot cocoa mixes too numerous to mention. They were all good, but none quite made the cut. I came across a variation of this recipe while perusing an old school cookbook of my husband's. With a tweak here and tweak there, I came up with this recipe. Our children have grown up with this Hot Chocolate mix and will accept no substitute.

3.4 lb. box of Nesquick
2 C powdered sugar
3 C powdered creamer
7 ½ C powdered milk

Stir ingredients together. Pour into airtight container. To use, mix ¼ C powder in mug with hot water.

Animal Crackers

Animal crackers and cocoa to drink, that is the finest of suppers I think; When I'm grown up and can have what I please, I think I shall always insist upon these. What do you choose when you're offered a treat? When Mother says, "what would you like best to eat?" Is it waffles and syrup, or cinnamon toast? It's cocoa and animals that I love the most!

The kitchen's the coziest place that I know; The kettle is singing, the stove is aglow, and there in the twilight, how jolly to see, the cocoa and animals waiting for me.

Daddy and Mother dine later in state, with Mary to cook for them, Susan to wait; But they don't have nearly as much fun as I, who eat in the kitchen with Nurse standing by; And Daddy once said, he would like to be me, having cocoa and animals once more for tea.

Christopher Morley

Lemon Curd

I love anything citrus, so when I was introduced to lemon curd for the first time, it was love at first taste. Knowing that I must make it for myself, I found this gem of a recipe. I expanded it quite a bit because I see little point in making just a wee bit of anything. I love to can it and put it on my shelf, awaiting just the right moment for it to take the center stage of our tea table.

1 ½ C butter
1 ½ C lemon juice
2 T lemon rind, grated
4 ½ C sugar
12 whole eggs
6 egg yolks

In a medium saucepan, melt the butter. Add lemon juice, lemon rind and sugar. Stir until the sugar has dissolved.

Beat together eggs and egg yolks, beating until thick. Blend into the sugar mixture.

Cook over medium heat, stirring constantly, until quite thick.

Cool and refrigerate.

TO PRESERVE
Pour lemon curd into sterilized jars and seal. Water bath can for 20 minutes.

 This canning method is not USDA approved and the recipe given is for informational purposes only – not for actual use.

Lemonade

During the hot summer months, we make it a habit to always have iced tea and lemonade on hand to offer parched guests. I always make my lemonade in a 1 gallon glass jar so that I have plenty.

2 C. sugar
2 C. lemon juice
15 C. water *{about}*

In a 1 gallon glass jar combine the sugar and lemon juice, stirring until the sugar has dissolved. Fill the jar about ½ full with water and continue to deep stir. Fill the jar just to the neck with remaining water. Stir again. Cover and refrigerate.

Party Nog

Although my husband refuses to taste anything with the word "Nog" in it, this recipe is a favorite of my children. We make it only once a year (I'm sure it is not something in which to indulge on a regular basis), but we look forward to it with great anticipation.

1 pkg. (3.4 oz) instant vanilla pudding mix
2 C. cold milk
1 to 2 tsp. vanilla
2 T. sugar
5 C. cold milk
1 C. evaporated milk *{or milk or cream}*

Combine pudding mix, 2 cups of milk, vanilla and sugar in a bowl and mix well. Pour into a half-gallon container with a tight fitting lid. Add 5 cups milk; cover and shake (or stir) well. Add evaporated milk (or cream). Stir well. Chill.

Potato Skins

These are so good that we could eat them as a main dish! When I am not wanting a lot of last minute work, I will make potato skins instead of baked potatoes. They are always a huge hit with my family and anyone else who happens to join us for dinner.

8 slices bacon
8 potatoes, scrubbed
Canola oil *{butter}*
Salt
1 ½ C cheddar Cheese, grated
1 C sour cream
4 Green Onions, sliced *{Optional}*

Preheat oven to 400°.

Wash potatoes and rub the skin liberally with canola oil (or butter). Bake for 45 minutes to 1 hour, until the potatoes are tender.

While you are waiting, fry up the bacon until it is crisp. Break into small pieces.

After the potatoes have baked, slice them in half lengthwise. Scoop out the flesh, leaving a little in the skins. Brush both side of the potato skins with canola oil. Salt both sides well.

Place the skins, cut side down on a pan and return to the oven. Bake for 7 minutes then turn potatoes to right side. Bake for 7 more minutes or until the skins are crispy.

Sprinkle cheese and bacon into each potato skin and return to the oven just until the cheese melts. Before serving, spoon 1 T of sour cream (optional) on each skin and sprinkle with sliced green onions.

Russian Tea

When I was a little girl, my mom made Russian Tea every fall and I looked forward to it with great anticipation. I've heard it called by many names including Friendship Tea and Amish Tea but I have always known it by the name of Russian Tea. I have seen many variations, but, of course, I like the one my mother made best of all.

Mix together:
1 C instant tea
1 ½ C Tang
1 C sugar
1 pkg. lemon Kool-Aid (without sugar)
1 tsp. ground cloves
½ tsp. cinnamon

Use 3 spoonfuls per mug. Add steaming hot water.

Sweet Iced Tea

In the summer, we are rarely found without a huge glass of iced tea in our hand. Although this is not nearly as sweet as true Southern sweet iced tea, it will do for the Redoubt States!

8 tea bags (I like Red Rose, but any bagged tea is fine)
Boiling water
1 C sugar

Tie 8 tea bags together and put in a 1 gallon glass jar. Pour enough boiling water into the jar to cover the tea bags and then some. Allow the tea to steep for 10 minutes and remove the bags. Stir in the sugar and continue to stir until the sugar goes into solution. Fill the jar (to the neck) with cold water. Cover and refrigerate.

The Perfect Cuppa Tea

Tea is an essential part of our existence. I can't imagine life without it. I have come to know that Tea Time really isn't about the tea at all, but about the ritual – the comfort. Although I really do prefer a good cup of tea, just about any cup shared with warm company will do. There are a few tricks that will make your tea truly wonderful....

- Always use freshly drawn water. If the water has been bubbling away on the stove for hours, the oxygen will be gone and will leave the tea quite flat and tasteless.
- Measure about 1 tsp. loose tea per cup and one for the pot. If you have a 6 cup tea pot, measure 7 tsp. of tea into the pot, strainer or tea sock.
- Tea bags will do, but loose tea does make a superior cup. I use a Chatsford tea pot which has a basket infuser. For my pots without built-in infusers, I use Tea Socks purchased from Upton Tea. As a last resort, I pour the freshly brewed tea through a tea strainer to strain out the leaves.
- Generally, a stout, black tea steeps (sits) for 5 minutes before removing the strainer. Green tea only steeps for 1 minute. Consult the packaging of your tea to determine steeping times.
- I always serve tea with Turbinado (raw) sugar and cream (which is really milk – real cream curdles). The Turbinado sugar gives the tea a wonderful, rich flavor and the milk smooths a black, stiff tea.
- Rooibos tea (which is really an infusion) is wonderful in the evening as it contains no caffeine. It is served with only sugar.
- Although this etiquette is disputable, I add sugar and milk and then add tea.

Welsh Rarebit

My mother's family is indeed of Welsh descent, however, we had never enjoyed the simple tea meal of Welsh Rarebit until I stumbled across a recipe when my children were small. Rarebit makes a wonderful late afternoon or early evening snack, particularly when a full-fledged meal is too heavy. It is equally welcome on a dreary winter day or a sultry summer evening.   It can be made with or without ale, however the ale does add a bit of spice.

¼ c English beer or ale **(or water or milk)**
1 tsp. dry mustard
¼ tsp. cayenne pepper
¼ tsp. Worcestershire sauce
2 C Cheddar cheese, grated **(or Farmhouse cheese)**
6 slices bread, sliced in half *{on the diagonal}*, toasted *{you can remove the crusts, if desired}.*

Combine ale, mustard, cayenne pepper and Worcestershire sauce in a medium saucepan.   Add cheese by the handfuls, stirring until the cheese is melted and smooth.

On a cookie sheet *{or baking pan}*, arrange toast triangles and pour cheese sauce over the toast. Broil until the cheese is bubbly and slightly browning, about 2 to 3 minutes.

Serve with a good cup of tea.

Quick Breads
Soft Wheat

Quick breads are the simplest of all breads to make because they use baking powder or baking soda as a leavening agent. Due to the fact that they don't require extra time to rise (leaven) they are perfect for a quick evening meal.

Soft wheat (wheat having a lower protein content – and a lower gluten content) is the wheat of choice for grinding and using in quick bread recipes. Soft white wheat, soft red wheat and golden wheat are all good choices for quick breads. Hard wheats can also be used in quick breads. Hard white, spelt and kamut are also fine choices. You should grind your flour on a fine setting (pastry flour) to get a fine, light crumb rather than a course, heavy bread. If you are using a small hand grinder that doesn't have a coarseness setting, it would be advisable to put the flour through the mill twice.

Quick breads require a soft hand. Unlike yeast breads, kneading is not generally required (or if it is, knead **just** until the dough is smooth, NO longer) for quick breads. Biscuits are stirred until mixed, kneaded once or twice (until the dough holds together) and then patted (I don't even use a rolling pin) flat and cut out. Pancakes and waffles are mixed until moist but are **not** beaten until smooth (the batter is generally lumpy). If you do beat the batter until silky and smooth, your pancakes will be tough as leather, requiring a knife just to cut!

NOTE: When grinding wheat berries into flour, you must use the flour within 18 hours or it will become rancid. You can grind extra flour to be used later if it is stored in the freezer until use. Wheat berries last indefinitely, but once the germ is cracked (during grinding) the flour will become rancid if not used quickly.

Angel Biscuits

This recipe came to me from my dear friend "Lady Day". She is one of the finest cooks I have ever known. She has been known to make everything from gourmet tea treats to humble stews on her wood cookstove. And truth be told, she has even rendered bear fat and boiled down animal carcasses in the confines of her pretty kitchen.

I use these biscuits in recipes that call for refrigerated, store-bought biscuits. They are light, flaky and incredibly good. They are equally wonderful as plain biscuits, served with your favorite soup, or as a tender crust for a main dish pie.

1 C. buttermilk **(or 1 C. (pwd) milk + 1 T lemon juice or vinegar)**
½ C. warm water
1 pkg. *{1 T.}* dry yeast
2 T. sugar **(or honey)**
4 C. flour **(or whole (soft) wheat flour)**
2 tsp. baking powder
1 tsp. salt
1/3 C. butter **(or shortening or lard)**

Heat milk, water and sugar until warm (about 110°) but not hot. Sprinkle with yeast, stir and allow to sit (sponge). Meanwhile, mix together flour, baking powder and salt. Cut in butter. Add milk/yeast mixture to dry ingredients, adding more milk until the dough becomes supple. Turn onto a floured surface and knead until smooth. Cut into biscuits. Place on greased baking sheets and allow to rise for 30 minutes.

Bake at 400° for 12 minutes.

Baking Powder Biscuits

Baking powder biscuits are one of my Dad's favorite foods, and a staple in most old-time households. The buttermilk in this recipe makes the biscuits light and airy – very tender. These are the go-to biscuits to accompany sausage gravy and are a perfect compliment to tea, when slathered in fresh butter and jam.

3 1/3 C flour *(or whole (soft) wheat)*
4 tsp. baking powder
1 tsp. salt
½ tsp. baking soda
½ C. shortening *(or butter)*
1 ½ C. buttermilk *(or 1 ½ C (pwd) milk + 1.5 T lemon juice or vinegar)*

In a mixing bowl, combine flour, baking powder, salt and baking soda. Cut in shortening until mixture resembles coarse crumbs. Add buttermilk; stir just until moistened. On a floured surface, gently knead dough until easy to handle. Roll out to about ½" thick. Cut into rounds.

Bake at 450° for 12 – 14 minutes or until golden brown. Serve warm.

Black Bottomed Muffins

Although we don't indulge in these often, they are always a sought-after treat. My friend, Julianne of Providence Lodge, gave me the recipe, which she remembers from her childhood.

Filling:
6 oz. cream cheese
1/3 C sugar
1 egg *(or 1T egg pwd + 3 T water)*
1 C chocolate chips

Combine cream cheese, sugar and egg. Mix in chocolate chips.

Muffin:
1 ½ C flour *(or whole (soft) wheat flour)*
1 C sugar **(or honey)**
¼ C cocoa
1 tsp. baking soda
½ tsp. salt
1 C water
1/3 C oil
1 T vinegar
1 tsp. vanilla

Mix all ingredients well.

Preheat oven to 350°

Fill paper lined muffin cups half full. Top with 1 tablespoon of the cream cheese filling.

Bake for 20 – 30 minutes. Cool. Store in an airtight container in the refrigerator.

Blueberry (Huckleberry) Buckle

The American Redoubt is famous for its ample Huckleberry crop, and I would be remiss if I failed to include at least one Huckleberry recipe. We love this buckle, although we use blueberries as often as we use huckleberries. I do have to admit that the flavor of this cake, when filled with huckleberries, is unparalleled.

½ C butter, softened *(or shortening)*
¾ C sugar **(or honey)**
1 egg *(or 1 T egg pwd + 3 T water)*
½ C milk *(or pwd milk)*
2 C flour *(or whole (soft) wheat flour)*
2 tsp. baking powdcr
¼ tsp. salt
1 C blueberries or huckleberries

Streusel:
½ C sugar
1/3 C flour **(or whole (soft) wheat flour)**
¼ C butter ,cold *(or shortening)*
1 C pecans *{optional}*

In a mixing bowl, cream together the butter and sugar. Beat in the egg and milk. Add the flour, baking powder and salt. Stir well. Fold in blueberries.

Meanwhile, to make the streusel, combine the sugar and flour. Cut in the butter until crumbly. Add pecans.

Pour the batter into a greased and floured 9" square baking pan. Sprinkle the streusel over the batter.

Bake buckle at 375° for 35 to 40 minutes or until a wooden pick inserted near the center comes out clean.

Butter Pecan Cakes

*These not-overly-sweet cakes store well and are always welcome
with a cup of coffee or tea. Their subtle flavor never competes,
making them lovely accompaniments to flavored beverages.*

1 C butter, softened *(or shortening)*
1 ½ C sugar **(or honey)**
2 tsp. vanilla
3 eggs *(or 3 T egg pwd + 9 T water)*
1 ¼ C milk *(or pwd milk)*
2 ¼ C flour *(or whole (soft) wheat flour)*
2 ½ tsp. baking powder
½ tsp. salt
½ C pecans, chopped

Beat together the butter and sugar. Add vanilla, eggs and milk.
Mix well. Stir in the flour, baking powder and salt. Add pecans.

Spoon into a greased and floured tartlet (or mini muffin) pan.

Bake at 350° for 12-15 minutes (or longer, depending on your
pan) or until lightly browned. Cool in pans on rack for 10
minutes. Remove from pans. Cool on rack completely.

Buttermilk Cornbread

We can't make a pot of beans without making a pan of cornbread to accompany it. Unlike true Southern Cornbread, this cornbread is sweet and very cake-like. We love it smothered in honey butter. Yum!

½ cube butter *(or shortening or lard)*
2/3 C sugar **(or honey)**
2 eggs *(or 2 T egg pwd + 6 T water)*
1 C buttermilk *(or 1 C (pwd) milk + 1 T lemon juice or vinegar)*
½ tsp. baking soda
1 C cornmeal *(or ground popcorn)*
1 C flour *(or whole (soft) wheat flour)*
½ tsp. salt

Preheat your oven to 375°. Grease an 8-inch cast iron skillet.

Melt the butter. Pour into a bowl, add sugar and stir. Add eggs and beat until well blended. Combine buttermilk with baking soda and stir the mixture into the bowl. Stir in cornmeal, flour and salt until well blended and few lumps remain. Pour batter into the prepared pan.

Bake in the preheated oven for 30 to 40 minutes or until a toothpick inserted in the center comes out clean.

Cake Doughnuts

While we love raised doughnuts, sometimes there is nothing quite as satisfying as an old-fashioned cake doughnut. These are the best we've ever had and we like the fact that they have at least a little whole-wheat flour in them. But, of course, the fact that we love to fry them in bear grease probably cancels out the health benefits of the whole wheat!

2 eggs *(or 2 T egg powder + 6 T water)*
1 C buttermilk *(or 1 C (pwd) milk + 1 T lemon juice or vinegar)*
1 C brown sugar **(or 1 C sugar + 4 T molasses)**
2 to 4 T butter, melted *(or shortening or vegetable oil)*
1 C whole-wheat flour {hard or soft wheat}
3 C flour *(or whole (soft or hard) wheat flour)*
1 tsp. baking powder
½ tsp. salt
¼ tsp. cinnamon
¼ tsp. nutmeg

Beat the eggs with the buttermilk until light. Add and beat in the sugar and melted butter. Mix the flours, baking soda, baking powder, salt and spices together. Blend with the liquid ingredients, mixing as little as possible. The dough will be sticky so turn it out onto a well-floured board. Roll (with a well-floured rolling pin) until it is between ¼ and ½ inch thick.

Cut the doughnuts with a doughnut cuter and allow them to rest while you heat a frying pan of shortening, vegetable oil, lard or bear grease to 365°F. The oil should be deep enough to allow the doughnuts to float. Fry the doughnuts, giving them room to expand, until they're golden brown, flip and allow to fry on the other side. Remove to a paper towel to drain.

As soon as they are cool enough, roll in a cinnamon and sugar mixture.

Chocolately-Chocolate Quick Bread

The applesauce in this bread keeps it moist for days. This bread is never dry and crumbly and the chocolate flavor is rich and full. Although wonderful, the frosting is not required to make this bread a decadent treat.

½ C. butter, softened *(or shortening)*
2/3 C. packed brown sugar *(or 2/3 C sugar + 2.5 T molasses)*
2 eggs *(or 2 T egg pwd + 6 T water)*
1 C. chocolate chips, melted
1 ½ C. applesauce
2 tsp. vanilla
2 ½ C. flour *(or whole (soft) wheat flour)*
1 tsp. baking powder
1 tsp. baking soda
1 tsp. salt
½ C. chocolate chips

Frosting:
½ C. chocolate chips
1 T. butter *(or shortening)*
2 to 3 T. cream *(or milk or water)*
½ C. confectioners sugar
¼ tsp. vanilla

In a mixing bowl, cream the butter and sugar. Add eggs and melted chocolate; mix well. Add applesauce and vanilla. Combine the flour baking powder, baking soda and salt; add to creamed mixture and mix well. Stir in chocolate chips.

Spoon the batter into four greased 5 ½" x 3" loaf pans. Bake at 350° for 35 – 40 minutes or until a toothpick inserted near the center comes out clean. Cool for 10 minutes before removing to wire racks to cool completely.

For the frosting, in a saucepan melt the chocolate chips with the butter; stir in cream. Remove from the heat; stir in powdered sugar, vanilla and salt. Drizzle over warm bread.

Chocolate Steamed Pudding

Steamed pudding is just the thing for a cold winter's afternoon. It merrily steams on the top of the wood cook stove while you go about your business and rewards you with chocolate perfection at days end. It is an old-fashioned pudding with the texture of a dense cake rather than the thick custard that we now associate with the term "pudding".

2 oz. (squares) unsweetened baking chocolate **(or 6 T cocoa pwd + 2 T butter (or shortening)**
1 tsp. butter **(or shortening)**
1 tsp. vanilla
1 egg **(or 1 T egg pwd + 3 T water)**
¾ C sugar **(or honey)**
1 C flour **(or whole (soft) wheat flour)**
½ tsp. salt
1 ½ tsp. baking powder
½ C milk **(or pwd milk)**

Melt the baking chocolate and butter over low heat (or in a double boiler). Add vanilla. In a separate mixing bowl, beat the egg until light and lemon colored. Add the sugar and beat until fluffy. Combine the chocolate and egg mixtures and stir in the flour, salt, baking powder and milk, just until blended.

Pour the batter into a greased steamed pudding mold (or a metal bowl or a one-pound coffee can covered with aluminum foil secured with a string or rubber band) and secure cover. Steam over simmering water in a covered kettle for 1 ½ hours.

HARD SAUCE
1 C sugar   1/3 C butter, softened
2 T grated orange rind   1 ½ tsp. orange extract

Mix together until smooth. Smooth into a small square container and chill. To serve, cut sauce into small squares and serve warm pudding with one square of sauce on top.

Coffee Cake Puffs

These are so simple to make that they are a perfect first baking project for children. They are homey and quick and somewhat addicting. We like them best when they are warm and fresh. Make sure you have a napkin – you will need it!

3 C flour **(or whole (soft) wheat flour)**
3 tsp. baking powder
1 tsp. salt
½ tsp. nutmeg
1 C sugar **(or honey)**
2/3 C butter **(or shortening)**
2 eggs **(or 2 T egg pwd + 6 T water)**
1 C milk **(or pwd milk)**

Topping:
1/2 C butter
1 ½ C sugar
3 tsp. cinnamon

Preheat oven to 350°. Lightly grease 12 muffin cups.

In a large bowl, cream together the sugar and the butter. Add the eggs, one at a time and beat well. Add the milk. Mix in the flour, baking powder, salt and nutmeg.

Fill each muffin cup 2/3 full. Bake for 20 to 25 minutes or until golden. Cool slightly and remove from muffin tins to cool further.

To make the topping:
Melt the butter in a bowl. In a separate container, combine the sugar and cinnamon. Dip the slightly cooled muffins in the butter then roll in the cinnamon/sugar mixture. Put on a plate and serve with tea or coffee.

Corn Chips

Yes, you can make corn chips at home! Although not quite the same as what you are used to with the bagged variety, these are a wholesome, hearty substitute.

1 C. yellow cornmeal **(or ground popcorn)**
2/3 C. flour **(or whole (soft) wheat flour)**
1 tsp. salt
1 tsp. baking powder
2 T. dry milk solids *{optional}*
½ C. water
¼ C. oil
½ tsp. Worcestershire sauce
1/8 tsp. Tabasco sauce

Preheat oven to 350°

In a large bowl combine the cornmeal, flour, salt, baking powder and milk solids. In a small bowl combine the water, oil, Worcestershire sauce and Tabasco sauce. Add liquids to the dry mixture and stir with a fork. Knead a little until smooth. Grease two cookie sheets (10x15") and sprinkle each with a little cornmeal. Divide the dough in half. Roll out each half directly onto cookie sheets with a floured rolling pin until the dough is as thin as a dime. Sprinkle lightly with paprika, garlic, onion or seasoned salt. Run rolling pin over once more (to impress the seasoning into the crackers). Prick with a fork. Cut into triangles or strips. Bake for 10 minutes or until lightly browned.

Flour Tortillas

Tortillas are a staple in our home and there is nothing to compare with a fresh, warm, homemade flour tortilla. You can replace ½ of the flour in this recipe with cornmeal or whole wheat flour – they will be no less delicious, but they will pack a nutritional whollop!

2 C. flour, un-sifted **(or whole (soft) wheat flour)**
1 tsp. salt
¼ C. lard or shortening **(or butter)**
½ C. lukewarm water

Combine in mixing bowl the flour and the salt. Cut in the lard or shortening with a pastry cutter until the particles are fine. Add warm water gradually. Toss with a fork to make a stiff dough. Form the dough into a ball and knead thoroughly on a lightly floured board until it is smooth and flecked with air bubbles. To make the dough easier to handle, grease the surface, cover tightly and refrigerate for 4 to 24 hours before using (or use right away). Let dough return to room temperature before rolling out.

Divide the dough into 8 balls for large tortillas or 11 balls for 8" tortillas. Roll as thin as possible on a lightly floured board, or between sheets of waxed paper. Drop onto a very hot ungreased griddle. Bake until freckled on one side (about 20 seconds). Lift the edge, turn and bake on the second side. Serve immediately, or cool tortillas, wrap airtight and refrigerate or freeze. To serve later, place in a tightly covered baking dish and warm in oven, or fry briefly in hot, shallow oil.

Irish Soda Bread

Irish Soda Bread is the quintessential survival bread. It is simple, no yeast to mess this, and uses very few ingredients. It can be made using white flour or freshly ground grain. It is hearty and perfect for both fresh eating and using later for toast and sandwiches. This bread requires no fat (other than to grease the pan) and bakes up quite nicely in a cast iron skillet in the wood cookstove.

4 C. flour **(or whole (soft) wheat flour)**
1 tsp. baking soda
1 tsp. baking powder
1 tsp. salt
2 T sugar
2 C buttermilk *{room temperature}* **(or 2 C (pwd) milk + 2 T lemon juice or vinegar)**

Preheat oven to 375°

Sift (or not) the flour, baking soda, baking powder and salt into a large bowl. Add sugar. Stir with a fork. Add buttermilk and stir until it forms a ball. Turn onto a lightly floured surface and knead for 2 minutes (do not knead longer – it will make the bread tough).

For dough - form into a ball and place in a well-buttered 8" cast iron skillet. If you don't have cast iron, you can use a cake or pie pan.   Press down slightly and, with a sharp knife, cut a cross in the top of the loaf.

Bake at 375° (or a medium/hot wood cookstove oven) for 35-40 minutes. (This bread does not require time to rise).

Orange Chocolate Chips Scones

Although we love scones topped with Devonshire cream, these scones are a nice change and need nothing extra. They are rich in flavor, with a light, flaky texture.

2 C flour **(or whole (soft) wheat flour)**
¼ C sugar **(or honey)**
2 tsp. baking powder
1 tsp. salt
½ C butter, cut into pieces **(or shortening)**
2 eggs, lightly beaten **(or 2 T egg pwd + 6 T water)**
3 T milk **(or orange juice or water)**
2 tsp. orange extract
1 tsp. grated orange peel
½ C chocolate Chips

Egg wash *{optional}*
1 egg yolk
1 tsp. water

1 T sugar

Preheat oven to 350°

Combine flour, sugar, baking powder and salt. Cut butter into the flour mixture. Add eggs, milk, orange extract and orange peel. Stir just until ingredients are moistened. Stir in chocolate chips.

Pat dough into 2 circles on a cookie sheet.   Brush with egg yolk and water. Sprinkle with sugar, cut into wedges. Separate the wedges to bake.

Bake 12 minutes or until done.

Pumpkin Bread

For those of you who like sweet quick-breads, this recipe is a winner. I happen to love pumpkin (and all of the spices that go with it), but the chocolate chips add a whole new dimension. It is wonderful warm, but perhaps even better cooled and slathered with butter – I can't quite decide!

½ C. butter, softened **(or shortening)**
2 2/3 C sugar **(or honey)**
4 eggs **(or 4 T egg pwd + ¾ C water)**
2 C. pumpkin *{16 oz. can}* **(or squash)**
2/3 C water
3 1/3 C flour **(whole (soft) wheat flour)**
2 tsp. baking soda
1 ½ tsp. salt
1 ½ tsp. baking powder
1 tsp. cinnamon
1 tsp. ground cloves
2/3 C chopped walnuts or pecans *{optional}*
1 ¼ C chocolate chips

Cream butter and sugar together; beat in eggs, pumpkin and water. Blend in dry ingredients; fold in nuts and chocolate chips. Divide and pour into 2 greased 9"x5" loaf pans; bake at 350° for 65 minutes.

Raspberry Scones

These scones are one of the reasons I grow raspberries! They are flavorful and hearty – perfect for afternoon tea.

2 C flour **(or whole (soft) wheat flour)**
3 T butter **(or shortening)**
¼ tsp. nutmeg
2 T sugar **(or honey)**
¼ c thick oats **(or regular cut)**
½ tsp. baking powder
½ tsp. baking soda
2 T honey **(or sugar or brown sugar)**
½ tsp. almond extract
½ C buttermilk **(or 1/2 C (pwd) milk + 1 T lemon juice or vinegar)**
1 C frozen raspberries **(or fresh or canned)**

Preheat oven to 375°. Grease a large cookie sheet.

Mix dry ingredients. Cut in butter with a pastry cutter. Pour in wet ingredients. Stir just until blended. Mix in frozen berries (or fresh). Scoop batter onto the cookies sheet in balls at least an inch apart.

Bake for 20 minutes until lightly browned.

Soda Crackers

If you are going to be making homemade cheese, you just have to have homemade crackers to go with it! This is a simple recipe that yields a crisp, tender cracker.

2 C. flour **(or whole (soft) wheat flour)**
1 tsp. salt
½ tsp. baking soda
2 T. butter **(or shortening or lard)**
2/3 C. sour milk or buttermilk **(or 2/3 C (pwd) milk + 1 T lemon juice or vinegar)**

Combine the flour, salt and baking soda in a bowl. Cut in butter with a pastry cutter. Stir in milk. Round dough into a ball and knead a few minutes. Divide the dough into several pieces and roll out very thin on a floured board. Lay sheets of dough on ungreased flat baking pans. Sprinkle with salt and prick with a fork. Cut into 1 ½ " squares with a sharp knife or pizza cutter. Bake at 375° for 10 – 12 minutes, or until lightly browned.

Scrumptious Scones

Scones are a staple in our home. However humble, the scone reveals its royal lineage when served warm on chipped china in a kitchen warmed by wood heat and sweet hospitality.

3 C flour **(or whole (soft) wheat flour)**
1/3 C sugar **(or honey)**
5 tsp. baking powder
1 tsp. salt
1 C (2 cubes) butter, chilled **(or shortening)**
1 large egg **(or 2 T. egg pwd + 3 T water)**
¾ C heavy cream **(or milk or pwd milk or yogurt)**
¼ C chopped pecans *{optional}*

In a mixing bowl, stir together the flour, sugar, baking powder and salt. Cut the butter into small pieces. Cut into the flour using a pastry cutter, until the mixture resembles course crumbles. Add pecans (if you are using) and stir them into the flour mixture. Mix the egg and cream together and add to the flour mixture. Stir together until just combined (overworking will result in flat, hard scones). Turn the dough out onto a kneading surface. Gather together, adding a little flour to keep the dough from sticking. Very gently, roll (with a rolling pin) or press (with your hands) into a 10" round (about ¾" thick), or roll into two 5" rounds. With a sharp knife, cut the round(s) into eight (or four) equal-size wedges. Place the wedges on a baking sheet. Put baking sheet in the refrigerator and chill for an hour or overnight. Allow to return almost to room temperature and bake for 22 minutes (for the large wedges) or 12 minutes (for the smaller wedges), until they're just starting to brown. Serve warm with Maple icing.

MAPLE ICING

3 ¾ C powdered sugar   4 T butter, melted **(or shortening)**
¼ C milk   Dash salt
2 tsp. maple extract

In a mixing bowl, stir all ingredients until smooth (I use an egg beater). Liberally smother cooled scones. Enjoy!

Upside-down Coffee Cake

I had never heard of an upside-down coffee cake until I stumbled upon this one. If I am out of fruit, the brown sugar, butter mixture alone is more than enough to dress up this cake. And I especially love the fact that it is completely at home in a cast iron skillet – you can't say that for many cakes!

TOPPING:
1 ½ C fresh/canned/frozen fruit *{well drained}* cranberries, apples, etc.
2 T chopped walnuts or pecans *{optional}*
2 T butter **(or shortening)**
½ C brown sugar, packed **(or 1/2 C. sugar + 2 T molasses)**
2 T milk **(or orange juice or water)**
¼ tsp. cinnamon

CAKE:
1 ½ C flour **(or whole (soft) wheat flour)**
½ tsp. salt
1 tsp. baking powder
1 C sugar **(or honey)**
1 tsp. vanilla extract
1 egg **(or 2 T egg pwd + 6 T water)**
½ C buttermilk **(or sour cream or yogurt or (pwd) milk)**

Preheat oven to 350°. Grease and flour a 9" cast iron skillet. In a small bowl, combine fruit and nuts. In a small saucepan, melt butter. Stir in brown sugar, milk (or orange juice) and cinnamon. Cook for 3 minutes, stirring constantly. Pour into the greased and floured skillet. Sprinkle with the fruit and nut mixture (the fruit and nuts are optional – cake is wonderful with just the brown sugar mixture).

For the Cake: Beat sugar and butter until creamy. Add vanilla, egg and buttermilk. Beat in flour, salt and baking powder until smooth. Spoon batter over the brown sugar/fruit mixture. Bake 40 minutes or until a toothpick inserted in center of cake comes out clean. Cool in pan for 5 minutes. Invert onto a plate to finish cooling.

Wheat Thins

When plain crackers won't do, these wheat thins are just the ticket. These are a favorite lunch-box treat of my husbands and a general all-around good cracker.

2 C. whole wheat flour
2 T. wheat germ **(or 2 T. whole wheat flour)**
1 tsp. salt
1 tsp. baking powder
2 T. brown sugar **(or 2 T sugar + ½ tsp. molasses)**
2 T. dry milk solids *{optional}*
6 T. butter **(or shortening or lard)**
½ C. water
1 T. molasses **(or honey)**

Preheat oven to 350°

Combine in a large bowl, whole wheat flour, wheat germ, salt, baking powder, brown sugar, dry milk solids. Cut in butter or lard with a pastry blender. In a small bowl combine water and molasses. Sir into flour mixture. Knead a little until smooth. Grease two cookie sheets (10x15") and sprinkle each with cornmeal. Divide dough in half. Roll out half of the dough directly onto the cookie sheet with floured rolling pin, rolling as thin as a dime. Sprinkle lightly with paprika, garlic, onion or seasoned salt. Run rolling pin over once more (to impress seasoning into crackers). Prick with fork. Cut into squares or triangles. Bake for 10 minutes or until lightly browned.

Zucchini Cupcakes with Caramel Frosting

This recipe is a family favorite! In fact, we love these wonderful treats so much that I grate and can pints upon pints of zucchini just so that we can indulge in these cupcakes all year long.

3 eggs **(or 3 T egg pwd + 9 T water)**
1 1/3 C sugar **(or honey)**
½ C vegetable oil
½ C orange juice **(or water)**
1 tsp. almond extract
2 ½ C flour **(or whole (soft) wheat flour)**
2 tsp. cinnamon
2 tsp. baking powder
1 tsp. baking soda
1 tsp. salt
½ tsp. ground cloves
1 ½ C shredded zucchini **(or carrots)**

Preheat oven to 350°

In mixing bowl, beat eggs, sugar, oil, orange juice (or water) and almond extract. Combine dry ingredients; add to the egg mixture and mix well. Add zucchini and mix well. Fill greased or paper-lined muffin cups two-thirds full. Bake for 20 – 25 minutes or until pick inserted in center come out clean. Cool for 10 minutes before removing to a wire rack.

Caramel Frosting:

1 C packed brown sugar **(or 1 C sugar + 4 T molasses)**
½ C butter **(or shortening)**
¼ C milk **(or pwd milk)**
1 tsp. vanilla extract
½ to 2 C confectioner's sugar

Combine brown sugar, butter and milk in a saucepan; bring to a boil over medium heat. Cook and stir for 2 minutes. Remove from the heat; stir in vanilla. Cool to lukewarm. Gradually beat in confectioner's sugar until frosting reaches spreading consistency.

Yeast Breads
Use Hard Wheat

Yeast breads are one of life's most sought after form of nourishment. A warm loaf, fresh from the oven evokes feelings of bliss and contentment. Bread is known as the staff of life – and rightfully so.

Through years of careful advertising, we have been led to believe that bread making is a time-consuming skill accessible only to the most dedicated of artisans. In reality there is nothing further from the truth. Every home baker can produce beautiful bread in her own kitchen with a little practice and a few trade secrets.

My bread making odyssey began when I was a child, learning at the elbow of my mother. Together, we would mix, knead and rise, anxiously awaiting the golden loaves to emerge from the oven. After years of "helping" mom, I thought I was an accomplished baker in my own right. And then I made my first batch of bread on my own. To say that it was a brick would be too kind. After years of helping my mom, my first loaves were about ½" thick and could have easily passed for sand paper.

Utterly despondent, I decided to change my approach. Rather than attempting another batch of wheat bread, I tried my hand at French bread. I put the ingredients together, just as my mother had taught me, making sure that the temperature of the water was just right. I added flour, stirred and finally turned the floury dough onto a kneading board. I kneaded and added flour until the dough became supple under my hand. I set the bread to rise, shaped it into loaves, slid it in the oven and waited with great anticipation. The timer rang, announcing that the judgment had been rendered. The bread was golden perfection! Success.

After many failures, I began adding more and more breads to my repertoire, first white bread then wheat breads, culminating in loaves made from freshly ground wheat.

Water Temperature: The temperature of the water (or any other liquid used for bread making) is critical to the successful rising of bread. If the water is too cool it won't encourage the yeast to grow. Water that is too hot will kill the yeast, producing a hard lump of a loaf. The perfect temperature to activate yeast is 110°. When I first began making bread, I used a candy thermometer to check the temperature of the liquid I was using. The longer I baked, the easier it was to know if the water was the right temp just by dipping my finger in the liquid. Essentially, your liquid has to be hot but not scalding.

Sponging: This is an old-time trick that I learned while trying to perfect baking with freshly ground wheat. Now I use it for all of my yeast breads. It is an effective insurance policy against bread failures and it produces a superior crumb in your bread. A sponge is simple. Combine all of your liquids in whatever you are mixing your bread in, whether it is a mixer or a bowl. Add your sweetener (be it sugar or honey) and your salt. Add any oils or eggs that your recipe calls for. Mix. Sprinkle with the called for amount of yeast. Mix. Add 1 or 2 cups of flour and mix again. Allow the sponge mixture (also known as "proof") to sit for ½ hour to 4 hours (the longer it sits the more "sour" it becomes). The mixture will get all bubbly as the yeast becomes active and begins to work. The benefits of sponging are that you will know that your yeast is active before you make bread and sponging softens the gluten, making for a tight, soft crumb.

NOTE: When grinding wheat berries into flour, you must use the flour within 18 hours or it will become rancid. You can grind extra flour to be used later if it is stored in the freezer until use. Wheat berries last indefinitely, but once the germ is cracked (during grinding) the flour will become rancid if not used quickly.

86

Better than Crispy Cream's Doughnuts

When fall is in the air, warm, wonderful homemade doughnuts are on the menu. A number of years ago, I searched for the "perfect" doughnut recipe and after a few failures, I settled on this method. They are easy to make, light as a feather and perfectly crispy on the outside and fluffy on the inside. The one problem that we have found with making our own doughnuts is that our children shun any doughnut that has been out of the fryer for more than 10 minutes! Spoiled kids!!

1 ¾ hot water (110°)
½ C sugar **(or honey)**
1 tsp. salt
2 eggs **(or 2 T. egg pwd + 6 T water)**
1/3 C shortening **(or butter or lard)**
1 T yeast
2 C sugar **(or honey)**
3 C flour **(or whole (hard) wheat flour)**

Combine the water, sugar, salt, eggs, shortening, yeast and sugar. Allow to "sponge" for ½ hours or until the mixture is bubbly. Stir in the flour. Knead until smooth and elastic.

Put dough in a greased bowl and cover and let rise until double (about 50 to 60 minutes).

Turn dough onto a floured surface. Gently roll dough to ½" thick with a floured rolling pin. Cut with a floured doughnut cutter.

Cover and let rise until double (about 30 to 40 minutes).

Heat oil to 350°. Slide doughnuts into hot oil with a wide spatula. Turn doughnuts as they rise. Fry about 1 minute on each side. Remove from oil. Dip in glaze.

DOUGHNUT GLAZE

1/3 C butter **(or shortening)**
2 C confectioner's sugar
1 ½ tsp. vanilla extract
4 – 6 T hot water

Melt the butter. Stir in the confectioners sugar and vanilla.
Add hot water 1 tablespoon at a time until you reach the
desired consistency.

If you would rather have maple doughnuts, skip the glazing
step and top with this frosting:

MAPLE FROSTING

½ C butter **(or shortening)**
3 C confectioner's sugar
2 tsp. maple flavoring

Cream together the butter and confectioners sugar. Add the
maple.

Beat until spreading consistency.

Carmel Pecan Rolls

When I was growing up, my mom made Cinnamon Rolls every year for Christmas breakfast. It was a tradition that my brother, dad and I looked forward to with great anticipation. When I started a family of my own I was compelled to carry on the Cinnamon roll tradition. Never being able to duplicate my moms perfect rolls, I had to expand my horizons and try new recipes. After stumbling across a variation of this recipe, it became our new favorite Christmas morning treat. Not only are these rolls full of cinnamon and sugar, they have the added benefit of being smothered in caramel and pecans.

2 C milk **(or pwd milk)**
½ C water
½ C sugar **(or honey)**
½ C butter **(or shortening)**
1/3 C cornmeal **(or ground popcorn)**
2 tsp. salt
2 eggs **(or 2 T egg pwd + 6 T water)**
2 T yeast
Allow to "sponge" for ½ hour
7 to 7 ½ C flour **(or whole (hard) wheat flour)**

In a saucepan, combine the milk, water, sugar, butter, cornmeal and salt, bring to a boil, stirring frequently. Set aside to cool to 110°.

When the mixture has cooled, add the eggs. Mix well. Add yeast and allow to "sponge" for ½ hour.

Stir in the flour. Knead until smooth. Transfer to a greased bowl, cover with a towel and let rise until double.

CARMEL TOPPING:
2 C brown sugar **(or 2 T sugar + 8 T molasses)**
½ C butter **(or shortening)**
½ C milk **(or pwd milk)**

Combine the sugar, butter and milk and bring to a boil.

Pour topping into two greased 13x9" pans.

Sprinkle with:
½ to 1 C chopped pecans

Divide dough in half. Roll dough (1/2 at a time) into a rectangle.

Spread with butter.

Sprinkle with:
½ C sugar *{I like to use brown sugar}*
2 tsp. cinnamon

Roll dough into a log and seal edges. Cut into 12 pieces and put into the prepared pan. Let rise until double. Bake at 375° for 20 to 25 minutes. Let cool for 1 minute. Invert onto a serving platter.

Cheese & Onion Loaf

These loaves come out crusty and savory, with a moist, dense crumb. Yum!! This bread is perfect paired with soups, stews or any other dish where a flavorful, savory bread is desired.

1 ½ C hot water *{about 110°}*
2 tsp. sugar **(or honey)**
1 T salt
1 T yeast
4 ¾ C flour **(or whole (hard/red) wheat flour)**
1 tsp. dry mustard
1 C Cheddar Cheese, shredded *{divided}*
2/3 C Cheddar Cheese, cubed **(or home canned cheese)**
1 medium-sized onion, finely chopped and sautéed

Mix together the water, sugar, salt and yeast. Allow to "sponge" for ½ hour. Add the flour and dry mustard. Mix in the cubed cheese and 2/3 C of the shredded cheese and onion.

Knead bread until elastic (about 10 minutes) and transfer into an oiled bowl. Allow to rise in a warm place until double in size (about 2 hours). Form into 1 large loaf (put in bread pan) and allow to rise until almost double.

Preheat the oven to 400°. While oven is heating, brush the top of the loaf with milk and sprinkle 1/3 C cheddar cheese on the top of the loaf.

Bake for 45 minutes to 1 hour or until loaf sounds hollow. Turn loaf onto wire rack (I have to loosen the crunchy cheese from the sides of pan to release loaf) and allow to cool completely.

Crumpets

In the winter, when the stove is bubbling along, I like to make crumpets to accompany our afternoon tea. Crumpets are quite unlike English Muffins, in that they are soft, almost chewy. They have pungent, yeasty flavor that is only enhanced by butter and jam. They are divine warm, just off the griddle, but are equally wonderful toasted or warmed in the oven. It is worth making a double batch, as they freeze well (however, ours never last long enough to make it to the freezer).

Although there are a few more steps in making crumpets than there are in typical yeast breads, they are not difficult. Crumpets are not split, like English Muffins, rather they are buttered on top (there are lots of little holes, allowing the butter to soak into the middle). In France, they call them "Les Eponges" or "Little Sponges" because of the way they absorb copious amounts of rich butter.

1 T yeast
½ tsp. sugar **(or honey)**
2 ¼ C hot water *{110°}*
3 C flour **(or whole (hard) wheat flour)**
¼ tsp. Cream of Tartar
2 tsp. salt
½ tsp. baking soda
½ C milk, lukewarm

In a small bowl, mix together the yeast, sugar and water. Let stand until foamy, 5 to 10 minutes. In a larger bowl, sift together the flour and cream of tartar.

Add the yeast mixture to the flour mixture to make a very thick, but smooth batter, beating with a spoon for 2 minutes. Cover the bowl with plastic wrap and let stand in a warm spot until the batter is doubled in volume, about 1 hour. Add the salt.

Beat the batter for about 1 minute. Cover the bowl and let stand in a warm spot until the batter increases in volume by about one-half, 15 to 20 minutes.

Gently stir the baking soda dissolved in milk into the batter. The batter should not be too stiff or your crumpets will be "blind" – without holes – so it is best to test one before cooking the whole batch.

Heat an ungreased, very clean griddle or frying pan over moderately low heat for about 3 minutes until moderately hot; your palm will feel warm when held 1 ½ inches above the griddle for about 30 seconds. Put a well-buttered crumpet ring on the griddle and heat for 15 seconds. Spoon or pour 1/3 cup of the batter into the ring. The amount of batter will depend on the size of your crumpet ring.

As soon as the batter is poured into the ring, it should begin to form bubbles. If bubbles do not form, add a little more lukewarm water (from the tap is fine), a tablespoon at a time, to the batter in the bowl and try again. If the batter is too thin and runs out under the ring, gently work in a little more flour and try again. As soon as the top surface is set and covered with bubbles, 7 to 8 minutes, the crumpet is ready to flip over. Cook the second, holey side of the crumpet for 2 to 3 minutes, or until pale golden.

Butter the crumpet rings well after each use.

French Bread

This was the first bread that I was allowed to make all by myself. My mom had gotten the recipe from a friend years before, so this bread was affectionately called "Andrea's French Bread". It had few ingredients, required little attention and rewarded the baker with unfailingly perfect results. Give it a try – you too can make wonderful, homemade, "from scratch" bread.

4 C water *{hot – about 110°}*
3 T sugar **(or honey)**
2 T salt
1/3 C olive oil **(or vegetable oil)**
2 T yeast
11 C flour, sifted **(or whole (hard) wheat flour)**

Combine the water, sugar, salt, olive oil and yeast. Allow to sit and "sponge" for ½ hour or more.

Add the flour. I begin with about 6 cups of sifted flour and add more flour from there. The dough should be slightly sticky but not stick to everything sticky. Knead until the dough is smooth (about 5 minutes if using a mixer with a dough hook or about 10 minutes if kneading by hand). Put into a greased bowl. Cover with a clean dish towel. Put in a warm place and let rise until the dough is double in size. Punch down, turn dough over so that the greased side is up, cover with a towel and let rise until almost double.

Punch down, cut into 3 equal pieces and shape into French style loaves. Place on cookies sheets, cut 3 diagonal slits in the tops of the loaves, cover with towel and let rise until double. Bake at 375° for 25 minutes or until bread sounds hollow when you tap on the bottom and the top is nicely browned.

Grandma Rowland's
White Bread

This is the bread that I grew up with (well, this and wheat bread). My mother made a huge batch of this white bread and a huge batch of half white half wheat bread every other week or so. After the bread had cooled, my dad carefully sliced each loaf, slid them into bread bags (we reused old bags) and stowed them in the freezer. Throughout the week, we had wonderful, homemade bread for everything from toast to sandwiches.

1 C milk, heated **(or pwd milk or water)**
1 ¾ C water
2 T yeast
1/3 C vegetable oil
1 egg **(or 1 T egg pwd + 3 T water)**
7 C flour **(or whole (hard) wheat flour)**
1½ tsp. salt
1/3 C honey **(or sugar)**

Heat milk, water, oil, salt and honey (110°). Add beaten egg. Add yeast and allow to sponge for ½ hour. Add flour. Knead until smooth. In greased bowl, let rise until double, covered with a clean tea towel. Punch down. Let rise until almost double.

Form into 3 loaves and put into 9"x5" bread pans. Let rise until double.

Bake at 400° for 25 minutes or until done.

Light Pizza Dough

Pizza is a Friday night institution in our home. Every Friday, our family anxiously awaits hot, savory pizza to enjoy with a family movie. Our favorite pizza is baked in our wood cook stove on perfectly seasoned cast iron. The crust is always perfect and sublimely wonderful!

1 ¾ C warm water
1 T sugar **(or honey)**
1 T yeast
¼ C olive oil **(or vegetable oil)**
1 T salt
5 C flour **(or whole (hard) wheat flour)**

Combine warm (110°) water with sugar, olive oil, salt and yeast. Allow to sponge for ½ hour or longer. Add flour, enough to form a soft dough. Knead until smooth and elastic. Allow to raise (thick crust) or immediately roll onto pizza pans (thin crust). Coat with olive oil and top with favorite pizza toppings. Bake at 425° for 25 minutes or until brown and bubbly.

When baking pizza in a wood cook stove, make sure to use cast iron skillets. The first 15 minutes of baking are done on the stove-top, over medium heat. This bakes the bottom of the crust, ensuring a baked crust by the time the pizza is done. After the first 15 minutes, slide skillets into the oven, placing them on the oven floor (or the lowest shelf). Bake on high heat until the cheese is melted and the pizza top nicely browned.

Oat Dinner Rolls

My dear friend Lady Day served these when we were over for dinner one evening and we were smitten. They are slightly sweet, very hearty and go wonderfully with just about any soup. These have become a family favorite.

2 ½ C water *{divided}*
1 C oats **(or thick cut rolled oats or multi-grain cereal)**
2/3 C brown sugar **(or 2/3 C sugar + 2 ½ T molasses)**
3 T butter **(or shortening or vegetable oil)**
1 ½ tsp. salt
2 T yeast
5 – 6 C flour **(or whole (hard) wheat flour)**

Boil 2 cups of water. Stir in oats and simmer breifly. Add sugar, butter, salt and the rest of the water. Cool to about 110°. Stir in the yeast and allow to sponge. Add the flour, 1 cup at a time. Knead until dough is elastic and not overly sticky.

Put the dough in a lightly greased bowl. Cover with a towel and allow to rise in a warm place until double. Punch down and let rise until almost double. Punch down again. Shape into rolls. Let rise.

Bake for 15 – 20 minutes in a preheated 350° oven.

Sheepherders Bread

This was the very first whole wheat bread that I ever made successfully. I had grown up thinking that you had to add white flour to whole wheat bread to make it work and be even remotely palatable. Boy, was I ever wrong! This bread was originally designed to be baked in a Dutch oven with the lid on over an open fire while tending sheep on the range. I have baked this in a cast iron Dutch oven in my wood cook stove and have been impressed by the results!

6 C hot water *{110°}*
1 C vegetable oil
1 C honey **(or sugar)**
4 tsp. salt
4 T yeast
18 C flour **(or whole (hard) wheat flour)**

Combine the water, oil, honey, salt and yeast. Allow to "sponge" ½ hour or longer. Add the flour.

Knead for 10 minutes (if you're are using a bread kneader, 5 minutes is sufficient). Put the dough into a greased bowl to rise. Cover with a clean towel. Let rise until double. Punch dough down. Let rise until almost double. Punch down again. Form into 4 loaves. Let rise until double. Bake at 400° for 30 minutes or until tests done. Cool on cooling racks.

Soft Giant Pretzels

My family LOVES these! Often, on a blustery winter afternoon, my daughters and I will whip up a batch of these large, soft beauties up to enjoy as an afternoon snack. I think they would be wonderful the next day, but they never make it that long in our house!

2 C 4 T hot water {110°}
6 T brown sugar **(or 6 T sugar + 1 T molasses)**
1 T yeast
6 C flour **(or whole (hard) wheat flour)**

Combine the water, brown sugar and yeast. Allow to "sponge" until bubbly. Add the flour. Knead until the dough is supple, add more flour if necessary.

Turn dough onto a lightly floured surface. Divide dough into 16 balls. Roll each into a 20" rope. Form into a pretzel shape. Place on a cookie sheet.

In a large saucepan, bring 2 quarts of water to a boil with ½ C baking soda (the soda gives the pretzels the characteristic "pretzel" taste and texture). Drop pretzels into the boiling water, two at a time. Boil for 10 – 15 seconds, turning over once. Remove with a slotted spoon; drain on a paper towel.

Place pretzels on greased baking sheets. Bake at 425° for 8 – 10 minutes. After you remove from the oven, spritz or lightly brush with water, sprinkle with salt.

Sweet Roll Dough

This is the recipe that my mother used for all of our dinner rolls as well as the Cinnamon Rolls that we eagerly anticipated every Christmas morning. This is my tried and true, go-to recipe for good old-fashioned dinner rolls.

½ C water *{110°}*
1 ½ C milk **(or water)**
½ C sugar **(or honey)**
2 tsp. salt
½ C butter **(or shortening)**
2 eggs **(or 2 T egg pwd. + 6 T water)**
2 T yeast
7 ½ C flour **(or whole (hard) wheat flour)**

Combine the water, milk, sugar, salt and butter. Heat to about 110°. Pour the mixture into a bowl or mixer and add the eggs and yeast. Mix well. Allow the mixture to "sponge" until bubbly. Add the flour.

Knead for 10 minutes or until smooth and elastic. Turn into a greased bowl. Let rise until double. Punch down. Let rise until almost double. Form into rolls (or make into cinnamon rolls). Allow to rise a third time. Heat oven to 375° and bake for 20 minutes or until done.

Whole Wheat Sandwich Bread

Homemade bread can be a little tricky. Particularly wheat. Often times, although tasty, the bread can be crumbly and course, making it difficult at best to make a decent sandwich. My goal in bread baking is to produce a wonderfully tasting, moist loaf with a fine crumb. You can use the wheat/white flour ratio in this recipe or all whole wheat – either way, you won't be disappointed.

3 C warm water *{110°}*
2 T active dry yeast
1/3 C honey **(or sugar)**
5 C bread flour **(or whole (hard) wheat flour)**
3 T butter, melted **(or shortening, vegetable oil)**
1/3 C honey *{yes, that is honey twice!}* **(sugar)**
1 T salt
3 ½ C whole wheat flour, freshly ground *{hard wheat}*
2 T melted butter *{optional}*

In a large bowl, mix warm water, yeast and 1/3 C honey. Add 5 cups bread flour and stir to combine. Allow to sponge for 30 minutes, or until big and bubbly.

Mix in 3 T melted butter, 1/3 C honey and salt. Stir in 2 cups whole wheat flour. Flour a flat surface and knead with whole wheat flour until the dough is not real sticky – just pulling away from the counter, but still sticky to touch. This may take an additional 2 to 4 cups of flour. Place in a greased bowl, turning once to coat the surface of the dough. Cover with a dishtowel. Let rise in a warm place until double. Punch down and divide into 3 loaves. Place in greased 9"x5" loaf pans, and allow to rise until dough has topped the pans by one inch.

Bake at 350° for 25 to 30 minutes; do not over bake. Lightly brush the tops of loaves with 2 T melted butter. Cool completely.

Yeast Cakes with Hops
(Homemade Yeast)

One thing I really don't want to run out of is yeast. My theory is that if we have a wee bit of yeast left, we can start a new batch and have fresh yeast indefinitely. This yeast can be made without a starter yeast, but if you do have a bit a yeast to begin with, the yeast will work very quickly.

1 C mashed potatoes	2 T sugar
1 C potato water	4 C cornmeal
1 C flour	1 T dried yeast
1 C dried hops	

Boil 3 or 4 peeled potatoes in unsalted water. When done, drain the potatoes and mash them well, but save the potato water to use later. Cover the hop blossoms with water and bring to a boil. Drain off the water and save it, too. If using dried yeast, allow the hops water to cool to 110°, add the yeast and allow to "sponge" or bubble.

Put flour in a pan and slowly stir in the potato water you saved. Be careful not to use too much water. Mix slowly so that the flour won't be lumpy. If the mixture is too liquidy it might be necessary to cook it until it is a thick paste-like dough.

Add mashed potatoes and sugar. Mix well and then slowly add the hop water until you have a medium soft dough. Let rise double. Then punch down and work in enough corn meal to make a stiff dough. Roll out the dough on a board to about 1/2 inch thick and cut into cakes, about 1" x 1". Let the cakes dry, turning them often to make sure they dry evenly. Hang them up in a muslin bag for a few days to make sure they won't mold. After this you can store them in fruit jars or however you wish.

To use, dissolve 1 cake per loaf in liquid prior to adding flour.

Breakfast Fare

I love breakfast. It truly is my favorite meal of the day. Generally, during the week, we survive on run-of-the-mill breakfast options like toast and homemade cereal, but come the weekend, we indulge in our morning favorites. Omelets, pancakes and the classic Farmers Breakfast are among our staple menu items. Occasionally we indulge in crepes or Sir Thomas (an English muffin, split, with Canadian Bacon and an over-easy egg) or some other scrumptious culinary treat.

When we have the time for a leisurely repast, we love nothing more than to fry up some bacon or sausage, make hash browns, toast and eggs and serve it up with a hot pot of tea. When we are pressed for time or are taking breakfast on the road, we opt for Scotch Eggs or a simple breakfast sandwich.

In the words of Father Badger (of the children's "Frances" book series) "There is nothing quite so cheery as an egg breakfast".

Amish Baked Oatmeal

I've always like oatmeal, but this cereal is out of this world! It much more closely resembles a warm, fresh from the oven oatmeal cookie than it does mushy porridge. Just one taste and you'll be hooked.

1 ½ C thick cut oats **(or thick cut or course ground wheat berries)**
½ C brown sugar **(or 1/2 C sugar + 2 T molasses or honey)**
½ C milk **(or pwd milk)**
¼ C melted butter **(or vegetable oil)**
1 egg **(or 1 T egg pwd + 3 T water)**
1 tsp. baking powder
1 tsp. cinnamon
¾ tsp. salt
1 tsp. vanilla extract

Combine all ingredients. Mix well. Spread evenly in a greased 13x9" baking pan. Bake at 350° for 25 to 30 minutes. Spoon into bowls and serve with warmed milk.

Breakfast Pockets

These are the perfect, all-in-one breakfast. They are hearty, filling and just right for an on-the-go morning. They are also popular for breakfast potlucks. If your guys are going out on patrol or the family is heading for a hike up the mountain, these are the energy food you want.

½ C water
¾ C milk **(or water)**
½ C oil **(or rendered bear or other animal fat)**
¼ C sugar **(or honey)**
1 tsp. salt
2 T yeast
1 egg **(or 1 T egg pwd + 3 T water)**
3 – 4 C flour **(or whole (hard) wheat flour)**

Filling
1 lb. pork sausage **(or bacon, sausage link etc.)**
½ C onion **(or chives)**
2 ½ C hash browns, cooked **(or cut/fried potatoes)**
7 eggs
3 T milk
½ tsp. salt
½ tsp. pepper
½ tsp. garlic salt
3 C shredded cheese *{optional}*

Heat water, milk, oil, sugar and salt to 110°. Beat in egg. Add yeast. Allow to sponge for ½ hour. Add flour to form a soft dough. Cover and let rise in warm place.

Cook sausage and onion over medium heat. Add cooked hash browns, eggs, milk and seasonings. Sprinkle with cheese; keep warm.

Divide dough into 14 pieces. Roll into 7 inch circles. Fill circles with filling. Seal edges.

Bake at 350° for 15 to 20 minutes or until golden brown.

Breakfast (or anytime) Potatoes

We are definitely a "potato family". We love them! Not only are these potatoes good with eggs and bacon, they equally wonderful with meatloaf or mock filet mignon. This is also a great way to use up left-over baked potatoes.

4 *{or more}* potatoes
1 large onion, diced
Bacon fat *{or oil – if you must}*
Salt
Pepper

Scrub and prick potatoes and bake them in a 375° oven for 45 minutes or until fork tender.

Dice potatoes (1 inch or so). Melt about 2 T bacon grease in a cast iron skillet and add the onion. Sauté until the onions begin to turn brown. Add the cooked, diced potatoes. Salt and pepper to taste. Cook without stirring for several minutes. Flip with a spatula (add more bacon grease if needed). Add more salt and pepper. Cook until all of the potatoes are crunchy and brown. Add bacon bits and chives, if desired.

Chunky Granola

One of my children's favorite treats is homemade granola mixed into homemade yogurt. This is our favorite granola recipe. It is very easy to adapt to whatever ingredients you have on hand and is especially good with a handful of chocolate chips added at the very end.

6 C. rolled oats **(or rolled wheat berries)**
½ C. pecans **(or other nuts)**
½ C. coconut
½ C. wheat germ *{optional}*
½ C. powdered milk *{optional to increase nutritional value}*
2/3 C. honey **(or sugar or brown sugar)**
2/3 C. oil **(or butter)**
1 tsp. vanilla
1 T. cinnamon (optional)
1-2 C. chocolate chips (optional)

Preheat oven to 350°

Place your rolled oats in an ungreased 9 x 13 pan and bake for 10 minutes. Remove from oven and stir in the nuts, coconut, wheat germ and powdered milk. Add the honey, oil, vanilla and cinnamon. Stir until thoroughly coated. Bake 10 – 15 minutes, stirring every 3 – 5 minutes until uniformly golden. Do not over-bake.

Let cool slightly and add chocolate chips (if desired), stirring well. Let cool completely in pan undisturbed, then break into chunks.

Cream of Wheat

When you are the proud owners of a milk cow, you choose recipes that use a lot of milk. Cream of Wheat is one such recipe! We had this so much when the children were younger that they began to despise Cream of Wheat. Now, it is once again a much anticipated breakfast treat!

4 ½ C milk **(or pwd milk)**
½ tsp. salt
¾ C Farina *{Cream of Wheat}*

Heat milk and salt to almost boiling. Add Farina slowly, stirring constantly. Maintain a low boil. Cook for 10 minutes or until thickened. Serve with brown sugar and milk.

Cream Waffles

Although I have used electric waffle irons for years, our favorite way to make waffles is in antique cast iron waffles makers on our wood cook stove. It takes some getting used to and the irons have to be perfectly seasoned, but the effort is well worth the final results!

2 eggs **(or 2 T egg pwd + 6 T water)**
2 C flour **(or whole (soft) wheat flour)**
4 tsp. baking powder
½ tsp. salt
2 tsp. sugar
1 ¾ C milk **(or water or pwd Milk)**
2 egg yolks, beaten **(or use mixed egg pwd)**
½ C butter, melted **(or vegetable oil)**

Separate the eggs (unless using powdered eggs. Beat the yolks and set aside. Beat the egg whites until stiff and set aside. Stir together the flour, baking powder, salt and sugar. Add the milk, egg yolks and butter. Stir well. Gently fold in the egg whites. Cook according to waffle iron instructions.

Egg and Ham Cakes

This is another favorite way to use up leftovers. You can use whatever leftover meat you have on hand and add wonderful things like chives, onions or mushrooms. This is one recipe that is limited only by your creativity.

1 C ham **(or sausage, bacon, etc.)**
1 C mashed potatoes
1 T parsley, chopped **(or chives)**
1 egg yolk *{optional}*
4 rashers *{pieces}* bacon
4 eggs

Finely dice the ham. Mix together the mashed potato, ham and parsley and add one egg yolk to bind. Divide the mixture into fourths. Shape each fourth into a round flat cake about one inch deep.

Wrap a rasher (piece) of bacon around each cake; fix with a toothpick. Place in an over-proof dish and bake in a moderate oven (350°) for 20 to 25 minutes. Poach or fry the remaining eggs and serve on the top of the cakes.

Eggs in Bread Cases

8 slices of bread
½ C butter, softened **(or bacon fat)**
4 eggs
4 rashers *{pieces}* bacon
salt & pepper

Spread the butter (or bacon fat) on slices of bread. Top each with a second slice of bread, from which an inner circle has been cut with a biscuit cutter. Spread butter on the top slice and break an egg into each circle. Sprinkle with salt and pepper. Place a rasher (piece) of bacon, rolled, on top of the eggs. Bake in a hot oven (400°) for seven minutes or until the egg is set.

Frittata

When I was a girl, my dad made the most wonderful omelets in the world. They were light and fluffy, packed with all kinds of good things. When I grew up and went out into the world, I happened to order an omelet in a restaurant, and much to my great surprise and consternation, they brought a flat, folded thing that bared no resemblance to the omelets of my youth. Years later, I came to find that the omelets my father had made were, in fact, not omelets, but frittatas. With our overabundance of eggs, frittatas are on our regular menu. Leftover bacon, sausage and ham are common features, as are onions, green peppers and cheese. Whatever we happen to have leftover in the fridge ends up in the skillet. I love making these on the wood cook stove best, but they work well in a regular oven too.

Melt a tablespoon (or so) of butter in a cast iron skillet.

Beat eggs (I use 14 eggs for a 10" skillet) with a bit of milk. Add diced meat, vegetables and cheese. Stir well. Pour into the heated skillet.

Cook (without stirring) over medium low heat until the eggs begin to set around the edges of the skillet. Once the eggs have set around the edges, put the skillet into a medium oven (350°) and cook until the eggs are set in the middle (eggs don't jiggle when you shake the skillet).

The frittata will be huge and puffy but will deflate as it cools. Slice and serve with toast and potatoes.

Grape Nuts

I detest Grape Nuts. When I was a little girl, my eyes proved bigger than my stomach and I poured myself a heaping bowl of Grape Nuts cereal. The moment I took a bite, I knew the error of my way. I hated it. But, by then, it was too late, my dad had walked into the kitchen. He saw me, pulled up to the kitchen table with a bowl roughly the size of a stock tank, full of cereal. And he expected me to eat it. All of it. Every bite was sheer torture, the cereal rolling around in my mouth like shards of sharpened gravel. But, under the watchful eye of my father, I ate that cereal. I ate it for breakfast. I ate it for lunch. I ate it for dinner – soggy milk and all. After that fateful day, I have never touched another bowl of Grape Nuts cereal. However, I came across this recipe, and, in honor of the father whom I love, I have added it to my collection. I do hope you enjoy Grape Nuts!

3 C. whole wheat flour
½ C. wheat germ **(or omit wheat germ and add ½ C. flour)**
1 C. brown sugar **(or 1 C sugar + 4 T molasses)**
2 C. buttermilk or sour milk **(or 2 C (pwd) milk + 2 T lemon juice or vinegar)**
1 tsp. baking soda
pinch salt

Combine ingredients in a large mixing bowl, beat until smooth.

Spread the dough on 2 large, greased cookie sheets. Bake at 350° for 25 – 30- minutes. Crumble by one of these methods:

1. While still warm, break into chunks and grate on a slaw cutter, or whirl briefly in a blender, about a cupful at a time.
2. Allow to cool thoroughly, then put through a fine grinder using the coarse plate.

Crisp in a 250° oven for 20 – 30 minutes. Store in an airtight container. Eat with milk. No added sugar needed.

German Pancake

When I first made this recipe, my family hated it! I baked it in a glass baking pan and served it smothered in canned apples topped with whipped cream. It was overpoweringly sweet and the consistency was rather slimy. Never one to give up on a perfectly good recipe, I tried it again. This time I used a cast iron skillet and rather than drowning it in toppings, I simply served it with maple syrup. It was an immediate success! The cast iron made the crust slightly crunchy, offsetting the chewy middle and the maple syrup highlighted the delicate flavor. It has become our Sunday morning standby.

8 Inch Skillet	16 Inch Skillet
¼ C butter, cubed	¾ C butter, cubed
1 C milk	3 C milk
4 eggs	12 eggs
½ tsp. vanilla ext.	1 ½ tsp. vanilla ext.
1 C flour	3 C flour
2 T sugar	6 T sugar

Place butter in a cast iron skillet; place pan in a 425° oven for 2 minutes or until better melts and pan is very hot. Combine milk, eggs and vanilla in a bowl. Stir in flour and sugar; beat until smooth. Pour into hot pan. Bake for 18-20 minutes or until puffed and brown on top.

Serve with warm syrup, dusted with confectioner sugar or fresh berries and whipped cream.

Pancakes

When I was growing up, my Dad was the master of the pancakes. I remember watching him drop water on the griddle to see if it was hot enough and watching the water as it danced to the edge. My Dad's pancakes were affectionately known as "gut-bombs" and were always perfect. They had a certain stick-to-your-ribs quality that was never to be duplicated simply because Dad didn't follow a recipe.

From time to time, my brother and I would go fishing before breakfast and bring home a bounty of Rainbow Trout. My Mom was more than happy to fry up the fish as long as we brought them to her perfectly cleaned. She would dredge them in flour, put them in a hot frying pan with a little oil, and cook them to perfection. While I loved fresh trout, what I remember most is my Dad eating them. He would cook up a batch of pancakes, fry an egg, lay it on top of the pancake, put the trout on top of the egg (breaking the yolk in the process) and then put syrup over the whole thing – oh, and let not forget – lots of pepper! I'm not sure, but I think, perhaps, that Dad's breakfast habits may have scarred me for life.

4 C. flour **(or whole (soft) wheat flour)**
8 tsp. baking powder
2 tsp. salt
4 C. milk **(or pwd Milk)**
4 T. oil
4 large eggs, beaten **(or 4 T egg pwd + 12 T water)**

Mix the dry ingredients in one bowl and the wet ingredients in another bowl. Stir them together until everything is moistened, leaving a few lumps. Pour onto hot griddle (water skips across griddle when sprinkled on) and cook on one side until the pancakes are full of "holes". Flip and cook until done.

Sausage Gravy & Biscuits

I didn't grow up eating biscuits and gravy. It was just not something that was in our repertoire of recipes. Anytime I saw biscuits and gravy being served at a restaurant it always looked so good that I knew that one day, I would have to give it a try myself. After I learned how to make hamburger gravy (by watching a friend) I knew the time had come to try my hand at sausage gravy. This is the recipe that I developed.

1 lb. bulk sausage **(or ground pork, turkey, rabbit ect.)**
½ C. butter **(or bacon grease)**
½ C. flour **(or whole (soft) wheat flour)**
4 – 5 C. milk **(or evaporated milk or pwd milk)**
Salt & Pepper to taste
1 recipe biscuits

In a large cast iron skillet over medium heat, brown the sausage until no longer pink. Do not drain. Add 1 cube (1/2 C) of butter. Allow butter to melt. Sprinkle the flour over the sausage/butter mixture and stir well (the butter and flour will have a very pasty consistency). Stir in 3 cups of milk, making sure there are no lumps (from the flour). Stir occasionally as the gravy thickens. Add more milk, according to the thickness of gravy you desire. Season liberally with salt and pepper. Serve over split, buttered biscuits.

Scotch Eggs

We do love eggs and when we discovered this recipe, we knew we were on to something. They are quite tasty warm but even better cold. Frequently, we will make them a day in advance of a family hike and take them on the road with us. They are full of protein and very filling, providing us with the perfect hiking meal. If you choose to eat them warm, they are traditionally served on a bed of lettuce with a dollop of mustard on the side.

1 quart of oil *{for frying}*
4 eggs
2 pounds pork sausage
4 C dried bread crumbs, seasoned
1 C flour
4 eggs, beaten

Preheat your oven to 350°. Heat oil in skillet to 375°. Place the eggs in a saucepan and cover with water. Bring to a boil. Cover, remove from heat and let eggs sit in hot water for 10 to 12 minutes. Remove from water, cool and peel.

Flatten the sausage and make a patty to surround each egg. Wrap each boiled egg in a sausage patty. Very lightly flour the sausage wrapped egg and coat with the beaten eggs. Roll in bread crumbs to cover evenly.

Deep fry (or pan fry while making sure each side is well cooked). Bake in the preheated oven for 10 minutes.

Eat warm, with mustard or chill and serve cold.

Scotch Scrapple

Although I present this recipe as it was written, I prefer to use leftovers. It is a wonderful use of resources, using up bits and pieces. This recipe is one that my Great-Grandmother made regularly when my dad was a little boy.

1 C oatmeal
1 ¼ C water
½ tsp. salt
½ C pork sausage meat **(or other leftover meat bits)**

Bring water and salt to a boil. Add the oatmeal to the boiling, salted water. Cook for 20 minutes or until thick, stirring constantly to prevent sticking.

Stir in the crumbled sausage meat and mix thoroughly. Season to taste. Pour into a narrow dish (or cleaned out coffee can) and leave overnight. Cut into slices, dip the slices in flour and fry in a little fat until brown on both sides.

Swedish Pancakes (Crepes)

My mother used to make these for special occasions and the occasional brunch. They were favorites when we were children and remain favorites with my children today.

1 C milk **(or pwd milk)**
2 T butter **(or vegetable oil)**
2 eggs **(or 2 T egg pwd + 6 T water)**
½ C flour **(or whole (soft) wheat flour)**
1 tsp. baking powder
½ tsp. salt

Heat the milk and butter in a saucepan over medium heat. Beat in the eggs, flour, baking powder and salt.

Pour batter onto a greased, low-sided skillet. Tip skillet to cover with batter. Cook over medium heat, turning once.

Soup

We love nothing better than a pot of soup on a cold winter's day. It is filling and comforting and full of goodness.

Generally, I plan the big meal of the week for Saturday and then schedule a soup, using the leftovers for Sunday. I have found that soup is a perfect Sunday dish. It is easily extended if extra guests happen to grace your table, and is perfectly complimented by a hearty loaf of homemade bread. Soup is a no-fuss, humble addition to your Sunday dinner table.

When I was growing up, my favorite soup chef was my Grandma Omie. She always started with leftovers from her refrigerator and added a little of this and a little of that until it was just right. Many afternoons I found myself on her doorstep, breathing in the heady aroma of her rich homemade soups. That scent always smelled like home, encompassing me with its warm goodness. Now that my Grandmother is gone, I love sharing her heritage and her story as I add a little of this and a little of that to my well-worn soup pot. My Grandmother's memory is alive in the hearts of my children as they partake of their inheritance – her soup.

Beef Cabbage Soup

This is our hands-down favorite winter soup. Cabbage keeps well in the cellar and is a staple of many winter-time recipes. This soup is flavorful and hearty – a real crowd pleaser when served with fresh, warm bread.

1 pound ground beef **(or venison, rabbit etc.)**
½ head cabbage, shredded
2 ribs celery, sliced **(or celerac)**
1 small bell pepper, cut into small pieces **(or dried peppers)**
1 medium diced onion **(or dried onions)**
2 C cooked kidney beans **(or (1) 16oz. can)**
2 C diced canned tomatoes **(or fresh)**
4 C water
2 T beef bouillon **(or pwd soup base)**
¼ tsp. garlic powder **(or 3 cloves fresh garlic)**
salt and pepper to taste

Brown ground beef and drain. Add remaining ingredients to the ground beef. Add more water to achieve desired consistency. Bring to a boil and simmer for at least one hour or until the veggies are tender.

Alternative Method
Left-over, cooked meat works well in this recipe. Often, I will use roast meat from a previous meal. Canned meat (either venison or beef) also works well.

For a quick meal, I can my beans in the pressure canner so they are ready to add to the soup without having to sit overnight. During the fall, I can tomatoes with onions and green peppers and add that to the soup rather than the individual ingredients. I make sure to add the liquid that the veggies have been canned in to add extra flavor.

Brown Onion Soup

Although humble, onion soup has a rich heritage. It is full flavored and satisfying and makes the most of but a few ingredients.

4 large onions
1 T sugar
Pepper
Salt
4 T butter **(or bacon grease)**
2 ½ pints beef stock or water **(or the two combined)**
French bread
Butter
Parmesan cheese, freshly grated **(or mozzarella)**

Peel and slice onions thinly. Separate the rings. Heat butter in a large saucepan with a little sugar; add the onion rings and cook them very, very gently over low heat, stirring constantly with a wooden spoon, until the rings are an even golden brown. Add beef stock gradually, stirring constantly until the soup begins to boil.   Then lower the heat; cover pan and simmer gently for 30 minutes. Just before serving, check and adjust the seasoning. Serve in heated soup tureen or in individual serving bowls, each one containing toasted, buttered rounds of French bread heaped with grated mozzarella cheese.

Brown onion soup may also be served "gratinee". When ready to serve, place thin round of toasted and buttered bread in a casserole; cover with freshly grated mozzarella cheese and pour onion soup over the toast. Sprinkle top with parmesan cheese and place casserole under grill or in hot oven until golden.

Nettle Broth

Nettles are extraordinarily high in iron and are one of the first greens of the year. This broth could prove to be the perfect nutritional supplement after a long, hard winter.

Chicken stock
Nettles
Barely
Pepper
Salt

Gather nettles and wash well and chop very finely (use gloves or the nettles will sting and itch for hours). Have some good stock in which you have cooked a sufficient quantity of pearl barely. Add chopped nettles, simmer till tender and season to taste.

Potato Soup

When we first moved into our "shouse", our meals consisted of very meager rations. This potato soup was a very constant companion. It is easily made with very few ingredients yet is very flavorful. You can make it as plain or as fancy as you want. It never fails to satisfy.

6 strips bacon, diced *{optional}* or *(bacon bits or canned bacon)*
1 qt. chicken broth *(or 1 qt. water with 1 ½ T soup base/bouillon)*
3 C cubed potatoes, peeled *(or 2 C dehydrated potato cubes)*
1 small carrot, grated *{optional}*
½ C onion, chopped *(or 1/4 C. dehydrated onions)*
½ tsp. celery seed *{optional}*
½ tsp. salt
½ tsp. pepper
3 T. flour *(or whole wheat flour or cornstarch)*
3 C. milk *(or pwd milk)*
2 C. cheddar cheese, cubed *{optional}* *(or canned cheese)*

In a large saucepan, cook bacon over medium heat until crisp. Using a slotted spoon, remove to paper towels; drain. Add the broth, vegetables and seasonings. Bring to a boil. Reduce heat; cover and simmer for 15 minutes or until potatoes are tender.

Combine the flour and milk until smooth; add to soup. Bring to a boil; cook and stir for 2 minutes. Add cheese; stir until cheese is melted and the soup is heated through.

Split Pea Soup

I love a warm bowl of Slit Pea soup. I have loved it since I was a little girl and was served my first bowl at an elderly friends home. This soup is very versatile – you can make it with or without meat, making is wonderfully cost effective.

1 lb. kielbasa or ham, cubed **(or canned ham chunks)**
1 lb. dried split peas **(or black-eyed peas)**
6 C water
1 C carrots, chopped *{optional}*
1 C celery, chopped *{optional}*
1 tsp. salt
½ tsp. pepper
2 bay leaves

Put the kielbasa or ham in a Dutch oven or large pot; add the remaining ingredients. Bring to a boil. Reduce heat; cover and simmer for 1 ¼ to 1 ½ hours or until peas are tender. Discard bay leaves.

Zesty Minestrone

Oh this is yummy! I love to make a big pot of soup on Sunday before we go to church so that we are welcomed by the spicy aroma of good food when we walk in the door after services. Add a loaf of French bread and this is the perfect Sunday afternoon dinner.

1 lb. Italian sausage, diced *(or canned bulk Italian sausage)*
2 tsp. oil
1 onion, chopped *(or 1/4 C dehydrated onions)*
1 green pepper, chopped *(or dehydrated pepper or canned peppers)*
3 cloves garlic, chopped *(or garlic powder)*
2 16-oz. cans whole tomatoes *(or 2 quarts home-canned)*
2 potatoes, chopped *(or dehydrated potato cubes)*
¼ c. fresh parsley, chopped
2 tsp. dried oregano
1 tsp. dried basil
½ tsp. red pepper flakes
salt and pepper to taste
1 qt. beef broth *(or 4 C water & 2 T beef soup base/bouillon)*
2 16 oz. cans kidney beans *(or 1 quart home-canned)*
1 C elbow macaroni, uncooked *(or ¼ recipe homemade pasta cut into 1" pieces)*

Sauté sausage in oil in a large saucepan; drain. Add onion, green pepper and garlic; cook 5 minutes. Pour in tomatoes, potatoes, spices and broth; bring to a boil. Reduce heat; simmer 30 minutes. Stir in beans and pasta; simmer an additional 20 minutes.

Main Dishes

These are the recipes that have shaped our family, our home. They are full of comfort and history and have become part of our heritage.

Most of our main dishes are extraordinarily simple, using nothing but ingredients found in most larders and pantries. We are not fancy folk, but we truly love good food. Although our recipes would never grace the fine china of a five star restaurant, they are quite comfortable filling humble stomachs and filling our cozy kitchen with the undeniable, wafting scent of home.

Beans with Bacon

Beans and bacon just seem to go together, don't they? This recipe is simple yet wonderfully filling and tasty.

2 ½ C dried navy beans
9 C water
1 pound bacon **(or canned bacon bits)**
2 onions, chopped
2 stalks celery, chopped *{optional}*
4 tsp. chicken bouillon **(or pwd soup base)**
1 bay leaf
1/3 tsp. salt
¼ tsp. pepper
1/3 tsp. cloves *{I don't add the cloves}*
1 can diced tomatoes **(or home canned)**
4 C water

Boil the beans in 9 cups of water and then let sit for one hour. Drain and set aside.

Cook the bacon to your desired texture (it can be soft or crisp, your choice). Drain, reserving ¼ cup bacon grease. Coarsely chop the bacon.

Add the onions and celery to the reserved grease and bacon and sauté until soft – do not drain. Add the chicken bouillon (or soup base), 4 cups water, beans, bay leaf, salt, pepper and cloves (if using) and simmer for 2 hours.

Stir in the tomatoes with their juice.

Serve with homemade bread or freshly baked cornbread.

Chicken Fried Steak

Every Once in a while we indulge in some good, old-fashioned, down home comfort food. Chicken Fried Steak is just such an indulgence. It really is quite simple to make and relatively quick. It is perfect if you need a full-out Sunday dinner on short notice.

Cube Steak
2 eggs **(or 2 T egg pwd. + 6 T water)**
1 ½ C milk **(or pwd milk)**
3 C flour
1 ½ tsp. salt **(or seasoning salt)**
½ tsp. pepper
1 tsp paprika
½ to ¾ C oil *{depending on the size of your skillet}*

Tenderize (with a hammer or tenderizer) cube steaks (as many as you want) to ½ inch thick.

Beat the eggs and milk together. In another bowl, mix together the flour, salt, pepper and paprika. Using tongs (or your fingers), dip the steaks in the egg mixture and then dredge steaks in the flour mixture. Dip the steaks in the egg mixture (again!) and dredge in the flour mixture (again!).

Heat the oil in a skillet on medium/high heat.

After you have dredged all of your steaks and the oil is hot, put steaks in oil (make sure they do not brown too fast – or turn the oil down). Fry for about 5 minutes then turn over. I always use two spatulas to turn the steaks, one to flip and the other to catch and ease the steaks into the oil. Cook for another 5 minutes. I will often turn the steaks another time or two to keep cooking them and making sure they are browned nicely on both sides. Remove to a serving platter. Serve with mashed potatoes and gravy.

Chicken Fajitas

These fajitas are a tasty, simple meal. I generally double the recipe because it is never enough to feed our hungry hoards.

4 T canola oil
2 T lemon juice
1 ½ tsp. seasoned salt
1 ½ tsp. dried oregano
1 ½ tsp. ground cumin
1 tsp. garlic powder
½ tsp. chili powder
½ tsp. paprika
½ tsp. crushed red pepper flakes {optional}
1 ½ pounds boneless, skinless chicken breast
2 T oil
1 medium sweet red pepper, julienned
1 medium green pepper, julienned
1 large onion, cut into rings

Combine the oil, lemon juice, salt, oregano, cumin, garlic, chili powder, paprika and crushed red pepper flakes in a sealable bag or bowl. Add the chicken breast, cut into thin strips. Turn to coat. Seal. Refrigerate for 1 to 4 hours.

In a large skillet, sauté in oil, red pepper, green pepper and onion. Cook until crisp tender. Remove from skillet and keep warm.

Discard marinade. In the same skillet, cook chicken over medium-high heat for 5-6 minutes or until no longer pink.

Return pepper mixture to pan; heat through.

Spoon filling down the center of tortillas; fold in half. Serve with cheese, taco sauce, salsa, guacamole or sour cream.

Chicken Strips

This is one of those dishes that we rarely have but it is often requested. When our children were smaller, one or more of them would request these chicken strips for their special birthday dinner. They are quick and tasty – so much better than those horrid, frozen store-bought concoctions!

1 C mayonnaise
2 tsp. onions {dried, minced}
2 tsp. dried mustard powder
1 C saltine crackers, crushed
2 lbs. chicken breast

Preheat oven to 425°

In a bowl, combine mayonnaise, onion and mustard. In another bowl, fill with crushed crackers. Cut chicken lengthwise into ¼ inch strips. Dip strips into mayonnaise mixture, then into the crackers. Place in a single layer on a large greased baking sheet. Bake at for 15 to 18 minutes or until juices run clear. (I like to bake for up to 20 minutes – we like our chicken strips to be crunchy).

Chicken Cashew Stir-Fry

Especially during the summer, when the vegetables are ripe in the garden, we love nothing better than a huge skillet full of crisp/tender stir fry. This is an easily adaptable recipe that we go to time after time.

1 ½ lbs. whole chicken breast
2 medium green peppers
4 green onions, julienned
Broccoli
Cauliflower
Whatever veggies are in season
1 C cashews
9 T soy sauce
3 T cornstarch
1 T sugar
1½ tsp. salt
1½ tsp. crushed red pepper
2 T cooking oil

Cut chicken & green peppers into 1" pieces – set aside. In a small bowl blend soy sauce and cornstarch, stir in sugar, salt and red pepper – set aside. Preheat wok or large skillet – add oil. Stir fry green peppers & onions (and any other veggies) 2 minutes (whatever looks right to you) and remove. Stir fry cashews 1-2 minutes (be careful, nuts burn pretty easily) and remove. You may need more oil. Add ½ of the chicken and stir fry 2 minutes (or til it looks good to you – browned) and remove. Stir fry the remaining chicken. Add all the chicken and soy mixture until thick. Add veggies and nuts. Cover and cook 1 minute. Serve over rice.

*The sauce can get thick quickly so you may have to add a little water.

Chicken (or Tuna or Turkey) Turnovers

These are a wonderful way to used canned chicken or leftover turkey meat. They are perfect for lunch, served with a clear-broth soup, or for late afternoon tea.

1 C. tuna or diced, cooked chicken or turkey **(or canned)**
1 C. shredded cheese **(or canned)**
¼ C. chopped celery **(or peppers, pickles)**
1 tsp. chives
Mayonnaise to moisten
Salt and pepper
1 recipe Angel biscuit dough

Combine the tuna, cheese, celery, chives and mayonnaise. Add salt and pepper to taste. Roll biscuit dough 1/8 to 1/4 " thick and cut into 4" rounds or squares. Place about 2 ½ T. filling on each; fold over and seal. Brush tops with melted butter (optional). Bake at 400° for 15 minutes. Serve with soup and salad.

Chinese Savory Beef

Although called "Chinese Savory Beef" more often than not, it is "Chinese Savory Venison" in our home. I can chunks of venison specifically for this recipe. When using canned meat, you just have to cook until everything is heated through, making this truly fast food.

2 T oil or minced fat from beef
2 lbs. beef, cut in 1 1/2 " squares *{may use tough meat or canned meat}*
1 onion, chopped **(or dried)**
2 cloves garlic, crushed **(or dried, canned or fresh)**
1 C soy sauce
1/8 tsp. pepper
6 C water

In a heavy Dutch oven, heat the oil. Add the beef and quickly fry until brown (I don't do this step if I am using canned meat). Add and quick-fry for a few minutes, the onions and garlic. Add soy sauce, pepper and water.

Bring to a boil. Reduce heat, cover and simmer for 3 hours. (I simmer mine for about 1 hour when the meat has been canned). Add more liquid if needed. Just before serving thicken with a small amount of cornstarch stirred into water. Serve over rice or noodles.

Colcannon

We love this Irish dish, which is perfect for using up leftovers. The combination of creamy potatoes, butter and cabbage is wonderful – very homey and comforting. Below is the original recipe, however, we always just mix together leftovers and love the results!

3 pounds potatoes, scrubbed **(or leftover mashed potatoes)**
2 cubes butter
1 ¼ C hot milk
black pepper
1 head cabbage, cored and finely chopped **(or leftover cabbage)**
1 pound *{or piece}* of ham or bacon **(or leftover meat)**
4 Scallions, finely chopped

Boil potatoes as for mashed potatoes. Drain and mash thoroughly to remove all of the lumps. Add 1 stick of butter, in pieces. Gradually add hot milk, stirring all the time. Season with a few grinds of black pepper.

Boil the cabbage in unsalted water until it turns a dark color. Add 2 T. of butter to tenderize it. Cover with a lid for 2 minutes. Drain thoroughly before returning it to the pot. Chop it into small pieces.

Put the ham in a large saucepan and cover with water. Bring to a boil and simmer for 45 minutes, until tender. Drain. Remove any fat and chop ham into small pieces.

Add cabbage, scallions and ham to the potatoes, stirring them gently. Serve in individual soup plates. Make an indentation on the top and put 1 tablespoon of butter into each indentation.

Crusty Mexican Bean Bake

I love the combination of flavors in this tried and true favorite. Most often I will make the recipe as it is written, however, I love to make the filling and wrap it in warmed tortillas and serve with rice. This is another recipe that takes well to tweaking!

Crust:
½ C. flour **(or whole (soft) wheat flour)**
½ tsp. salt
½ tsp. baking powder
2 T. shortening or butter **(or lard, bacon grease)**
½ C. sour cream or yogurt *{increase flour by 2 T. if using yogurt}*
(or thick sweet cream)
1 egg, beaten **(or 1 T egg pwd + 3 T water)**

Stir ingredients together. The batter may be slightly lumpy. Spread thinly with the back of a spoon on the bottom and sides of a shallow, greased 2-qt. casserole. Set aside.

Filling:
¾ lb. ground beef **(or other ground meat)**
½ C. chopped onion **(or dehydrated onion)**
1 tsp. salt
2 tsp. chili powder
½ tsp. Tabasco sauce **(or other hot pepper sauce)**
2 C. undrained cooked kidney beans *{I like to use home-canned}*
¾ C. (6 oz.) tomato paste

Brown the hamburger in a skillet along with the onion. Add remaining ingredients and heat through. Spoon the filling into the crust and bake at 350° for 30 minutes.

Crusty Pup Corn Dogs

We don't indulge in fried foods often, but this recipe is one of our few exceptions! This is the best homemade corn dog recipe ever. These, along with onion rings, will prove to be real crowd pleasers.

1 C cornmeal **(or ground popcorn)**
1 ¾ C flour **(or whole (soft) wheat flour)**
2 tsp. baking powder
2 tsp. salt
1 egg **(or 1 T egg pwd + 3 T water)**
1/3 C sugar *{shaken off}* **(or honey)**
milk
hot dogs *{8}*
wooden skewers

Combine cornmeal, flour, baking powder, salt, egg and sugar. Add milk until batter has a pancake type consistency. Dry off the hot dogs with a paper towel. Coat with flour and put skewer through hot dog.

Heat oil to 370°

Dip hot dogs in batter to coat evenly. Fry until golden (about 2 ½ minutes).

*Too much milk and the batter won't stay on the hot dogs. Too little milk and your batter will crack when fried.

Double Crust Barbeque Pie

This recipe came from my friend, Lady Day. She and I have swapped recipes for so long that it is hard to remember where they originated. Although not a fancy meal, this is perfect for a busy evening or makes a hearty lunch.

1 recipe "Angle Biscuits"

2 lbs. hamburger
1 medium onion, chopped **(or dehydrated onions)**
Barbeque sauce

Brown and drain the hamburger. Add the onion and barbeque sauce (use enough sauce to make the meat very moist).

Roll out ½ of the biscuit dough on a cookie sheet. Spoon the meat filling onto the dough.

Cover generously with:
Grated cheddar cheese **(or canned)**

Roll out the other half of the biscuit dough and cover the meat. Seal edges.

Bake at 350° until well browned.

Enchiladas

These are simple, good and hearty enchiladas. Although we don't eat a lot of "Mexican" food, we find these to just hit the spot.

¾ lb. ground beef
1 onion, chopped **(or dehydrated onion)**
2 C. refried beans
1 tsp. salt
1/8 tsp. garlic powder
12 tortillas
2 C. shredded cheese **(or canned)**

1 recipe Chili-Tomato Sauce

Brown hamburger in skillet with onion. Drain fat. Stir in refried beans, salt and garlic powder.

Heat chili-tomato sauce and pour about ½ into an ungreased, shallow 3 qt. baking dish. Place about 1/3 C. beef-bean filling on each tortilla and roll to close. Place, flap side down in the sauce in the bottom of the baking dish. Pour remaining sauce evenly over the tortillas. Cover with shredded cheese. Bake, uncovered at 350° for 15-20 minutes, or until thoroughly heated through.

Fettuccine Alfredo

This simple pasta and sauce is nothing short of spectacular. When making this wonderful sauce we will accept nothing less than homemade pasta – anything less just isn't fitting. Served alongside French bread and salad, it is simply divine. Oh, and making your own Parmesan cheese only intensifies the perfection.

One batch homemade Fettuccine

For the Sauce:
½ C butter
2/3 C heavy cream
1 ¼ C grated Parmesan cheese
¼ tsp. salt
dash of pepper

Heat the butter and the cream in a saucepan until butter is melted. Remove from the heat. Add 1 cup Parmesan cheese, salt and pepper. Stir until the sauce is blended and fairly smooth.

Add to drained noodles and toss until they are well coated. Sprinkle with remaining cheese.

Greek Chicken Kabobs

In the summer, we love nothing more than a light meal cooked on the barbeque. To us, this is the taste of summer!

In small bowl, mix together:
½ C olive oil
¼ C lemon juice
2 cloves garlic, minced **(or dehydrated garlic or canned)**
2 T Dijon mustard
2 T dried oregano
1 tsp. dried thyme
1 tsp. black pepper
salt

In a large sealable bag or bowl place:
1 red bell pepper, cut into 2" pieces
1 green bell pepper, cut into 2" pieces
1 large sweet onion, peeled and cut into wedges
2 pounds skinless, boneless chicken breast halves, cut into cubes

Add marinade to bowl or bag. Mix to coat and seal bowl or bag. Refrigerate 4 to 24 hours.

Discard marinade and thread the meat and vegetables onto skewers, leaving a small space between each item.

Lightly oil the grill grate. Grill skewers for 10 minutes, turning as needed or until meat is cooked through and vegetables are tender.

*In the winter, we will marinade the meat and veggies, skip the skewers and stir fry this mixture in a skillet and serve it over a bed of rice. Yum!

Hare Haselet

*If you are looking for a great rabbit or hare recipe, this is for you.
Simple yet satisfying.*

1 hare (or rabbit)
½ lb. bacon
¼ small loaf bread, cubed
1 Onion
1 C flour
Dried Herbs
Pepper
Salt

Cut the meat off the bones and mince. Add bread, bacon, onion,
all minced, flour and season with herbs, pepper and salt. Mix
well together and form into two big rolls. Put into a greased
dish with a slice of bacon on each roll and cover. Bake in a
moderate (350°) oven for two hours.

Hoppin' John

We tried this recipe on a whim and it proved to become a family favorite! It is so wonderful, in fact, that we began canning bacon specifically to we could use it in this recipe. Our preferred Cajun seasoning is Cajun's Choice, which we stock in 5 gallon buckets.

1/3 pound of bacon, or 1 diced ham hock plus 2 T oil **(or canned bacon or ham)**
1 celery stalk, diced *{optional}*
1 small onion, diced **(or dehydrated onion)**
1 small green pepper, diced **(or dehydrated peppers)**
2 garlic cloves *{optional}*
2 C black-eyed peas
1 bay leaf
2 tsp. dried thyme
1 heaping tsp. Cajun seasoning
Salt

If you are using bacon, cut it into small pieces and cook it slowly in a medium pot over medium-low heat. If you are using a ham hock, heat the oil in the pot and add the diced ham hock. Once the bacon is crispy (or the oil is hot), increase the heat to medium-high and add the celery, onion and green pepper and sauté until they begin to brown, about 4-5 minutes. Add the garlic, stir well and cook for another 1-2 minutes.

Add the black-eyed peas, bay leaf, thyme, Cajun seasoning and salt and enough water to cover. Add water as you cook until you get the consistency you desire. Simmer for 1 to 2 hours or until the peas become soft.

Serve Hoppin' John in a bowl over rice. We like to add a lot of water so that the Hoppin' John is soupy rather than thick – we like lots of "sauce".

Joe's Special (Enola Gay Version)

When I was fresh out of high school, I moved to Seattle to live the "high life". During an excursion to a restaurant that I considered "upper class", I came across a menu item called "Joe's Special". It was basically beef, sautéed with spinach and onions with eggs poured over the top and scrambled. I didn't order it because I detested cooked spinach, however, I did come home and come up with a recipe all my own!

1 lb. ground beef **(or ground venison, etc.)**
1 onion, chopped **(or dehydrated onion)**
¼ C. butter **(or bacon grease)**
2 C. broccoli, chopped in bite sizes
14 eggs, beaten

In a large skillet, brown hamburger – drain. Add butter and onion, and sauté. Add chopped broccoli and beaten eggs. Stir well and cover. Cook on medium, stirring frequently, until broccoli is tender and eggs are set. Serve with toast or biscuits.

Macaroni & Cheese

I'm sure that everyone has their favorite mac & cheese recipe, and this is mine. I was informed by a San Francisco city boy that this was honest-to-goodness "soul food". In my ignorance, I asked what on earth "Soul Food" was – his reply was less than satisfactory, so I guess I'll just have to guess!

2 16oz. pkg. elbow macaroni **(or 1" slices of homemade noodles)**
8 C cheddar cheese, grated & divided **(or home canned cheese)**
3 T butter **(or bacon fat, lard, oil, shortening)**
3 T flour
¾ tsp. mustard powder
1 T garlic powder
1 ½ C. milk **(or pwd milk)**
1 tsp. salt

Cook macaroni according to package directions or make your own noodles and cut 1" long. Grate cheese and set 2 cups aside to sprinkle on the top of the macaroni.

In a medium saucepan, melt butter. Add flour and cook and stir until there are no lumps. Add mustard powder, garlic powder and salt. Whisk in milk, making sure to whisk out any lumps. Cook over medium heat, stirring frequently as the mixture thickens. After the sauce has thickened, add 6 cups grated cheddar cheese and stir until the cheese has melted.

Pour your prepared noodles into a 10"x15" pan. Pour cheese sauce over the noodles and stir until well coated. Sprinkle the remaining 2 cups of cheese over the top of the macaroni.

Bake at 350° for 30 minutes or until lightly browned.

Mandarin Rice Bake

This dish is a perfect way to use left-over ham. I rarely use canned soup, preferring a homemade white sauce, but the canned variety can be used in a pinch. I serve this with steamed veggies and a crusty loaf of bread.

¾ C. raw rice
1 ½ C. boiling water
½ tsp. salt
1 ½ - 2 C. cubed ham or other leftover meat **(or canned ham)**
1 ½ C. chopped celery *{optional}*
1 C. chopped onion **(or dehydrated onion)**
½ C. chopped green pepper **(or dehydrated peppers)**
1 C. white sauce with chicken **(or condensed cream of chicken/mushroom soup)**
2 T. soy sauce

In a greased 2 qt. casserole add rice, boiling water and salt. Over rice mixture add, ham, celery, onion and green pepper. Stir in white sauce or soup and soy sauce. Cover and bake at 350° for 1 hour and 15 minutes.

Mock Filet Mignon

This is one of our all-time favorite recipes. You can practically hear your arteries hardening while you eat it, but it is worth every bite!

In a large bowl, combine:
1 ½ pounds ground beef
2 C cooked rice *{we use leftovers}*
1 C onion, diced **(or dehydrated onion)**
1 T Worcestershire sauce
1 ½ tsp. salt
¼ tsp. garlic powder
¼ tsp. pepper
Mix well
Rashers *{strips}* of bacon

Shape into six (we often make 8 smaller patties) patties. Wrap a strip of bacon around each patty; fasten with a toothpick. Place in an ungreased shallow baking dish. Bake at 450° for 30 minutes or until meat is no longer pink.

New Potatoes and Ham

When I was growing up, my mother made a version of this meal that was our favorite. Her version consisted of thinly sliced potato rounds and Spam instead of ham. It was so flavorful! By the time I was grown, Spam had become outdated and I was looking for a way to use leftover ham chunks. This has all of the flavor of my Mom's version with a little extra.

8 – 12 small, whole new potatoes
3 green onions, chopped **(or dehydrated onions)**
2 T. butter **(or bacon fat)**
2 T. flour **(or whole (soft) wheat flour)**
1 ½ C. vegetable liquid and milk
salt and pepper
1 – 2 C. cubed, cooked ham **(or canned)**
½ C. grated cheese *{we like Parmesan}*

Scrub and cook the potatoes in boiling, salted water until partially tender. Add onions. Continue cooking until vegetables are tender. Drain, reserving liquid. Make a white sauce with the butter, flour and vegetable liquid and milk. Season with salt and pepper. Pour the sauce over the vegetables. Add the ham and cheese. Heat through and serve.

Norwegian Meatballs

What a wonderful winter meal these little meatballs make! They just beg to be eaten in front of a crackling fire with oil lamps providing the only lighting. We love the old-fashioned flavor of these meatballs and they are an especial treat when you put them on top of homemade noodles.

Meatballs:
1 onion, diced **(or dehydrated onion)**
1 egg, beaten **(or 1 T egg pwd + 3 T water)**
1 T. cornstarch **(or 1 T flour)**
1 tsp. salt
¼ tsp. ground nutmeg
¼ tsp. ground allspice
¼ tsp. ground ginger
Pepper
1 ½ lbs. ground beef **(or other ground meat)**
4 T. butter **(or bacon fat)**

Gravy:
2 T. butter **(or bacon fat)**
4 T. flour **(or whole (soft) wheat flour)**
2 C. beef broth **(or water flavored with bouillon or soup base)**
1 C. milk or half and half cream **(or pwd milk)**
Salt and pepper to taste

In a bowl, combine the onion, egg, cornstarch, salt and spices. Add beef; mix well. Shape into 1 ½" meatballs. In a large skillet over medium heat, brown the meatballs in the butter, half at a time, for 10 minutes or until the meat is no longer pink. Turn to brown evenly. Remove to paper towels to drain, reserving 1 T. drippings in the skillet. For gravy, add butter to drippings. Stir in flour. Add broth and cream; cook and stir for 2 minutes or until thickened and bubbly. Season with salt and pepper. Reduce heat to low. Return meatballs to skillet; heat through.

Pasta

Pasta is one of our favorite meals and nothing can quite compare with the homemade variety. Years ago, I rolled out pasta with my rolling pin, but no matter how hard I tried, I could never make it anything but thick noodles. After buying a hand-crank pasta machine at a yard sale, I began making pasta in earnest! It turns out wonderfully and is the perfect accompaniment to your own special sauce.

1 1/3 to 1 ½ C flour **(or whole (soft) wheat flour)**
¼ tsp. salt
2 large eggs **(or 2 T egg pwd + 6 T water)**
2 tsp. olive oil **(or vegetable oil)**

Mix together the flour and salt. Make a well in the center and break into it 2 large eggs. Add the olive oil.

Gradually draw the flour into the eggs with a fork and beat lightly. Continue until the flour has absorbed all the egg. Work in a little additional flour if the mixture is exceptionally moist, but don't overdo it. If you are not sure about the amount of flour to add, push your finger into the ball of dough as far as its center. When you pull it out, it should feel somewhat sticky, but not moist. If it feels moist, work in a little more flour.

Let the dough rest for a few minutes to give the flour a chance to absorb the liquid. To do this, cover the dough with a damp towel and let it rest for at least 10 minutes but up to 30 minutes.

Lightly dust the pasta with flour and flatten it out with your hands. Feed the dough through your pasta machine and flatten and knead until the dough takes on the consistency of suede leather. At this point you can begin to adjust your machine down one notch at a time until you have the right thickness for the pasta you are making.

Cut, boil and serve.

Pork Sausage Casserole

This is one of the VERY few casseroles my husband will eat. It is really very economical and when made with home-canned chicken broth, incredibly flavorful. If I think my broth does not have very much flavor, I will add a little chicken soup mix or bouillon to the mix.

1 lb. bulk pork sausage **(or home-canned sausage)**
1 onion, chopped **(or dehydrated onion)**
2 C. raw rice
1 C. celery, chopped *{optional}*
½ tsp. poultry seasoning
3 ½ C. boiling chicken broth **(or water if using soup base)**
1 ½ T. chicken bullion **(or chicken soup base)**

Brown the sausage and onion in skillet. Drain fat and add rice, celery, onion, poultry seasoning and chicken broth. Pour into a casserole or dutch oven. Bake at 350° for one hour.

Porcupine Meatballs

Once, when we had friends visiting from the city, their young son asked what we were having for dinner (while feasting on these meatballs). Our daughter informed him that these were Porcupine Meatballs. Our guest looked up with big eyes and gulped "Porcupine?". No, we heartily assured him, they were plain old beef – however, he didn't take another bite of his meatball and maintained a strict vegetarian diet throughout the duration of his visit.

These tasty meatballs are good made with just about any kind of meat, however, we have never tried porcupine.

1 lb. ground beef
½ C rice, uncooked
½ C water
1/3 C onion, diced **(or dehydrated onion)**
1 tsp. salt
½ tsp. celery salt *{optional}*
½ tsp. garlic powder
1/3 tsp. pepper

Sauce *
2 C tomato sauce **(or 1 can)**
1 C water
2 tsp. Worcestershire sauce

Mix hamburger with rice, ½ C water and onion, celery salt, garlic powder and pepper. Shape into meatballs (about 3"). Place in a baking dish. Mix remaining ingredients, pour over meatballs. Cover and cook at 350° for 45 minutes. Uncover and cook 15 minutes longer. Serve over rice.

*Often, I will double the sauce recipe so that there is plenty to pour over rice.

Skillet Beef and Lentils

When we first moved into "Little Shouse on the Prairie" we had very little money. I had to make every dollar stretch as far as I could. We had stored foods for Y2K, and among those buckets of food were large amounts of lentils. And so, I got creative. This dish was so tasty that it became a mainstay – even after the meager first years of off-grid living where behind us.

4 C water
1 ½ C. lentils, rinsed
2 T. butter **(or bacon fat or lard)**
2 onions, chopped **(or dehydrated onion)**
1 clove garlic, minced **(or dehydrated garlic)**
1 lb. ground beef **(or venison or rabbit or bear, etc.)**
2 T. beef soup base **(or 2 beef bouillon cubes)**
2 T. white rice
1 tsp. salt
1 tsp. garlic **(or dehydrated garlic)**
2 T. chives, dried *{optional}*
½ tsp. pepper

In a saucepan, bring water to a boil. Add lentils and cook for 20 minutes. Drain, reserving the liquid. In a deep skillet, sauté the onions and garlic in the butter. Stir in ground beef. Brown well and add 2 1/3 C. of the reserved liquid and the beef soup base (bouillon). Cover and simmer for 10 minutes. Stir in the lentils, rice, salt, garlic, chives and pepper. Bring to a b oil, reduce heat and cover and simmer for 30 minutes, or until lentils are rice are tender and liquid is absorbed (add more liquid, if necessary). Serve with crusty whole wheat bread.

Stuffed Bell Peppers

*My Grandma "Omie" used to make these when I was a little girl –
and I hated them! Then, one day when the bell peppers where
huge and ripe on the vine, my mouth started watering for these
flavors of my youth. Go figure!*

4 green or red bell peppers
Salt
5 T olive oil **(or vegetable oil)**
1 medium onion, peeled and chopped **(or dehydrated onion)**
1 clove garlic, peeled and chopped **(or dehydrated garlic)**
1 lb. ground beef **(or venison or rabbit or bear, etc.)**
1 ½ C cooked rice
1 C chopped tomatoes **(or canned tomatoes)**
1 tsp. oregano
Pepper
½ C ketchup
½ tsp. Worcestershire Sauce
Dash of Tabasco sauce

Bring a large pot of water to a boil over high heat. Meanwhile,
cut top off peppers from the stem and remove seeds. Add
several generous pinches of salt to the water, then add peppers
and boil, using a spoon to keep peppers completely submerged,
until brilliant green (or red) and their flesh slightly softened.
Drain, set aside to cool.

Preheat oven to 350°. Heat 4 T of the oil in a large skillet over
medium heat. Add onions and garlic, and cook, stirring often,
until soft and translucent. Remove skillet from heat, add meat,
rice, tomatoes and oregano and seasonings. Mix well.

Drizzle remaining 1 T oil inside peppers, arrange cut side up in
a baking dish. Stuff peppers with filling. Combine ketchup,
Worcestershire sauce, Tabasco sauce and cup of water in a
small bowl, then spoon over filling. Add ¼ cup water to the
baking dish. Place in the oven and bake for 40-50 minutes, or
until the internal temperature is 150° to 160°.

Sweet & Sour Pork

This dish is perfect for using bits of leftover pork roast or even pork chops. It is full of flavor and is perfect when you have a taste for an Asian dinner.

Marinade:
1 egg, beaten **(or 1 T egg pwd. + 3 T water)**
1 T. sugar
1 tsp. salt
1 T. soy sauce
1 lb. lean pork, cubed **(or chicken, grouse or turkey, etc.)**
1 clove garlic, minced **(or dehydrated garlic)**
1 green pepper, cut into chunks **(or reconstituted dehydrated peppers)**
1 onion, cut into wedges **(or reconstituted dehydrated onions)**
¼ C. pineapple chunks drained *{reserve juice}*
Sauce:
6 T. vinegar
6 T. brown sugar **(or 6 T sugar + ½ T molasses)**
4 T. soy sauce
2 T. cornstarch **(or 2 T flour)**
1 ½ C. pineapple juice
4 T. oil

Combine marinade ingredients in a bowl. Add cubed pork and allow to stand for 20-30 minutes. Combine the garlic, green pepper, onion and pineapple chunks and set aside.

Combine the sauce ingredients and set aside.

Heat the 4 T. of oil in a large skillet or wok. Dredge pork cubes in cornstarch and fry on all side until brown. Remove from the skillet and keep warm. Pour off excess fat if necessary, leaving about 2 T. Stir fry garlic, peppers and onions for 2 – 3 minutes. Add pineapple chunks and sauce ingredients. Cook just until sauce thickens and clears. Return pork to the skillet, heat to bubbling and serve immediately with hot rice. Onions and peppers should be partially crisp.

Tourtiere
(Meat Pie)

Although my husband is not a great fan of meat pies, I love them. This is by far my favorite. This is the traditional Christmas pie from Quebec and its roots trace to medieval France. In New England you will often hear it pronounced "toocheer".

1 double pie crust
1 ½ lbs ground pork **(or beef, venison, bear, etc.)**
½ lb. diced potato **(or dehydrated potato cubes)**
1 large onion, chopped **(or dehydrated onions)**
1 C water
½ tsp. salt
¼ tsp. allspice
¼ tsp. nutmeg
¼ tsp. savory
¼ tsp. black pepper
egg wash made by beating 1 egg with 1 T water *{optional}*

Prepare whatever pie dough you choose and chill it while you make the filling.

Place the ground pork, onion, water and spices (the medieval influence) in a saucepan and bring to a boil. Turn down to a simmer and cook uncovered for 25 to 30 minutes. Stir it frequently to keep it from sticking. You want the liquid to cook down to prevent the filling from being too soupy.

While the filling cooks, roll out two rounds of pie dough. Line a 9" pie pan with one. Brush the bottom with some of the egg wash to keep it from getting soggy while it cooks.

Pour the filling into the pie shell. Cover with the second circle of dough and crimp the edges. Cut vents in the top and brush with the egg wash.

Bake for 10 minutes at 500°; then turn the heat down to 375° and bake for 20 to 25 minutes more.

Cookies & Bars
Soft or Durham Wheat

I love to bake cookies. I always have. When I was a girl, I would whip up a batch of Chocolate No-Bake cookies when my family would develop a sweet tooth. The holidays always brought with them a mad rush of cookie making as my Mom prepared for Thanksgiving munching and Christmas visiting. Every year, Mom and I would make Chocolate Chip Cookies, Grandma Adam's Chocolate Drop Cookies and Sugar Cookies cut in the shapes of Christmas Trees and Silver Bells. Our neighbors anxiously awaited my Mom's cookie platters. Each person had their favorite and some even made requests.

When I grew up and had a family of my own, I too, continued the cookie tradition. I used the same recipes that my mother had used, and her mother had used before her. As my children and I rolled out cookie dough, listening to the same Christmas music my mother and I had listened to, we built on the foundation begun generations before.

As our family grew, so did our cookie repertoire. Now, not only did we make chocolate chip, sugar and oatmeal cookies, we discovered filled cookies, shortbread cookies and layer cookies. Now we maintain a full house and a full cookie jar!

One thing that we have found is that cookies are very forgiving. The temperature is generally not overly critical, making cookies a perfect candidate for wood cook stove baking. Cookies were the very first baked goods that I found the courage to experiment with in my wood cook stove. What I found is that cookies baked in a wood fire oven are absolutely divine! They are soft and chewy in the center and slightly crunchy on the outside. Chewy and crunchy - the perfect cookie combination. One caution however, although cookies are forgiving, baking in too low of an oven will produce rock hard cookies that are impossible to eat without first being soaked in a cup of tea or mug of coffee.

Because cookies generally require either baking soda or baking powder, they work quite nicely with soft white or Durham wheat. They do not require as much gluten as yeast breads in order to maintain their shape and structure. The soft white wheat has a more subtle flavor than does the hard red wheat and doesn't interfere with the other flavors that make cookies wonderful.

When I bake cookies, I use the amount of flour listed in the recipe merely as a guide. I always start with less flour than is recommended, slowly adding more until the dough is the correct consistency. The amount of flour that is needed depends on many factors, including the humidity in the air. I often add more flour than the recipe indicates. If the dough is sticky, I add flour just until the dough no longer sticks to my hands, but is still soft. If not enough flour has been added, the cookies will spread all over the cookie sheet and be flat as pancakes. If too much flour has been added, they retain the shape they were when they were put on the cookie sheet and will be as hard as rocks. Generally I roll the cookies dough around in my hand to make round balls (for drop cookies) before I put them on the baking sheets. Doing this gives me a good idea as to the condition of the dough. I always bake a test sheet with 3 cookies and adjust my flour as needed.

Apple Harvest Cookies

Our friend "Old Cowboy" refers to these as "Old-Timey Cookies".
They are soft, moist and full of spices. They are one of our
favorite fall cookies. I always have to adjust the amount of flour,
depending on the humidity. I end up adding a cup or cup and a
half more flour – just enough to help the cookies hold their
shape. The dough should be sticky, but not messy sticky.

½ C shortening **(or butter)**
1 ½ C packed brown sugar **(or 1 ½ C sugar + 6 T molasses)**
1 egg **(or 1 T egg pwd. + 3 T water)**
¼ C milk **(or apple juice or water)**
2 C flour **(or whole (soft) wheat flour)**
1 tsp. baking soda
1 tsp. ground cinnamon
1 tsp. ground cloves
½ tsp. ground nutmeg
1 C chopped, peeled apples or pears **(or canned or rehydrated dried fruit)**

In a large mixing bowl, cream together the shortening, brown sugar, egg and milk. Stir in the flour, baking soda, cinnamon, cloves and nutmeg. Add the chopped apple.

Drop batter by heaping teaspoon full onto greased baking sheets. Bake at 400° for 10 to 12 minutes. Remove to wire racks. Combine glaze ingredients and spread over cookies while warm.

Vanilla Glaze:
1 ½ C confectioners sugar
1 T butter, melted *{optional}*
¼ tsp. vanilla extract
½ tsp. salt
2 ½ T milk

Mix together the confectioners sugar, butter, vanilla, salt and milk. Drizzle over the cooled cookies.

Blond Brownies

When we just have to have chocolate chip cookies but I'm not in the mood to bake multiple cookie sheets full, I am inclined to bake these wonderful Blond Brownies. They are thicker than typical cookies, which makes them wonderfully chewy yet they retain all of the tasty goodness of the American Classic.

2/3 C butter **(or shortening)**
2 ¼ C brown sugar, packed **(2 ¼ C sugar + 12 T molasses)**
3 eggs **(3 T egg pwd. + 9 T water)**
2 tsp. vanilla extract
2 ½ C flour **(or whole (soft) wheat flour)**
2½ tsp. baking powder
½ tsp. salt
1 to 2 C chocolate chips

Preheat oven to 350°

Cream the butter and sugar together until they're very light. Add the eggs and beat in thoroughly, one at a time. Blend in the vanilla.

Mix the dry ingredients together. Blend the butter mixture with the flour mixture. Fold in the chocolate chips.

Spoon the dough into a lightly greased, 9 x 13-inch baking pan (or use two 8 x 8-inch cake pans).

Bake for 25 to 30 minutes. Cool, cut into squares and serve.

Chewy Gingersnaps

There is nothing quite as homey as gingersnaps in the winter. These are a chewy variety (no good for gingerbread men). They keep well and the flavor improves with age.

1 ½ C butter, softened **(or shortening)**
2 C sugar **(or honey)**
2 eggs **(or 2 T egg pwd. + 4 T water)**
½ C molasses
4 ½ C flour **(or whole (soft) wheat flour)**
3 tsp. baking soda
2 tsp. cinnamon
1 tsp. ginger
1 tsp. cloves
½ tsp. salt
½ tsp. nutmeg

In a mixing bowl, cream together the butter and sugar. Add the eggs and beat well. Mix in the molasses. Add the flour, baking soda, cinnamon, ginger, cloves, salt and nutmeg. Mix well.

Refrigerate for 1 hour or until dough is easy to handle.

Roll into 1" balls; roll in sugar. Place 2" apart on ungreased baking sheets. Bake at 350° for 8 – 12 minutes or until puffy and lightly browned. Cool for 1 minute before removing to wire rack.

Chinese Almond Cookies

While out at a Chinese Buffet with my parents, my Dad confessed that he absolutely loved the almond cookies they served. Deciding to surprise my Dad the next time they came to visit, I tracked down a recipe that I thought looked like his favorites. They were, and a new family favorite was born!

½ C butter **(or shortening)**
½ C sugar **(or honey)**
1 egg **(or 1 T egg pwd. + 3 T water)**
2 tsp. almond extract
1 ¼ C flour **(or whole (soft) wheat flour)**
½ C ground almonds

Cream together the butter and sugar. Add the egg and almond extract. Stir in the flour and ground almonds.

Roll dough into 1 ½" balls and place on cookie sheet about 2" apart. Bake at 400° for 5 to 8 minutes or until lightly browned.

Cool on cooling rack.

Chocolate Drop Cookies

What follows is a family treasure. This recipe has been passed down for generations in our family – the original recipe having been modernized relatively recently, by my Great Grandmother. These cookies are a part of my heritage. They were a coveted part of every Christmas Plate my mother presented to neighbors. They were at every family reunion, every special tea party and occasionally made their appearance to entice the appetite of someone who was under the weather. These cookies are a taste of our home.

One thing I must tell you - a requirement for making Chocolate Drop cookies is frosting them on the bottom. Yes, you read that right – the bottom must be frosted. My Great Grandmother, my Grandmother and my Mother all frost their cookies on the bottom (as do I, of course). Really, when you think about it, this makes perfect sense. The bottoms are nice and flat and imminently spreadable. We frost the bottoms of every frosted cookies we make, be they Chocolate Drops, Sugar Cookies or whatever else catches our fancy.

1 C brown sugar **(or 1 C sugar + 4 T molasses)**
½ C butter, softened **(or shortening)**
1 egg **(or 1 T egg pwd. + 3 T water)**
½ C milk **(or pwd. Milk)**
1 tsp. vanilla extract
1 ¾ C flour **(or whole (soft) wheat flour)**
6 T cocoa
½ tsp. baking soda

Cream together the brown sugar and butter. Add the egg, milk and vanilla extract. Mix thoroughly. Add the flour, baking cocoa and baking soda. Mix just until combined.

Drop batter by the teaspoon full onto a greased cookie sheet (or a cookie sheet that has been well seasoned.) Bake at 350° for 8 – 12 minutes or until done (cookies will spring back when gently touched).

Chocolate Drop Cookie Frosting

2 T butter, melted **(or shortening)**
1 tsp. vanilla extract
2 T milk **(or pwd. milk)**
2 C powdered sugar
3 T cocoa powder

Mix the butter, vanilla extract and mix. Add the powdered sugar and cocoa powder. Beat until thoroughly mixed. Add milk until spreading consistency has been achieved.

Chocolate Chip Cookies

This recipe is probably redundant for most folks – but since it is our go-to chocolate chip cookie recipe I couldn't leave it out. This recipe produces those lovely, thick, soft cookies that we all love. If your cookies spread too thin, add a bit more flour (the dough should be slightly tacky but not stick to your hands). If your cookies are hard, too much flour was added. I always take mine out of the oven when they just START to brown, ensuring soft, barely done cookies.

1 C butter, softened **(or shortening)**
¾ C brown sugar, packed **(or ¾ sugar + 2 ½ T molasses)**
¾ C granulated sugar *(or honey)*
1 tsp. vanilla extract
2 eggs **(or 2 T egg pwd + 6 T water)**
3 C flour **(or whole (soft) wheat flour)**
1 tsp. baking soda
1 tsp. salt
2 C chocolate chips

Cream together the butter, brown sugar and granulated sugar. Add the vanilla extract and eggs. Mix well. Add the flour, baking soda and salt. Mix well. Add chocolate chips.

The dough should be soft but not sticky. If it sticks to your fingers, add a little flour. Continue adding flour until the dough no longer sticks, but be careful not to add too much flour or your cookies will be hard.

Roll into 1 ½ inch balls and place on an ungreased cookie sheet. Bake at 375° for 9 to 11 minutes or until lightly browned. If you like soft cookies, be sure not to over bake.

Note: This dough also works well wrapped up, stored in the fridge or freezer and made into fresh cookies later. It is wonderful to make one sheet of cookies at a time and always have warm, fresh out of the oven cookies in the blink of an eye.

Cowboy Cookies

One of my favorite cookies to make when I want to fill the cookie jar (and have a few left over to give to folks in the neighborhood) are Cowboy Cookies. I have no idea why they are called Cowboy Cookies but I do know that my favorite Cowgirl loves 'em! They are simple, good and are especially easy to make with stored foods. I always make a double batch.

1 C butter, softened **(or shortening)**
1 ½ C brown sugar **(or 1 ½ C sugar + 6 T molasses)**
½ C sugar **(or honey)**
2 eggs **(or 2 T egg pwd. + 6 T water)**
1 ½ tsp vanilla
2 C flour **(or whole (soft) wheat flour)**
1 tsp. baking soda
½ tsp. salt
2 C oatmeal
2 C chocolate chips
1 C flaked coconut **(or dried coconut)**

In a mixing bowl, cream together the butter, brown sugar and sugar. Add the eggs and vanilla. Beat until fluffy. Add the flour, baking soda and salt and mix. Stir in the oatmeal, chocolate chips and coconut.

Drop by tablespoons onto greased cookie sheets. Bake at 350° for 12 minutes or until golden brown.

Dad's Layer Cookies

These are one of our preeminent Christmas cookies. Many years ago, before we were married, someone in the neighborhood presented my husband with these cookies during the Christmas season. He loved them, however, they weren't quite right. They had a saltine cracker crust and walnuts rather than pecans. My husband quickly fixed the recipe and they have been a Christmas staple ever since. They are somewhat homely, but once you've taken the first bite, you will be hooked. Cut them in small squares because they are rich (and addictive)!

1 C graham crackers crumbs
4 T butter, melted
1 C pecans
1 C chocolate chips
1 C coconut
1 can sweetened condensed milk

Combine the graham cracker crumbs and butter. Stir until moist. Press firmly into the bottom of a 9x9 pan. Layer the remaining ingredients in order – pecans, chocolate chips and coconut. Pour the sweetened condensed milk over the top, making sure the surface is covered.

Bake at 350° for 20 minutes or until top is lightly browned.

Cool completely before cutting.

Filled Oatmeal Cookies
a.k.a. Survival Bars

*The original filled oatmeal recipe called for a raisin filling,
however, we much prefer jam. Our favorite is Blackberry jam,
however, Raspberry runs a close second. You could even mix up
fresh berries (in season) and fill the cookies with berries right off
the vine. These cookies require no fresh ingredients and are
perfect for a quick breakfast. They are very similar to todays
popular breakfast bars.*

1 ½ C shortening **(or butter)**
1 ½ C brown sugar **(or 1 ½ C sugar + 6 T molasses)**
1 ½ tsp. vanilla extract
1 ½ tsp. baking soda mixed with 6 T. hot water
3 C oatmeal *{I use thick cut oats}*
3 C flour **(or whole (soft) wheat flour)**
¼ tsp. nutmeg
1 ½ tsp. salt.

Combine shortening, sugar and vanilla. Mix well. Add soda in
water, nutmeg, salt and flour. Stir in oatmeal. Add more water
or flour to make a nice, workable dough. Roll out thin. Cut out
with round cookie or biscuit cutter (or whatever shape you
like). Lay cookies on a cookie sheet, place desired filling on the
(1 tsp. or so) and top with another cookie (there is no need to
seal the edges). Bake at 350° for 8 to 10 minutes or until
lightly browned.

German Chocolate Cake Cookies

When you just have to have chocolate cookies but want the crunch of a little something extra, these fill the bill. If you take care not to over bake them, they will stay soft for days in the cookie jar, making them excellent "everyday" cookies.

1 C butter, softened **(or shortening)**
1 C brown sugar **(or 1 C sugar + 4 T molasses)**
1 C granulated sugar **(or honey)**
2 tsp. vanilla extract
2 large eggs **(or 2 T egg pwd. + 6 T water)**
2 ¼ C flour **(or whole (soft) wheat flour)**
½ C unsweetened baking cocoa
1 tsp. baking soda
pinch salt
1 C semi-sweet chocolate chips
1 C shredded sweetened coconut **(or dried coconut)**
1 C chopped pecans

Cream together the butter, brown sugar and granulated sugar. Add the vanilla extract and the eggs. Mix in the flour, cocoa and baking soda. Add the chocolate chips, coconut and pecans.

Drop the dough by tablespoonful's onto the prepared baking sheets and bake at 375° for 8 to 10 minutes. Cool on a baking rack.

Graham Crackers

Sometimes, in the winter, we'll bake up a big batch of these crackers and sit in front of the crackling fire with warm Graham crackers and steaming mugs of homemade cocoa. Nothing could be cozier!

1 C whole wheat flour, freshly ground *{soft/white wheat}*
1 C all-purpose flour **(or all whole wheat flour)**
¼ C sugar
½ tsp. salt
1 tsp. cinnamon
1 tsp. baking powder
1 egg **(or 1 T egg pwd. + 3 T water)**
¼ C oil
¼ C honey
2 to 3 T milk *{approximately}*

Preheat your oven to 350°

In a mixing bowl, combine the dry ingredients. Beat the egg until light, adding the vegetable oil, honey and 2 tablespoons of the milk. Stir into the dry ingredients until you have a fairly stiff dough.

Turn the dough onto a floured surface and knead gently until it holds together. Roll it out until it is about 1/8" thick. Cut into 2" squares (or use your favorite cookie cutter), prick with a fork and place on a barely greased cookie sheet. Brush the tops with milk (and cinnamon sugar if you are so inclined) and bake for 15 to 20 minutes.

Great Grandma Adam's Sugar Cookies

These are the sugar cookies I grew up with. I have tried many alternatives, thinking I should dress things up a bit, but I always come back to this time-honored favorite.

1 C butter, softened **(or shortening)**
1 ¼ C sugar **(or honey)**
3 eggs **(or 3 T egg pwd. + 9 T water)**
1 tsp. vanilla extract
3 C **flour (or whole (soft) wheat flour)**
1 tsp. baking powder
¼ tsp. salt

Preheat oven to 350°

Cream together the butter and sugar. Add eggs, one at a time. Beat in vanilla extract. Add flour, baking powder and salt. Mix until combined.

Refrigerate until ready to roll out – or roll out immediately. Roll to ¼" thick and cut with cookie cutters, according to season. Bake for 7 – 10 minutes or just until edges are beginning to brown.

Homemade Girl Scout Cookies

These homemade Girl Scout cookies are very similar to the thin mint cookies that the Girl Scouts sell. They are wonderful but so easy! Another option is to leave out the peppermint flavoring, sandwich a layer of peanut butter between two crackers and dip the sandwich in chocolate. Yum!

Melt in double boiler or saucepan on low:
2 C chocolate chips *{semi-sweet or milk chocolate}*
2 tsp. Crisco *{to make the chocolate smooth – add more as necessary}*
Take off heat

Add and stir to combine:
1 tsp. peppermint extract *{or more to taste}*

Dip, one at a time, in chocolate mixture:
Ritz Crackers *{or other butter crackers}*

Place crackers on wax paper until the chocolate hardens. I usually put the cookie sheets in the freezer and then transfer the cookies to a box or tin for storage. I like to store them in the refrigerator or freezer, just so the chocolate doesn't melt on your hands.

Long Range Reconnaissance Patrol Bars (LRRP Bars)
(Also known as Granola Bars)

These hearty bars keep for a very long time and provide an instant meal. They are packed with carbs and protein, making you able to stay energized on long range patrols (or even shorter ones). We make these for every hike we embark upon and they never make it home.

Preheat oven to 350°

Butter an 8 by 12 inch baking dish and line it with parchment or tin foil.

On a cookie sheet, toss together:
2 C old-fashioned oats
1 C sliced almonds
1 C shredded coconut, loosely packed **(or dried coconut)**
Bake for 10 to 12 minutes, stirring occasionally, until lightly browned.

Tranfer mixture to a large mixing bowl.

Stir in:
½ C toasted wheat germ **(or multi-grain cereal)**

Reduce oven to 300°

In small saucepan, combine:
3 T butter
2/3 C honey **(or sugar)**
¼ C brown sugar **(or ¼ C sugar + 1 T molasses)**
1 ½ tsp. vanilla extract
¼ tsp. salt
Bring to boil over medium heat. Cook and stir for a minute, then pour over the toasted oatmeal mixture.

Add:
½ C chopped apple slices **(or dried dates, or raisins etc.)**
½ C chocolate chips *{optional}*
½ C dried cranberries
Stir well

Butter an 8x12" baking dish and line it with tin foil.

Pour mixture into prepared pan. Wet your fingers and lightly press the mixture evenly into the pan. Bake at 350° for 25 to 30 minutes, until golden brown. Cool for at least 2 to 3 hours before cutting into squares. Serve at room temperature.

Madeleines

These French cookies are one of our very favorite tea treats. They are light, buttery and simply divine when paired with a stout cup of English Breakfast. Maid Elizabeth (our eldest daughter) generally makes the batter early in the day and pops them into the oven just in time for our afternoon cup of tea.

½ C butter
1 C flour **(or whole (soft) wheat flour)**
½ tsp. baking powder
1/8 tsp. salt
3 large eggs, at room temperature **(or 3 T egg pwd. + 9 T water)**
2/3 C sugar **(or honey)**
1 tsp. vanilla extract
Beat to combine

Melt the butter and set aside. Allow to cool while mixing up the batter. In a small bowl, whisk the flour, baking powder and salt until well blended. Set aside. Beat the eggs and sugar until the mixture has tripled in volume and forms a thick ribbon (about 5 minutes). Add the vanilla extract. Beat to combine.

Sift a small amount of the flour mixture over the egg mixture and, using a large rubber spatula, fold the flour mixture into the beaten eggs to lighten it. Sift the rest of the flour over egg mixture and fold in, being sure not to over-mix the batter or it will deflate.

Whisk a small amount of the egg mixture into the melted butter to lighten it. Then fold in the cooled, melted butter in three additions. Cover and refrigerate for at least 30 minutes or several hours, until slightly firm.

Position rack in the center of the oven and preheat to 375°. Generously butter two 12 mold madeleine pans. Dust the mold with flour and tap out the excess.

Drop a generous tablespoonful of the batter into the center of each prepared mold, leaving the batter mounded in the center.

Bake the Madeleines for 11 to 13 minutes, until the edges are golden brown and the centers spring back when lightly touched. Do not over bake these cookies or they will be dry.

Remove the pans from the oven and rap each pan sharply against a countertop to release the Madeleines. Transfer smooth side down on wire racks to cool. Dust with confectioners sugar to serve.

Peanut Butter/Chocolate Chip Cookies

When we are craving that wonderful combination of peanut butter and chocolate, these are the cookies we turn to. They are rich and wonderful – especially good warm, fresh from the oven!

¾ C peanut butter
½ C butter **(or shortening)**
1 ¼ C brown sugar, packed **(or 1 ¼ C sugar + 5 T molasses)**
3 T milk **(or pwd milk)**
1 T vanilla extract
1 egg **(or 1 T egg pwd. + 3 T water)**
2 C flour **(or whole (soft) wheat flour)**
¾ tsp. salt
¾ tsp. baking soda

Cream together peanut butter, butter and brown sugar. Stir in milk, vanilla extract and egg. Add flour, salt and baking soda and mix to combine.

Roll into 1" balls and place 2" apart on cookie sheets. Bake at 375° for 7 – 8 minutes or until just beginning to brown.

Remove to cooling rack.

Simply Perfect Shortbread

This treasure came to me by way of my dear friend Lady Day. It is the perfect accompaniment to a cup of tea or perhaps a mug of coffee.

4 cubes butter (2 C) , softened **(or shortening*)**
1 C granulated sugar
4 C flour **(or whole (soft) wheat flour)**
2 tsp. almond flavoring

Mix together all ingredients. Form dough into a roll and wrap in waxed paper or plastic wrap. Chill the roll in the refrigerator (an hour or overnight). Slice the dough into cookies and bake at 350° for 20 to 30 minutes or until lightly browned on the bottom. Do not overbake!

* This recipe really is better with real butter. Although you can substitute shortening, I don't recommend it.

Turtle Bars

Oh, my goodness! I don't even know what to say about these bars, other than that they are out of this world. The original recipe is of Irish origin, where they are served at every coffee shop throughout the country. The Irish version has a shortbread crust and broken-up pretzels instead of pecans. We tweaked the recipe a bit and came up with this take on the original classic.

Base:
1 ¼ C butter, softened
¾ C sugar
2 ½ C flour

Caramel Layer:
½ C butter
14 oz. can sweetened condensed milk
½ C brown sugar
2 T corn syrup
1 tsp. vanilla extract
1 C pecan pieces

Chocolate Topping:
6 T butter, melted
1 C milk chocolate chips

Preheat oven to 350°. Grease a 13x9" pan. In pan, combine the butter, sugar and flour. Press into your prepared pan. Bake for 15 – 20 minutes or until firm and golden. Remove from the oven to cool.

To make the caramel, combine the butter, sweetened condensed milk, brown sugar and corn syrup in a heavy-based saucepan. Place over medium heat and stir continuously until boiling. Boil for 6-7 minutes, till caramel thickens enough to leave the side of the pan, stirring all the time.

Remove from heat and add the vanilla extract, stirring well.
Fold in pecan pieces. Spread caramel carefully over the cooled
crust with a knife.

When caramel has set, melt butter and chocolate in a double
boiler over low heat. Remove from heat and stir till smooth.
Cool slightly before spreading over caramel layer with a knife.
When chocolate is firm and set, cut into squares.

White Chocolate Cranberry Cookies

Our eldest daughter loves white chocolate chips and I love dried cranberries. These cookies are the perfect combination of both!

½ C butter **(or shortening)**
½ C brown sugar **(or ½ C sugar + 2 T molasses)**
½ C sugar **(or honey)**
1 egg **(or 1 T egg pwd + 3 T water)**
1 T vanilla
1 ½ C flour **(or whole (soft) wheat flour)**
½ tsp. baking soda
¾ C white chocolate chips
1 C Craisins *{dried cranberries}*

Cream together the butter, brown sugar and sugar. Beat in the egg and vanilla extract. Add the flour, baking soda, white chocolate chips and craisins.

Drop by teaspoon full onto prepared baking sheets. Bake at 350° for 8 – 10 minutes or just beginning to brown.

White Chocolate Macadamia Nut Cookies

Here is another white chocolate chip recipe. We love the flavor of these cookies, however we don't indulge in them very often. Macadamia nuts are not one of our stored foods items.

2 C butter **(or shortening)**
3 C sugar **(or honey)**
4 eggs **(or 4 T egg pwd. + 12 T water)**
4 tsp. vanilla extract
5 C flour **(or whole (soft) wheat flour)**
2 tsp. baking soda
2 tsp. salt
2 C white chocolate chips
1 C macadamia nuts, chopped

Preheat oven to 375°

In a medium bowl, cream together the butter and sugar. Stir in the egg and vanilla. Combine the flour, baking soda and salt, stir into the creamed mixture. Finally, stir in the white chocolate chips and nuts. Drop cookies by heaping teaspoonful onto an ungreased cookie sheet, about 2" apart.

Bake for 8 to 10 minutes until lightly browned. Cool on wire racks. When cool, store in an airtight container.

White Wedding Cookies

I'm sure just about everyone has their own version of these flaky, slightly nutty, wonderful little cookies. These are a favorite of both my husband and my father. We especially love them with afternoon tea.

1 C butter, softened **(or shortening*)**
½ C confectioners' sugar
1 tsp. vanilla extract
2 C flour **(or whole (soft) wheat flour)**
¼ tsp. salt
1 tsp. baking powder
¾ C toasted pecans, finely chopped

In a large bowl, cream together the butter, confectioners' sugar and vanilla extract until light and fluffy. Gradually stir in the flour, salt and baking powder. Add pecans.

If dough is too sticky to handle, refrigerate until firm. Break off 1 inch pieces of dough. Roll into balls.

Place on ungreased baking sheets, 2 inches apart. Bake at 350° for 10 to 12 minutes or until set but still pale in color.

Cool slightly, then roll in confectioners sugar. When cookies are completely cooled, roll in confectioners sugar again.

* This recipe really is better with real butter. Although passable with shortening, I don't recommend it.

Pies & Cakes
Soft or Durham Wheat

When baking cakes or pies, most any flour works. Because cakes call for baking powder and pie crusts require no leavening agents at all, soft wheat flours are quite acceptable. The soft wheats yield a lighter textures and color than their hard wheat counterparts, producing a finer cake or pie crust. Although hard wheat can be used, they will produce a dense, "nutty flavored" final product.   If you must use hard wheat flour, choose a recipe that contains a lot of spices, as the "wheaty" flavor will be masked by the spices.

As you sift through these recipes, you will notice that there are far more pie recipes than cake. I am cake challenged. I'd like to think that the fault lies not with me, but with the fact that I haven't had an oven with a regulated temperature for over 14 years, however, if I am truly honest with myself, I have to admit that I'm just not a skilled cake baker. Thankfully, my inadequacies are lost on my family – they much prefer pies to cakes – and I do just fine making pies.

Our very favorite pies are berry pies, followed by pear crumb. I didn't put in recipes for common pies, such as berry, apple or cherry (you can find those in any cook book), but only those that we have come across or created over the years that have become family favorites.

I also included a few pie crust recipes. I'm sure everyone has their own favorites – these are mine.

Best Pecan Pie

All of the men in my life love their pie! Without a doubt, my husband, father and sons would rather have pie than cake any day. I came up with this recipe specifically to make into tartlets to send with my husband to work. They make the perfect afternoon pick-me-up.

9" pie shell – prebaked

1/3 C butter
1 C packed brown sugar **(or 1 C sugar + 4 T molasses)**
¼ C granulated sugar **(or honey)**
¼ tsp. salt
3 eggs
1/3 C corn syrup
1 T vanilla
2 C small pecan halves

Melt the butter in a medium saucepan. Mix in the brown sugar, granulated sugar and salt. Beat in eggs, one at a time. Add corn syrup and vanilla and mix well.

Place saucepan over very low heat. Cook and stir constantly with wire whisk until mixture is hot and looks shiny, about 6-7 minutes. You have to stir constantly so the mixture cooks evenly and the eggs don't scramble on the bottom of the pan. Stir in pecans.

Pour pecan mixture into the prepared pie crust.

Bake at 300° until the center feels set but soft when touched with your finger and moves slightly when the pie is gently jiggled, about 40 – 45 minutes

Breakfast Coffee Cake

I dug this recipe up from an old English cookbook and was hooked after I made it for the first time. I never make a single batch, always preferring to make a large cake in a Bundt pan. The sour cream renders this cake incredibly moist, unlike most coffee cakes. It keeps well, with the flavor actually improving over time (not that it ever lasts more than a day in our home!). Although called a coffee cake, I prefer mine with a lovely cup o' tea.

CAKE:
8 T butter, softened **(or shortening)**
1 C sugar **(or honey)**
1 tsp. vanilla extract
1 ½ C flour **(or whole (soft) wheat flour)**
1 tsp. baking powder
½ tsp. baking soda
pinch of salt
1 C sour cream **(or yogurt or milk or pwd milk)**
2 large eggs **(or 2 T egg pwd + 6 T water)**

TOPPING:
½ C walnuts or pecans, coarsely chopped *{optional}*
¼ C brown sugar, packed **(or ¼ C sugar + 1 T molasses)**
1 T ground cinnamon

Heat the oven to 375°. Grease and flour a loaf pan (or grease and line with waxed paper). Mix all the topping ingredients in a small bowl until blended. Set aside.

To make the cake: Beat together the butter, sugar and vanilla until the mixture is pale yellow and fluffy. Add the sour cream and eggs and beat into the butter mixture. Add the flour, baking powder, baking soda and salt. Mix until the batter is thoroughly combined. The batter will be quite soft. Spoon half the batter into the prepared pan. Sprinkle half of the topping over the batter. Spoon the remaining batter into the pan.

Evenly sprinkle the remaining topping over the batter and press it lightly into the surface.

Bake the cake for 45 to 55 minutes, or until it is lightly browned and a wooden pick inserted in the center comes out clean. Cool the cake in the pan on a wire rack for about 30 minutes. After the cake has cooled, carefully turn it out of the pan, remove the waxed paper from the bottom (if waxed paper was used) and put upright on a serving planter. Cut slices and serve warm.

NOTE: This recipe can be doubled and baked in a tube pan or Bundt pan. Increase the baking time to 1 hr. 10 minutes.

Buttermilk Pie Crust

This pie crust never fails to please. It holds together very well, making it easy to roll out and is perfectly flaky.

3 C flour **(or whole (soft) wheat flour)**
1 tsp. salt
½ C shortening **(or lard or butter)**
½ C chilled butter **(or shortening or lard)**
½ C buttermilk **(or (pwd) milk with 1 ½tsp. lemon juice or vinegar)**

Mix together the flour and salt. Using a pastry cutter, cut in the shortening and butter. Using a fork, stir in the buttermilk. Stir until dough forms a ball. You may add a little more buttermilk if necessary to gather up the crumbs.

Divide the dough into two disks, wrap and chill. Roll on a lightly floured surface.

Candy Bar Pie

This is just a sheer indulgence that really, probably, shouldn't be legal, but, here it is anyway. We rarely make this sublime treat, but when we do it doesn't last longer than 5 minutes! Hmmm.

6 chocolate bars (1.45 oz.)
1 carton (1 ½ C) whipped cream, whipped
1 T. vanilla
1 graham cracker crust (9")

In a double boiler, melt chocolate bars. Fold in the whipped cream. Stir in vanilla. Spoon into pie crust. Chill until ready to serve.

Chocolate Chip Pie

This is one of THOSE pies – you know, the ones that you don't make very often but when you do, your family is wrapped around your little finger. Use this recipe with discretion!

½ C flour **(or whole (soft) wheat flour)**
½ C sugar **(or honey)**
½ C brown sugar, packed **(or ½ C sugar + 2 T molasses)**
2 eggs, beaten **(or 2 T egg pwd + 6 T water)**
¾ C butter, softened)
1 C semi-sweet chocolate chips
1 C shopped walnuts *{or pecans}*
9" pie crust, unbaked

Blend flour, sugar and brown sugar into eggs; add butter, mixing well. Fold in chocolate chips and walnuts; pour into pie crust. Bake at 325° for 55 to 60 minutes or until knife inserted into middle of pie comes out clean.

Fried Apple Pie Pastry/ Pasty Dough

For years I searched for the perfect crust for fried fruit pies, only to be disappointed time and again. When I used regular pie crust, the results were dismal – the crusts crumbled, were too thick and never held together. Every attempt I made seemed to bring me a little closer to an acceptable crust, but perfection alluded me. Finally, on a whim, tried a pasty crust recipe rather than a pie crust recipe. It was fabulous! Finally, an easy to make easy to handle, perfect crust for fried hand pies. We fill these pies with everything from blackberries to apples to pears – whatever we can think of. We limit ourselves to making these about two times a year, otherwise, none of our clothes would fit!

1 C butter **(or shortening)**
1 ¼ C boiling water
1 tsp. salt
3 T sugar *{omit if you are using for meat pies}* **(or honey)**
4 ½ to 5 C flour **(or whole (soft) wheat flour)**

Cut up the butter and put it into a medium bowl. Stir in boiling water and stir until the butter has melted. Add the salt, sugar and flour. Stir until the dough forms a soft ball. Wrap in plastic and refrigerate while making your filling.

Cut into 16 equal pieces and roll out on floured board.

Lots of Pie Crust

Come Thanksgiving or any other holiday that requires a lot of pies, this is the pie crust recipe that I use. It makes 4 single crust pies or 2 double crust pies, with trimmings left over! It does brown quickly, so be sure to watch it during that last little bit of baking.

1 egg **(or 1 T egg pwd. + 3 T water)**
1 T vinegar
½ C ice water
4 C flour **(or whole (soft) wheat flour)**
1 T sugar
2 tsp. salt
1 ¾ C shortening **(or butter or lard)**

Beat the egg with the vinegar and water and set aside.

Combine the flour, sugar, salt. Cut in the shortening or butter with a pastry cutter until the chunks are the size of small peas.

Slowly pour the egg, vinegar and water mixture into the flour mixture (add more water if necessary) until the dough forms a ball. Roll out immediately or cover with plastic wrap and store in refrigerator until ready for use.

Maple Nut Pie

We love the flavor of maple, and the combination of maple and nuts is classic. This pie always delivers sweet perfection.

2 eggs, beaten **(or 2 T egg pwd. + 6 T water)**
1 C real maple syrup **(or 1 C corn syrup + 1 T maple extract)**
2 tsp. maple extract **(or 1 T rum)**
½ tsp. vanilla extract
2 T melted butter **(or shortening)**
2 T **flour (or whole (soft) wheat flour)**
¼ tsp. salt
1/8 tsp. cinnamon
1/8 tsp. ground nutmeg
2 C roughly chopped walnuts *{or pecans}*

Mix together the eggs, maple syrup, maple extract, vanilla extract and butter. Sprinkle with flour, salt, cinnamon and nutmeg. Whisk until smooth. Spread the walnuts in the bottom of a prepared pie shell. Pour the maple syrup/egg mixture over the walnuts.

Place in the preheated oven on the middle rack. Place a cookie sheet on the rack underneath to catch any drips.

Bake at 375° for 40 to 45 minutes. Halfway through the baking time, you may want to tent (with foil) the pie to prevent over-browning of the crust.

The surface of the pie may crack while cooking – that's fine. It will deflate while cooling.

Pear Crumb Pie

*Next to Blackberry pie, this is my husband's all-time favorite.
Every fall we gather as many pears as we can and bottle them up
so that we can enjoy this pie at a moment's notice. Apple pie is
nice, but this pear pie is out of this world. We find that this
makes a lovely breakfast as well as a fine dessert.*

9" unbaked pie shell

½ C brown sugar, packed **(or ½ C sugar + 2 T molasses)**
2 T cornstarch
½ tsp. cinnamon
¼ tsp. ginger
1/8 tsp. salt
Dash nutmeg
6 C thinly sliced, peeled pears **(or 2 quart jars canned pears)**
1 T lemon juice

Topping
2/3 C flour **(or whole (soft) wheat flour)**
1/3 C brown sugar, **packed (or 1/3 C sugar + 1 T + 1 tsp.
molasses)**
1/3 C butter, cold

Combine filling ingredients, spoon into the prepared crust.
Bake at 400° for 25 minutes. For topping, combine flour and
brown sugar; cut in butter until crumbly. Sprinkle over filling.
Bake 40 minutes longer. Cover edges with foil during the last
15 minutes to prevent overbrowning if necessary.

Poppy Seed Pound Cake

Our oldest daughter, Elizabeth, loves making pound cakes. They are one of her many specialties. She found this original "pound" cake recipe (a pound of butter, a pound of sugar, a pound of flour....) and incorporated her favorite flavors, Almond and Poppy seeds.

2 C butter *{1 pound}* **(or shortening)**
2 ¼ C sugar *{1 pound}*
9 large egg yolks *{1 pound}*
1 C milk **(or pwd. Milk)**
3 T brandy or sherry *{optional – we never use this}*
2 tsp. vanilla or almond *{our favorite}* flavoring
4 C flour *{1 pound}* **(or whole (soft) wheat flour)**
1 T baking powder
1 tsp. salt
¼ C poppy seeds
9 egg whites beaten until stiff

Cream together the butter and sugar (the longer you beat the butter and sugar, the lighter the cake). Mix in the egg yolks, milk, brandy and vanilla. Add the flour, baking powder, salt and poppy seeds and stir to combine. Fold in the egg whites.

Pour into a lightly greased and floured tube pan or two 5x9 inch bread pans and bake at 350° for about 1 hour or until the top surface of the cake springs back when you press on it gently with your fingers.

Allow the cake to cool in the pan for 10 minutes before turning onto a cooling rack. Let the cake cool thoroughly after it is done, cover and store for a couple of days to allow the flavor to mature.

NOTE: *You do not have to separate the eggs and whip the whites. You can just add 9 eggs and call it good. We like to separate the eggs so that the cake is a little lighter.*

Candy & Confections

When I was growing up, our family had very little money. We never had soda pop, very rarely had candy and considered fresh milk celebration worthy. We never felt deprived, but considered all indulges great treats.

Every Christmas, my Vashon Island grandmother would put together a package of homemade candy and ship it to our family in the hinterboonies. Turtles, Chocolate Covered Cherries and peanut brittle filled the box. The arrival of grandma's package heralded the arrival of the Christmas Season and we looked forward to it with great anticipation.

My mother kept grandma's treasure of candy carefully hidden (under lock and key) in a corner of her unheated bedroom and brought it out every evening, to the great anticipation of my brother and I.

When I grew up, long after my grandmother had ceased sending her Christmas candy packages, I decided that I had to try candy making for myself. Starting with Grandma's Turtle recipe, I began our own family Christmas candy traditions. Over the years, we have added many recipes to our repertoire, each child having their own favorite.

I hope you enjoy making candy as much as we have. May you have new Christmas traditions in your future!

*NOTE: I didn't offer any ingredient substitutions for the candy and confection section because candy has to be full of "bad for you stuff" to be really good!

Better-than-York Peppermint Patties

Our daughter Serenity loves peppermint. When she was little, I was the candy maker in the family, but just as soon as she was old enough, she kicked me out of the kitchen and took over the candy making (at least the peppermint patty making)! These are her all-time favorites. They are rich and pepperminty and are always gone in a flash. I like to keep them in the refrigerator so they are cool and refreshing.

1 egg white
4 C confectioners sugar
½ C light corn syrup
1 to 1 ½ tsp. peppermint extract *{to taste}*

Beat the egg white until frothy but not stiff. Slowly add the confectioners sugar. Add the corn syrup and peppermint extract.

Knead until it has the consistency of dough. Add more sugar if necessary, until the mixture is no longer sticky.

Roll out the peppermint dough on a surface dusted with cornstarch, with a rolling pin dusted with cornstarch to 1/4 " thick. Cut out rounds with a cookie cutter. Put on cookie sheets in the fridge for 45 minutes.

Melt over low heat or in a double boiler:
1 12oz. bag semi-sweet chocolate chips
2 tsp. Crisco (not butter)

Dip peppermint patties in chocolate, turn to coat. Chill patties until firm (30 minutes).

I keep these peppermint patties in the refrigerator and serve chilled.

Caramel Corn (Microwave)

Years ago, I went to a Tupperware party at a friends house. Now, truth be told, I am not a Tupperware kind of girl, so I didn't come home with any new plastic gadgets, however, I did come home with a killer recipe. Our hostess made caramel corn – in a MICROWAVE! no less, and it was awesome. I wrangled the recipe from her and have been spoiling my family with it ever since. It always turns out perfectly, takes very few ingredients and is lightening fast, and really, is better than any recipe we have tried. It is cheating, I suppose, using the microwave, but is sure is convenient, especially if you are feeding hoards of locusts (our pet name for children when we have large gatherings). Try it – you won't be disappointed!

1 C popcorn {kernels, to be popped}
1 C brown sugar
1 C butter
¼ C corn syrup
½ tsp. baking soda

Pop the popcorn and place in a paper grocery bag. In a large, microwave safe bowl, combine the brown sugar, butter and corn syrup. Microwave for 5 minutes, stirring halfway through. Add the baking soda to the caramel mixture. Stir well. This will significantly change the consistency of the caramel.

Pour the caramel mixture over the popcorn in the paper bag. Stir through the popcorn. Fold the bag and put in the microwave for 1 minute. Mix popcorn again and put in the microwave for 1 more minute. Pour the popcorn into a serving bowl. Allow the caramel corn to sit for about ½ an hour to harden. Break into chunks and enjoy.

Grandma Rowland's Turtles

These are the Turtles that I remember from my childhood (with a bit of tweaking here and there).

2 C. Pecan Halves
1 recipe "The BEST Caramel"
2 C. Milk Chocolate Chips
2 T shortening or parafin

Butter a 10"x15" pan.

Make 1 recipe caramel. While still hot, add the pecans to the caramel mixture. Pour into prepared pan. Allow to cool and harden. Cut into 1 ½" squares.

Melt chocolate chips and shortening in a double boiler or in the microwave. Dip each square into the melted chocolate mixture and set on a waxed paper lined cookie sheet to cool.

Allow to cool completely (either at room temperature or put the cookie sheet in the refrigerator) and package in tins, Tupperware or boxes.

Peanut Brittle

Making goodies together has become a wonderful family tradition. We put on our favorite Christmas music, push up our sleeves and have a blast. We have found that we can make our treats as easily on our wood cook stove as we can on the gas and electric stoves of our past. The work is a little hotter (the wood stove has to be really hot to get that candy to 300°!), but we just take turns stirring and then stepping outside in the sub-freezing temperatures to cool off.

Butter 2 cookie sheets and warm in oven (about 250°)

Combine and set aside:
1 ½ tsp. baking soda
1 tsp. water
1 tsp. vanilla extract

In medium pot combine:
1 ½ C granulated sugar
1 C water
1 C corn syrup

Heat mixture to 240°, on medium/high heat

Stir in:
3 T butter
2 C raw peanuts

Stir constantly until mixture reaches 300°

Take off heat

Pour in:
Baking soda, water, vanilla mixture
Stir vigorously
Quickly pour onto cookie sheets

Let cool and break into pieces

"Mounds" Candy

I came across this little recipe years ago and changed it a bit to mimic "Mounds" bars. Oh, we love this! Our Southern friends always help themselves to a handful when they come to visit during the Christmas season. They are quick and easy to make and I love the fact that they use nothing more than standard pantry items.

¼ C butter
3 C flaked coconut
2 C confectioners' sugar
¼ c half-and-half cream *{or cream or milk}*
2 C semisweet chocolate chips
2 tsp. shortening

lightly butter a 9x9" baking pan, set aside.

In a saucepan, cook butter over medium-low heat until golden brown (this makes the candy really good!), about 5 minutes. Remove from the heat; stir in the coconut, sugar and cream. Press into the prepared pan. Refrigerate until the candy is easy to cut. Slice into 1x2" rectangles. Put candies on a waxed paper lined cookie sheet and return to the refrigerator to harden.

On low heat (or in a double boiler) melt chocolate chips with 4 tsp. shortening. Dip each piece of candy in melted chocolate and cover completely. Return to wax paper and refrigerate to harden. Store in an airtight container in the refrigerator or a cool room.

The BEST Caramel

When I was little, my grandmother made boxes of candy at Christmas time and sent them through the mail to our family. They were always waited upon with great anticipation. My favorite candy, out the many varieties she sent, were the Turtles. Grandma used Kraft caramels for her turtles, but I wanted to make my own so that I didn't have to open all of those little candies. After trying many different recipes, I came across this version. It is the ONE!

1 C butter
2 C brown sugar
1 C corn syrup
1 14 oz. can sweetened condensed milk
2 tsp. vanilla

In a saucepan, over medium heat, bring the butter, brown sugar, corn syrup and sweetened condensed milk to a boil. Cook and stir constantly until the mixture reaches 248° (it takes about 30 to 40 minutes). Remove from the heat. Stir in the vanilla.

Pour into a buttered pan to cool. Cut into squares and wrap in waxed paper.

FOR CARAMEL APPLES

Heat candy to 250° (if you exceed 250° the caramel will be too hard to eat).

Insert wooden sticks into 8 – 10 apples. Dip each apple into slightly cooled caramel mixture. Turn to coat. Set on buttered, sugared wax paper.

Salads, Sides & Sauces

This little section turned into a dumping ground for all of the recipes I couldn't put anywhere else. I mean, really, putting salad dressing, onion rings and refried beans all in the same section? But, try as I might, I just couldn't come up with enough recipes to put all like things together and so we ended up with "Salads, Sides & Sauces".

Some of these recipes I use frequently, others are only for certain times of the year. Generally, during the summer, I have one of these salads in my refrigerator, waiting to accompany any hot weather meal. The stuffing recipe is the same recipe used by my myself, my mother, my grandmother and my great-grandmother. It is nothing fancy, but to our family it tastes like home.

If you have ever wanted to know how to make your own Worcestershire Sauce, the recipe is here, along with the best onion ring recipe we have every used.

Enjoy real renaissance living as you pick greens from your garden, slather them in salad dressing you made yourself and top it off with homemade croutons. Now that's living!

Amish Macaroni Salad

*I've never been fond of macaroni salad that is full of vinegar –
just too sour for my taste. I found this recipe and it has become a
summer staple for our family. No picnic is complete without it!*

2 C uncooked elbow macaroni
3 hard boiled eggs, peeled and chopped
1 small onion, chopped
3 stalks celery, chopped
1 small red bell pepper, seeded and chopped
2 T dill pickle relish
2 C mayonnaise
3 T prepared mustard
¼ C granulated sugar
2 ¼ tsp. white vinegar
¼ tsp. salt

Bring a pot of lightly salted water to a boil and add the
uncooked macaroni. Cook for 8 to 10 minutes or until tender.
Drain and set aside to cool.

In a large bowl, stir together the boiled eggs, onion, celery, red
pepper and pickle relish. In a small bowl, stir together the
mayonnaise, mustard, sugar, vinegar and salt. Pour over the
vegetables and stir in macaroni until well blended.

Cover and chill for at least 1 hour before serving.

*You can add cubes of cheese just before serving if you would
like.

Basic Baked Beans

Serenity (our 2nd daughter) loves bakes beans. I try to make up a big batch, eat what we can and pressure can the rest. It is wonderful to be able to grab a jar off the shelf and have an instant meal.

1 lb. navy beans
2 qt. water
½ C. molasses
¼ C. ketchup (optional)
1 tsp. mustard
2 tsp. salt
¼ tsp. pepper
1 onion, chopped
2 slices bacon, chopped (or salt pork)
bean liquid to cover

Soak the beans overnight. In the same liquid, bring the beans to a boil and simmer until tender, about 1 ½ hours. Drain, reserving liquid.

Preheat oven to 275° to 300°

Combine the cooked beans, molasses, ketchup, mustard, salt, pepper, onion and bacon. Cover with the reserved bean liquid. Bake for 4 – 8 hours, adding liquid occasionally if necessary. Cover during the first half of the baking time then uncover.

Caesar Salad Dressing

Who doesn't love a tangy Caesar Salad? This is a simple dressing – just keep adding garlic until you get it right!

2 T Dijon mustard
1 T balsamic vinegar
1 tsp. Worcestershire sauce
2 cloves fresh garlic
1 ½ T lemon juice
½ C olive oil
¼ C grated Parmesan
Dash salt
Cream or milk

Put the mustard, vinegar, Worcestershire, garlic and lemon juice into a blender. Pulse to combine. With the blender on low, slowly add the olive oil. Add the Parmesan and salt and mix. Add enough cream or milk to thin to your favorite consistency. Store in refrigerator.

Chili-Tomato Sauce

This is wonderful over enchiladas, however, I think you could probably find a lot of other uses for it too!

2 T. oil
1 onion, minced
3 ½ C. tomato sauce
2 cloves garlic, minced
1 – 2 T. chili powder
¼ tsp. dried oregano
1 tsp. salt

Sauté the onion in the oil. When the onion is just yellow, not brown add the tomato sauce, garlic, chili powder, oregano and salt. Cover and simmer at least 30 minutes, stirring frequently. Use for tacos or enchiladas.

French Dressing

Another simple dressing that perfectly compliments summer greens. I love the fact that I always have all of the ingredients in the pantry.

1 T. grated onion
1 tsp. salt
2 T. sugar
2 T. vinegar
½ C. canola oil
½ C. ketchup
2 T. lemon juice
1 tsp. paprika

Shake, beat or whirl in blender. Keeps well in the refrigerator.

Herbed Rice Pilaf

I began making this rice pilaf when I was still a new cook. Over the years I have adjusted the recipe and used what I had in the cupboard. Occasionally I still use the original recipe, but more often than not, I tweak it to suit our needs. It is a wonderful, light side dish perfect for summer meals.

1 C rice
¾ C onion, diced
2 ½ C water
2 T parsley
¼ tsp. sage

1 C celery, diced
¼ C butter
1 pkg. chicken noodle soup mix *
1 ½ tsp. thyme
¼ tsp. pepper

In a large skillet, cook the rice, celery and onion in butter, stirring constantly, until rice is browned. Stir in the next six ingredients, bring to a boil. Reduce heat; cover and simmer for 15 minutes. Remove from the heat and let stand, covered, for 10 minutes.

  *Often, I don't have packaged soup mix. Instead I use 1 ½ T chicken bouillon and a handful of crunched up angle hair pasta.

Spicy Bacon Vinaigrette

This is my very favorite salad dressing. The bacon adds that "little extra". The bacon combined with the French dressing flavor is unparalleled.

Blend together until smooth:
1/3 C ketchup
½ C white vinegar
2/3 C sugar
1 clove garlic, minced
salt and pepper to taste
½ C olive oil

Add:
½ lb. bacon, crisply cooked and crumbled
1 green onion, chopped

Stir or shake well. Store in refrigerator.

Homemade Croutons

Croutons are wonderful on salads and a nice addition to homemade soups. I like to use homemade French bread (after it's a few days old) and spice it up with various seasonings.

½ C butter *{1 cube}*
1 or 2 cloves of garlic, minced
Chives
Italian spices *{or whatever suits your fancy}*
1 loaf day old French bread *{or white or wheat bread}*, cubed.

Melt butter in skillet. Add garlic, chives and Italian spices and sauté for about 1 minute. Add cubed bread. Stir bread to coat.

Put coated bread onto cookies sheets and put into a 300° oven for about 20 minutes or until toasted and dry.

These will keep for weeks in a sealed jar or plastic bag.

Onion Rings

If you are looking for crispy, sweet, perfect onion rings, this is the recipe for you. Although we don't indulge in these often, they are always a treat.

3 sweet onions, thickly sliced and separated into rings
1 ½ tsp. baking powder
1 C flour
1 tsp. salt
1 egg
2/3 C water
½ T lemon juice
1 T butter, melted
oil for deep frying

Soak onion rings in ice water for ½ hour; pat dry with paper towels and set aside. Sift baking powder, flour and salt together; set aside. Combine egg, water and lemon juice; beat well. Stir into flour mixture until just blended; add butter. Dip onion rings into batter; drop into 375° oil and fry 2 minutes on each side. Drain.

Maple Syrup

Although we love real maple syrup, it is not always in our budget. We find this to be a fine substitution – much like the imitation syrup you can buy in the grocery store.

2/3 C brown sugar
1 C water
2 T. butter
1/3 C sugar
1 tsp. maple extract

Boil together brown sugar and water. Cook granulated sugar on a low flame until it melts and begins to color Add the brown sugar mixture, stirring until smooth and thick. Mix in butter and maple. This will keep for a week in the refrigerator.

Mayonnaise I

We go through a lot of mayonnaise and wouldn't want to be without a few recipes of our own. Try them both and see which is to your liking.

2 raw egg yolks
2 T vinegar
½ C olive oil
½ tsp. mustard
1 tsp. sugar
½ tsp. salt
pinch of cayenne pepper

Put egg yolks in a bowl and beat lightly with sugar, salt, mustard and cayenne. Add oil a teaspoon at a time. Stir well, one direction until mixture is thick and creamy. Add vinegar a drop at a time. This mayonnaise must be made in a cool place. It is best to stand the bowl in cold water. Store in a cool place. Before using, whipped cream may be added.

Mayonnaise II

2 eggs
1 ½ tsp. salt
1 tsp. dry mustard
½ tsp. paprika
2 T. lemon juice
½ C. oil *{canola or other}*
2 T. vinegar
1 ½ C oil *{canola or other}*

In the blender, whirl together the eggs, salt, dry mustard and paprika. With a spatula, clean the sides of the blender and add lemon juice. Start blender, remove cover and very slowly pour in ½ C oil. Add vinegar. Very slowly, with blender running, add 1 ½ C. oil. Store in the refrigerator.

Mexican Refried Beans

I love this simple refried bean recipe. It can be made in minutes (once the beans have been cooked) and used in so many recipes. I don't recommend canning refried beans, however, I like to can dry beans and then quickly mix up a batch of the refried beans from the canned beans.

1 lb. dried pinto, pink or kidney beans
6 C. water
2 onions, chopped *{optional}*
½ C. hot bacon drippings **(or butter or lard)**
Salt to taste

Soak the beans overnight.   Add 6 cups of water and 2 chopped onions. Bring to a boil, cover and simmer slowly until the beans are tender, about 3 hours. Mash beans with a potato masher. Add bacon, lard or butter and salt. Mix well; continue cooking, stirring frequently until beans are thickened and the fat is absorbed. Serve at once or refrigerate for later use.

"The" Mustard Recipe

A number of years ago, a friend of mine, Julianne of Providence Lodge, shared the most wonderful mustard recipe with me. It had been the secret recipe of her "other mother", who had kept the recipe close to her until the grave. Upon her death, the recipe was given as a favor to those who attended her funeral. We love this mustard with roast beef, venison or with fresh, warm soft pretzels.

½ C sifted flour
¼ C sugar
1/8 tsp. salt
½ C dry mustard *{or ¼ for those not so brave}*
¾ cider vinegar

Mix together and enjoy!

Potato Filling

These are little more than leftover mashed potatoes, but I find the added ingredients make it a whole new meal.

¼ C. butter **(or bacon grease)**
1 C. celery, chopped
1 C. onion, chopped **(or dehydrated onions)**
4 medium potatoes, peeled
1 egg, beaten **(or 1 T. egg pwd. + 3 T water)**
2 slices bread, torn into small pieces

Pare and boil the potatoes in salted water. While the potatoes are boiling sauté the celery and onion in butter. When the potatoes are done prepare them as for mashed potatoes. After potatoes have been mashed, mix in the egg, bread and vegetables. Season with salt and pepper to taste. Put into a greased baking dish. Bake for 1 hour at 350°. Cover for the first half hour, uncover for the remaining time.

NOTE: I prefer to use leftover mashed potatoes for this dish rather than peeling new ones.

Three-Bean Salad

This is an old-fashioned salad, just right for hot summer days. During the summer, I rely on big batches of this salad, pasta salad and potato salad to keep me out of the kitchen on hot summer days.

Choose 2 C. each of three kinds of cooked, drained beans

Cut green beans
Cut yellow beans
Soy beans
Red kidney beans
Green lima beans
Great northern or navy beans
Chick-peas or garbanzos

1 onion, finely chopped
1 green pepper, chopped
½ C. canola oil
½ C. vinegar
½ C. sugar
1 tsp. salt
¼ tsp. pepper

In a large bowl toss beans with the onion and green pepper. Combine the canola oil, vinegar, sugar, salt and pepper and pour over the bean mixture.

Chill before serving. The flavor improves with marinating overnight or longer.

Turkey/Chicken Stuffing

I can practically smell this spicy, savory stuffing now- oh and it makes my mouth water! Every Thanksgiving, my house is filled with the aroma of mom's sausage stuffing. This has been the stuffing that our family has used since time immemorium – no Thanksgiving would be complete without it!

2 quarts bread crumbs
1 lb. sausage, ground
4 medium onions, diced **(or dehydrated onions)**
1 ½ T salt
4 T poultry seasoning
¾ C butter *{1 ½ Cubes}* **(or bacon grease)**
3 – 4 C celery, diced
1 ½ tsp. pepper

Brown sausage in large skillet. When brown, add butter, then add celery and onions. Cook over medium heat for about ½ hour.

Put bread crumbs in large bowl. Add salt, pepper and poultry seasoning. Mix well.

Allow sausage, onion and celery mixture cool, then pour over bread crumbs and mix well. Let cool awhile longer. Add cold water (or turkey or chicken broth), a little at a time, until it's the way you want it, approximately 2 cups. If cooked outside the turkey, cook 1 hour at 350° and cover with drippings.

White Sauce

I use white sauce as the base for so many things. It is the basis for the cheese sauce in my Macaroni and Cheese, the condensed chicken soup in the Mandarin Rice Bake and so many more. White sauce is just the beginning – from here, you can go anywhere!

2 T. butter **(or bacon grease or vegetable oil)**
2 T. flour
1 C. milk

Melt butter in saucepan over low/medium heat. When the butter is melted, add the flour and whisk to combine. Cook briefly before adding milk. Whisk milk into flour mixture and stir until thickened.

NOTE*: This is a basic white sauce recipe that can be altered endlessly. When making white sauce that will be a base for cheese sauce, add a pinch of ground mustard powder. If using instead of Cream of Chicken soup, add a tsp. of chicken bouillon or soup base. If using instead of Cream of Mushroom soup add a handful of diced mushrooms. The variations are endless, use your imagination.*

Worcestershire Sauce

We add just a bit of Worcestershire sauce to a number of dishes.
Oh how excited I was when I discovered I could make my own!

2 T ground pepper
1 C molasses *{not blackstrap molasses}*
1 ½ tsp. cloves
1 ½ tsp. powdered mace
1 ½ tsp. cayenne pepper
1 ½ tsp. garlic
2 medium onions
8 C vinegar

Put mixture into a jar and let it stand for two weeks, closely covered. Stir the mixture daily. At the end of two weeks, boil it for 20 minutes and strain through muslin or cheesecloth. When cold, bottle and cork.

Chapter V

Canning & Food Preservation

My very first pressure canner came from my grandmother, along with her stock of canning jars (she would never buy them if they cost more than a nickel). She had canned extensively from her bountiful orchard on Vashon Island, but had come to the point in her life that required her to downsize.

Although my mother had canned when I was little, I was not particularly familiar with the practice. After my grandmother gifted me with her canner, I dug up some books and dove headfirst into the world of food preservation.

My first foray into canning came in the form of green beans. My mother had canned her beans whole rather than cut. I loved the way they looked in the jar, so stately and uniform. After our first garden provided a bumper bean crop, I set to work. That first year, I canned 75 quarts of green beans. I loved the way they looked on the shelf, mingled with the applesauce and raspberry jam. Soon, peaches, pears, pickles and cabbage lined the shelves, along with canned dried beans, chicken stock and cheddar cheese.

The more I canned, the more I loved it. When my family moved "off-grid", I found how truly valuable my food preservation skills were. Living with no electricity meant no refrigeration. No freezer. I began to rely on home canning to feed my family in the most economical, healthful manner possible.

Although our circumstances have improved over the years, I am all the more convinced that home canning is an essential part of life. It allows me great flexibility in meal planning and doesn't require electricity, earning high points in my book.

Note: Pressure canning requires care and safe practices. Once, early in my canning career, I used my pressure canner to water bath can some jars of juice (don't ask!). My pressure canner was taller than my water bath canner, so I filled it up with water, set the lid on top (not locking it down – I was just water bath canning, after all) and went on about my business. A few minutes after the water was as a rapid boil, I went to the canner to check on my juice. Not thinking about the steam that had built up, I lifted the lid. The canner literally exploded, the canner lid hitting the ceiling. I was covered in boiling water, burned down my entire front. After checking on my sleeping baby, I rushed upstairs, turned cold water on in the shower and stood under the spray, clothes and all. Going to the hospital, I was treated for 2nd degree burns, put on pain killers and sent home. By the grace of God, only my hand blistered and the pain was manageable.

That was my wake-up call. Never again have I been lax in my canning practices. A pressure canner is safe and effective so long as it is used according to instructions. Can safely.

Basic Pressure Canning Instructions:
(Please read the manufacturers instruction that came with your pressure canner)

1. Place rack in bottom of canner and add boiling water to a depth of 1 inch for small canners and 2 inches for large canner.
2. As each jar is filled and cap firmly tightened, set it on the rack in the canner to keep hot. Pack only enough jars at one time to fill canner. Set jars apart so steam can circulate freely.
3. Adjust the cover of the canner and fasten securely.
4. Exhaust canner. Adjust heat to high, leave the petcock (steam valve) open and let steam escape freely for 7 to 10 minutes. Close petcock/steam valve. When required amount of pressure is shown on gauge, start counting processing time. Adjust the heat to keep pressure steady.
5. Process for the required length of time.
6. When processing time is up, remove canner from heat. Let canner stand until pressure gauge returns to zero. Open petcock/steam valve gradually. If no steam escapes, remove cover.
7. Remove jars from canner.

Basic Water Bath Canning Instructions

(Please read the manufacturers instructions that came with your canning kettle)

1. Before you prepare food to be processed, place the water bath canner on the heat with sufficient water to cover the jars at least one inch over the top. This permits water to be heating while the food is being prepared. Water should be boiling when jars of food are placed into it.

2. Prepared only enough jars of food at one time to fill the canner.

3. Place the jars of food on the rack in the canner far enough apart to allow the circulation of water around them. If water does not cover the jars at least one inch over the top, add boiling water to this height. Start counting processing time as soon as the water in canner reaches a good rolling boil. Keep the water boiling all during the processing period. If water boils down add sufficient boiling water to keep it at the required height.

4. Process the required length of time.

5. As soon as the processing time is up, remove jars from the canner.

CONVENIENCE FOODS

Baked Beans
Pressure Canner

4 C navy beans
½ lb. salt pork or bacon, cut into small pieces
4 tsp. salt
4 T molasses
6 tsp. prepared mustard
1 ½ C catsup
8 T brown sugar
2 C onion, chopped

Wash beans thoroughly. Cover with cold water and soak overnight. Boil in same water 45 minutes. Drain beans, saving the liquid. Add all ingredients to beans along with 2 cups of reserved bean liquid. Mix well. Pack into jars to within 1 inch of the top. Put on cap, screw band firmly tight. Yield: 8 pints

Process: Pints   60 minutes
              Quarts   60 minutes

              10 pounds pressure

Bunny Sausage
Pressure Canner

6 lbs. rabbit meat, ground
2 small onions, minced
2 T salt
2 tsp. pepper
¼ tsp. paprika
1 bay leaf
½ tsp. ground sage
½ C ground crackers or bread crumbs
1 or 2 eggs, well beaten
¾ C milk

Mix well together and mold into small cakes and fry until nicely browned. Pack into clean jars to within 1 inch of the top and add 3 or 4 tablespoons of grease in which the cakes were fried. Put on cap, screwing band firmly tight.

Process:	Pints	75 minutes
	Quarts	90 minutes
	10 pounds pressure	

Chicken A La King
Pressure Canner

*NOTE: ALTHOUGH THIS RECIPE ORGINATED IN A KERR CANNING PAMPHLET, RECIPES USING A GRAVY ARE NO LONGER ADVISED FOR HOME CANNING. THIS RECIPE IS INCLUDED FOR EDUCATIONAL PURPOSES ONLY.

1 five pound chicken
4 T flour
1 T salt
2 red peppers, chopped
1 quart chicken broth
1 red pepper, chopped

Cut chicken into pieces, add 3 quarts water and cook until tender. Cool, remove meat from bones and cut into small pieces. Dissolve the flour and the salt in a little of the cold broth and add to the remainder of the broth which has been heated. Cook until slightly thickened, stirring to keep free from lumps. Add peppers and chicken. Heat to boiling and fill jars to within one inch of the top. Put on cap, screw band firmly tight. Yield: 5 pints.

Process:	Pints	75 minutes
	Quarts	90 minutes
	10 pounds pressure	

Chili Beans
Pressure Canner

1 C onion, chopped
6 T chili powder
2 T salt
¼ tsp. pepper
1 red pepper
1 pint canned tomatoes
2 pounds beans (pinto or red kidney)
 7 ½ C boiling water

Wash beans thoroughly. Cover with cold water and soak overnight. Drain off the water the beans were soaked in. Combine the rest of the ingredients (including beans) and boil for 5 minutes. Pack hot into jars to within ½ inch of the top.

Process: Pints   60 minutes
              Quarts   60 minutes

              10 pounds pressure

Dried Beans or Peas, any variety

Pressure Canner

I love to home-can beans! A little work on the front end saves all the work on the back end. When the wood cook stove is boiling along in the winter, I will put a huge pot of beans on to soak and spend the next day canning them. It is a wonderful system! We always have canned beans at the ready for spur-of-them moment bean dishes. This is what we call "fast food"!

Wash beans and soak in cold water overnight. Boil beans 15 minutes. Pack loosely in jars to within 2 inches of top. Add 1 teaspoon salt to each quart jar. Fill jar to within ½ inch of the top with the water in which the beans were boiled. Put on cap, screw band firmly tight.

Process: Pints   60 minutes
            Quarts   60 minutes

            10 pounds pressure

Green Tomato Salsa
Water Bath

5 C chopped green tomatoes
1 ½ C long green chili's, seeded and chopped
½ C jalapenos, seeded and chopped fine
4 C onion, chopped
1 ½ C lemon juice (1/2 lemon juice/1/2 vinegar)
6 cloves garlic, chopped fine
1 T ground cumin
2 T salt
1 tsp. pepper
cilantro

Combine all ingredients in a large saucepan and bring to a boil. Reduce heat and simmer for 10 minutes. Ladle into hot pint jars, leaving ½" headspace.

Water bath can for 20 minutes.

Head Cheese
Pressure Canner

6 pounds chopped meat
3 T salt
4 tsp. pepper
2 tsp. red pepper
2 ½ tsp. allspice
3 tsp. cloves
2 quarts broth in which meat is boiled

Clean hog's head by removing snout, eyes, ears, brains and all skin. Trim off all fat. Cut head into pieces and soak in salt water (1/2 C salt to 1 gallon water) for 3 to 5 hours to draw out all blood. Drain from salt solution and wash well in clear water. Heart, tongue and other meat trimmings may be cooked with head meat. Cover meat with hot water and boil until meat can be removed from bones. Remove all meat from bones. Strain broth and measure. Finely chop meat. Add salt, pepper and spices to meat and mix thoroughly with broth. Cook mixture 15 minutes. Pack in jars to within 1 inch of the top.

Process:	Pints	75 minutes
	Quarts	90 minutes

10 pounds pressure

Spaghetti Sauce
Pressure Canner

3 lbs. ground beef (or ground Italian sausage or a combination)
3 cloves garlic, finely chopped
1 ½ C onions, chopped
3 quarts canned tomatoes (home canned, preferably)
3 tsp. salt
1 ½ tsp. paprika
1 ½ tsp. pepper
3 bay leaves, crumbled

Brown ground beef (or sausage), onion and garlic. Put tomatoes through sieve. Add all ingredients and cook about 30 minutes. Ladle into jars to within 1 inch of the top. Put on cap, screw band firmly tight. Yield: 6 pints

Process:	Pints	75 minutes
	Quarts	90 minutes
	10 pounds pressure	

FRUIT

How to Make Syrup

Make syrup according to sweetness desired. Boil sugar and water together until sugar is dissolved. Juice of the fruit may be used in place of water. Keep syrup hot but do not let it boil down.

	Sugar (cups)	Water (cups)	Used For
Thin	1	3	Small, soft fruits
Medium	1	2	Peaches, apples, pears, sour berries
Heavy	1	1	All sour fruits or those to be extra sweet

Syrup should be boiling when poured over fruits.

Apples
Water Bath

Select uniform apples. Wash, pare and core. Cut into desired size. If peeled fruit is to stand several minutes before precooking, drop it into mild salt solution to prevent discoloration. Drain. Boil 3 to 5 minutes in a medium syrup. Pack into sterilized jars to within ½ inch of the top. Fill to within ½ inch of top of jar with boiling syrup.

Process:	Pints	20 minutes
	Quarts	25 minutes

Apple Sauce
Water Bath

20 large apples
4 C water
2 ½ C sugar

Wash apples. Quarter, core and remove all bruised pieces. If cut fruit is to stand several minutes before cooking, drop into mild salt solution to prevent discoloration. Drain. Add water and cook until soft. Press through sieve or colander to remove skins. Add sugar and bring to boil. Pack while BOILING HOT into jars to within ½ inch of the top. Put on cap.

Process: Pints   25 minutes
               Quarts   25 minutes

Berries
Water Bath

Blackberries, Blueberries, Boysenberries, Gooseberries, Huckleberries, Loganberries. **All berries except cranberries and strawberries**. Wash berries and pick over carefully. Pack into jars to within ½ inch of top. Fill to within 1 ½ inches of top of jar with boiling syrup.

Process: Pints   15 minutes
               Quarts   20 minutes

Cherries
Water Bath

Wash, stem, pit if desired. Pack into jars to within ½ inch of the top. Fill to within 1 ½ inches of top of jar with boiling syrup (use a syrup appropriate to the sweetness of the cherry).

Process:	Pints	20 minutes
	Quarts	20 minutes

Cranberries
Water Bath

Wash and remove stems from cranberries. Drop into boiling heavy syrup. Boil 3 minutes. Pack into sterilized jars to within ½ inch of the top. Fill to within ½ inch of top of jar with boiling syrup.

Process:	Pints	10 minutes
	Quarts	10 minutes

Cranberry Sauce
Water Bath

1 quart cranberries
1 C water
2 C sugar

Pick over and wash berries. Add water and cook until berries are soft. Press through fine sieve. Add sugar and boil another 3 minutes. Pour into sterilized jars to within ½ inch of top.

Process:	Pints	10 minutes
	Quarts	10 minutes

Grapes
Water Bath

Remove stems. Wash grapes. Pack tightly into jars without crushing, to within ½ inch of top. Fill to within 1 ½ inches of the top of the jar with boiling syrup.

Process: Pints   20 minutes
                   Quarts   20 minutes

Grapefruit/Orange/Pomelo
Water Bath

To remove peel, place whole fruit in pan of boiling water. Let stand 3 minutes. Plunge into cold water. Peel. Remove all white membrane. Run a thin knife between pulp and skin of each section and lift out whole. Pack solidly into jars to within ½ inch of the top. Add boiling syrup to within ½ inch of the top of the jar.

Process: Pints   20 minutes
                   Quarts   20 minutes

Peaches
Water Bath

Select ripe firm peaches. Remove peel by floating in boiling water briefly (2 minutes) and then plunging into cold water. Peels will slide off easily (if peach is properly ripened). Remove pits. If peeled fruit is to stand several minutes before packing, drop it into a mild salt solution to prevent discoloration. Drain.

Pack halves or slices into jars to within ½ inch of the top. Fill to within 1 ½ inches of the top of the jar with boiling syrup.

Process: Pints   20 minutes
              Quarts   25 minutes

Pears
Water Bath

Remove peel, core and cut into halves or quarters (or slices, for pies). If peeled fruit is to stand several minutes before precooking, drop into mild salt solution to prevent discoloration. Drain.

Pack to within ½ inch of the top of the jar. Fill to within 1 ½ inches of the top of the jar with boiling syrup.

Process: Pints   25 minutes
              Quarts   30 minutes

Pineapple
Water Bath

Wash pineapple. Slice, peel, remove eyes and core. Leave slices whole or cut into chunks. Pack into jars to within ½ inch of the top. Fill to within 1 ½ inches of the top of the jar with boiling syrup.

Process: Pints   30 minutes
            Quarts   30 minutes

Plums
Water Bath

Select plums that are not too ripe. Wash and prick skin with needle to prevent bursting (or cut fruit in half). Pack into jars to within ½ inch of the top. Fill to within 1½ inches of the top of the jar with boiling syrup.

Process: Pints   20 minutes
            Quarts   25 minutes

Rhubarb
Water Bath

Wash and cut into 1 inch lengths. Pack tightly into jars to within ½ inch of the top. Fill with boiling syrup to within 1 ½ inches of the top of the jar.

Process: Pints   15 minutes
            Quarts   15 minutes

Strawberries
Water Bath

1 C sugar
2 pounds strawberries (6 heaping cups)
½ C strawberry juice

Boil the sugar and juice together (obtain juice by crushing and heating some of the softer berries). Cool and add the whole strawberries, then boil for 3 minutes. Cover the pot and set aside for at least 4 hours. Pack into jars to within ½ inch of the top.

Process:	Pints	15 minutes
	Quarts	15 minutes

JAMS/JELLIES

Apple Pectin
Water Bath

Today, Pectin comes to us in tidy little boxes that we pick up at the supermarket when jam season rolls around. Our grandmothers knew a different way. The following recipe gives directions for extracting pectin from apples (Crabapples are full of pectin) for use in other jam and jelly recipes. It really doesn't take much time and the results are truly spectacular. If ever a time comes that we don't have the modern conveniences to which we have become so accustomed, we will want to know the ways of our grandmothers. This is just a little taste....

7 large apples (preferably crabapples)
4 C water
2 T lemon juice

Wash tart apples. Cut in pieces but do not peel. Add water and lemon juice. Boil for 40 minutes. Press through jelly bag (or cheesecloth), then strain juice through a flannel bag without pressure. Boil juice rapidly 15 minutes. Pour boiling juice into sterilized jars and seal.

Process:　　　Pint　　　　　5 minutes

Use for jelly making from such fruits as peaches, strawberries, cherries, etc., or any fruits that are lacking in pectin. Add 1 cup apple pectin for each cup of fruit juice used. Usually ¾ cup sugar to 1 cup of the combined juices is correct, or test combined juices for pectin content.

Berry Jam
Water Bath

Wash and pick over berries. Crush and measure berries and juice. Heat through. Add ¾ cup sugar for each cup berries and juice. Cook, stirring frequently, until thick. Pour into sterilized jars to within ¼ inch of top. Put on cap, screw band firmly tight.

Process: Pints/Quarts   10 minutes

Crab Apple Jelly
Water Bath

Crab apples are found in abundance in much of the United States. They are often found along abandoned train tacks and near old farmsteads. Year after year these wonderful little fruits fall to the ground and provide fodder for the local wildlife, however, with a little work, they can become a welcome staple of your homestead pantry.

Wash and remove blossom end. Cut into quarters without peeling. Barely cover with water and boil until the fruit is tender. Press through a jelly bag (or cheesecloth) and strain. Measure juice and bring to a boil. Add ¾ cup of sugar for each cup of juice and boil rapidly to jelly stage. Pour into sterilized jars. Fill to within ½ inch of the top. Put on cap, screw band firmly tight.

Process: Pints/Quarts   5 minutes

Cranberry Jam, *Spiced*
Water Bath

8 C cranberries (2 pounds)
1 C water
1 C vinegar
1 tsp. ground cinnamon
½ tsp. ground cloves
½ tsp. ground allspice
6 C sugar

Mash cranberries lightly; add vinegar and water. Cook until soft. Put through course strainer; add spices and sugar, cook 8 minutes, or until thick, stirring often. Pour into sterilized jars to within ¼ in of the top. Put on cap, screw band firmly tight.

Process: Pints/Quarts   10 minutes

Jelly Making
Water Bath

TESTING FOR THE JELLY POINT
Bring jelly to a full, rolling boil that cannot be stirred down. Dip a spoon in the boiling jelly. As it nears the jellying point it will drop from the side of the spoon in two drips. When the drops run together and slide off in a sheet from the side of the spoon, the jelly is finished and should be removed from the heat at once.

A candy or jelly thermometer may be used. The temperature of the boiling juice at the jellying point will be from 220° to 222° at sea level. At higher altitudes the temperature will be lower.

Remove the foam from the jelly and pour at once into sterilized jars. Fill to thin ½ inch of the top of the jar.

Process: 5 minutes in boiling water bath

PECTIN
Pectin is a substance in fruits that, when heated and combined with fruit acid and sugar, causes the fruit juice to congeal or "jell". Not all fruit contains pectin, but you may extract pectin from fruits such as apples, plums, etc. and combine it with other fruit juices, or use commercial pectin. When using commercial pectin, be sure to follow the recipe that comes with the pectin.

TO TEST JUICE FOR PECTIN
The juice may be tested to determine whether it contains sufficient pectin to make jelly. The amount of pectin will indicate the amount of sugar to be used.

Mix 2 tablespoons sugar, 1 tablespoon Epsom salts, 2 tablespoons cooked fruit juice. Stir well and let stand for 20 minutes. If mixture forms into a semi-solid mass the juice contains sufficient pectin.

240

TO TEST FOR ACID
Juice high in pectin may lack acid to make good jelly. The fruit juice should be as tart as one teaspoon lemon juice mixed with 3 tablespoons of water. If necessary, lemon juice may be added to the fruit juice. Usually one tablespoon lemon juice to each cup of fruit juice is sufficient.

ADDING THE SUGAR
The amount of sugar to be added will be determined by the pectin content of the juice.

JUICES	SUGAR (for 1 cup juice)
High in pectin	¾ C sugar
Low in pectin	½ C sugar

Juice should always be boiling when the sugar is added. Boil jelly as rapidly as possible.

PREPARING THE FRUIT
- Select a mixture of slightly under-ripe and ripe fruit
- Wash fruit
- Cut hard fruit (apples, quinces) into pieces. Slightly crush berries
- Add enough water to barely cover hard fruits. Berries and grapes need only enough water to start them cooking. Boil until fruit is tender
- Pour the hot, cooked fruit at once into a jelly bag (or cheesecloth) and let drip. When done dripping, press jelly bag. Re-strain juice through a clean jelly bag (or cheesecloth) to make juice as clear as possible
- Jellies and preserves made in small batches turn out better. Don't use more than 6 to 8 cups of juice at a time. Unsweetened fruit juices may be canned and made into jellies later.

Raspberry Orange Conserve

I have always been fascinated by conserves (jam with nuts added) but couldn't find one to suit my fancy. One summer, when the berries were ripe and I had a bowl full of oranges on the counter, I decided to combine them and came up with this recipe. It was love at first taste!

Wash and crush:
4 C raspberries

Liquefy in blender:
2 C oranges (peeled, discard peel and pith)

Measure the raspberries and orange pulp into a large pot.

Add:
1 box pectin (or 6 T bulk pectin)
Stir well

Begin heating berries on medium/high heat, stirring frequently. Bring to a rolling boil (a boil that cannot be stirred down).

Add:
8 ½ C sugar (all at once)
Stir until the sugar dissolves and bring the mixture back up to a rolling boil, stirring constantly.

Add:
¼ C nut meats (I love pecans or walnuts)
Boil for 2 minutes. Ladle into sterilized canning jars, cap off and process for 10 minutes in a water bath.

Winter Jam
Water Bath

3 C cranberries
1 ½ C diced, peeled apples
1 ½ C water
1 ½ C crushed pineapple (undrained)
2 T lemon juice
3 ½ C sugar

Cook the cranberries and apples in the water until they are clear and tender. Press fruit through sieve to remove cranberry skins. Measure, there should be 3 cups of pulp. Add pineapple, lemon juice and sugar. Mix well and boil rapidly until thick and clear (about 6 to 8 minutes). Pour into sterilized jars to within ¼ inch of the top. Put on cap, screw band firmly tight.

Process: Pints/Quarts   10 minutes

MEAT

Butchering Charts
Whitetail Deer Venison Yield Chart

GIRTH	LIVE WEIGHT	FIELD DRESSED	YIELD
24"	55 lbs.	38 lbs.	28 lbs.
25"	61 lbs.	43 lbs.	27 lbs.
26"	66 lbs.	49 lbs.	30 lbs.
27"	71 lbs.	53 lbs.	31 lbs.
28"	77 lbs.	59 lbs.	34 lbs.
29"	82 lbs.	64 lbs.	36 lbs.
30"	90 lbs.	70 lbs.	39 lbs.
31"	98 lbs.	74 lbs.	42 lbs.
32"	102 lbs.	80 lbs.	45 lbs.
33"	110 lbs.	87 lbs.	50 lbs.
34"	118 lbs.	91 lbs.	54 lbs.
35"	126 lbs.	99 lbs.	57 lbs.
36"	135 lbs.	104 lbs.	61 lbs.
37"	146 lbs.	115 lbs.	66 lbs.
38"	157 lbs.	126 lbs.	71 lbs.
39"	169 lbs.	135 lbs.	74 lbs.
40"	182 lbs.	144 lbs.	80 lbs.
41"	195 lbs.	156 lbs.	88 lbs.
42"	210 lbs.	170 lbs.	94 lbs.
43"	228 lbs.	182 lbs.	103 lb.
44"	244 lbs.	198 lbs.	110 lb.
45"	267 lbs.	214 lbs.	120 lb.
46"	290 lbs.	233 lbs.	130 lb.
47"	310 lbs.	251 lbs.	139 lb.
48"	340 lbs.	272 lbs.	153 lb.

Venison Butchering Chart

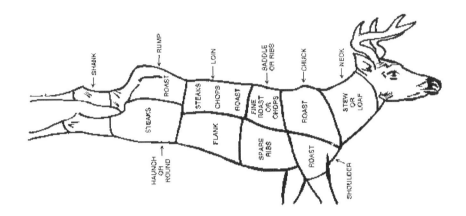

Beef Yield Chart

LIVE WEIGHT	CARCASS WEIGHT	YEILD
1030 lbs.	650 lbs.	488 lbs.
1110 lbs.	700 lbs.	525 lbs.
1200 lbs.	750 lbs.	562 lbs.
1270 lbs.	800 lbs.	600 lbs.
1350 lbs.	850 lbs.	638 lbs.

Beef Butchering Chart

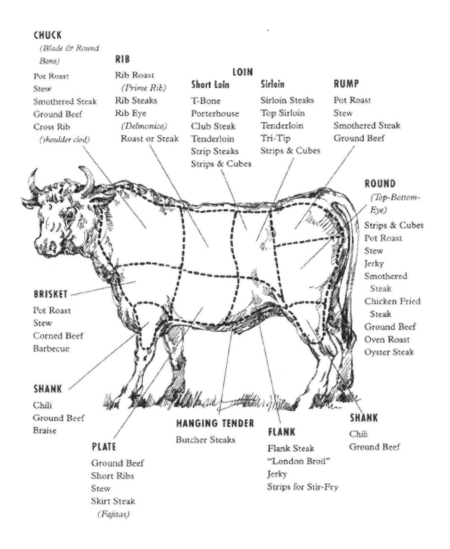

CHUCK
(Blade & Round Bone)
Pot Roast
Stew
Smothered Steak
Ground Beef
Cross Rib
(shoulder clod)

RIB
Rib Roast
(Prime Rib)
Rib Steaks
Rib Eye
(Delmonica)
Roast or Steak

LOIN

Short Loin
T-Bone
Porterhouse
Club Steak
Tenderloin
Strip Steaks
Strips & Cubes

Sirloin
Sirloin Steaks
Top Sirloin
Tenderloin
Tri-Tip
Strips & Cubes

RUMP
Pot Roast
Stew
Smothered Steak
Ground Beef

ROUND
(Top-Bottom-Eye)
Strips & Cubes
Pot Roast
Stew
Jerky
Smothered
 Steak
Chicken Fried
 Steak
Ground Beef
Oven Roast
Oyster Steak

BRISKET
Pot Roast
Stew
Corned Beef
Barbecue

SHANK
Chili
Ground Beef
Braise

PLATE
Ground Beef
Short Ribs
Stew
Skirt Steak
(Fajitas)

HANGING TENDER
Butcher Steaks

FLANK
Flank Steak
"London Broil"
Jerky
Strips for Stir-Fry

SHANK
Chili
Ground Beef

Hog Butchering Chart

LOIN

Roasts & Chops
(Blade, Center, & Sirloin)
Back Ribs
Boneless Top Loin
Tenderloin
Strips, Cubes, & Cutlets
Country Style Ribs

SHOULDER or "BOSTON BUTT"

Roast
Steaks
Cubes
Strip
Sausage

FRESH LEG OR HAM

Ham (whole)
Ham Slices
Cutlets
Scallops
Roasts
Strips & Cubes

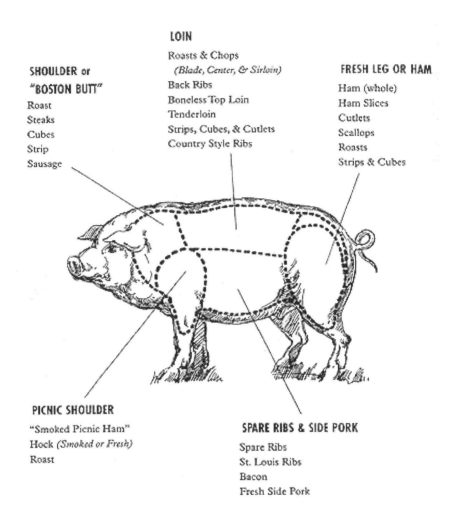

PICNIC SHOULDER

"Smoked Picnic Ham"
Hock *(Smoked or Fresh)*
Roast

SPARE RIBS & SIDE PORK

Spare Ribs
St. Louis Ribs
Bacon
Fresh Side Pork

Chicken Butchering Chart

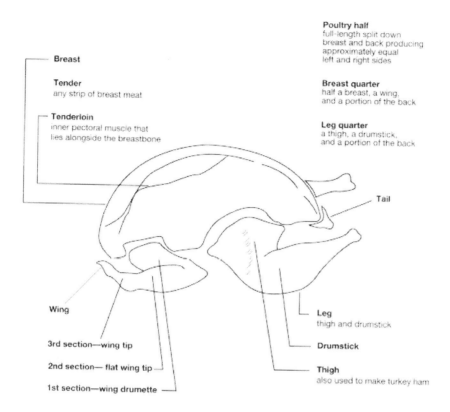

Breast

Tender
any strip of breast meat

Tenderloin
inner pectoral muscle that
lies alongside the breastbone

Poultry half
full-length split down
breast and back producing
approximately equal
left and right sides

Breast quarter
half a breast, a wing,
and a portion of the back

Leg quarter
a thigh, a drumstick,
and a portion of the back

Tail

Wing

3rd section—wing tip

2nd section— flat wing tip

1st section—wing drumette

Leg
thigh and drumstick

Drumstick

Thigh
also used to make turkey ham

249

Rendering Fat
Bear, Deer, Cow, Goat, Pig, Elk, etc.

Fat from deer, sheep, beef and bison is considered tallow, while fat from pig and bear is considered lard, however, processing it is the same.

Cut the fat, gathered during butchering, into 1" to 1 ½" squares. Make sure you don't leave any hair in the fat (you want high quality lard or tallow). Fill a large stock pot (or two or three, depending on how much fat you have to render) about ¼ to 1/3 full. Rendering fat will splatter, so you don't want to fill your pot too full. If you are using a conventional stove, you don't want to deal with the mess and if you are using your wood cook stove (as I do), you don't want to start a fire.

Turn your burner on high (or get your wood box filled and cranking out the heat) and put your stock pot(s) over the hot spot. Stir occasionally. You really don't have to stir very often, just enough to keep the fat from sticking to the bottom of the pot.

As the fat begins to melt, the chunks of fat/meat will grow smaller and begin to brown. These are the cracklings (you know, the ones that Laura talked about in the *Little House on the Prairie* books). Some folks like them sprinkled with a little bit of salt and other people use them to flavor soup or corn bread. If you have no taste for cracklings, your chickens will love them.

After the cracklings are quite brown, but not burned, and your pot is rather heavy with oil, it is time to strain the fat into canning jars (or a shallow pan, if you are planning on using your tallow for candle making). Take the pot(s) off the stove and remove the cracklings with a slotted spoon. When you have removed most of the big chunks you can then strain the oil through a fine mesh strainer or a couple of layers of fine cheesecloth.

After the fat (tallow) has been poured into sterilized jars, cap them off and put them in your water bath canner and process for 20 minutes. You can now use your rendered fat in multiple ways. You can use it in place of vegetable oil in recipes. You can use it as frying oil. You can let it harden (in the refrigerator or other cool place) and use it in place of shortening in biscuits, pie crust or whatever you need it for.

If you intend to use your tallow for candle-making, or soap-making you can process the fat a bit further (to remove impurities and water). Break it up into a small pan, place the pan in a larger pan filled partially with water. Heat the water and melt the tallow. Let it heat (on very low heat) until any retained moisture is evaporated off. Let it cool slightly and strain it through coffee filters or fine cheesecloth into clean, dry canning jars.

*Tallow candles are considerably softer than their wax counterparts. They will burn quickly – use caution.

Bacon
Pressure Canner

A few years ago, we splurged and bought a couple of cases of canned bacon. It was great. We loved having bacon on the shelf. It was quick and tasty but it was terribly expensive. Although too expensive for everyday use, it got me to thinking – if bacon can be canned commercially, why couldn't I can it at home? After researching methods combined with the experience of using commercially canned bacon, I figured I was ready to try it for myself. Here is my method.

1. Clean jars and prepare the pressure canner.
2. Lay a piece of parchment paper on the counter, about 16" long.
3. Lay strips of bacon (thick cut works best) on the parchment paper (about 10 or 11 pieces) and top with another piece of parchment paper.
4. Fold the paper (along with the bacon) in half and roll tightly from one end to the other (it should be small enough to fit into a wide mouth canning jar).
5. Slide into a wide mouthed canning jar and seal. Do not add salt or water.
6. Can at 10 pounds of pressure for 90 minutes.

Chicken and Game Birds
Pressure Canner

Dress fowl and allow to cool. Cut in convenient pieces. Boil until meat can be removed from the bones; pack meat in jars to within 1 inch from the top. Add 1 tsp. salt to each quart jar if desired. Add 4 T of the hot broth.

Process: Pints   75 minutes
            Quarts   90 minutes

            10 pounds pressure

Chicken, Raw Pack
Pressure Canner

Wash chicken in cold water. Cut into pieces and pack into jars to within 1 inch of the top of the jar, without precooking. Add 1 tsp. salt to each quart jar. Do not add liquid.

Process: Pints   75 minutes
                       Quarts   90 minutes

                       10 pounds pressure

Cured Beef (or Venison), Quick Method
For use in hot weather or if needed for immediate use

Rub the meat thoroughly with a rather large quantity of fine salt, with a little saltpeter. Using two sticks, prop it over a tub or pan of water, placing a good quantity of salt on the upper side. Turn it once after twelve hours, laying additional salt on the turned-up side. It will be cured in twenty-four hours. If you need the meat immediately, you can squirt a salt brine into all of the crevices using a large syringe. If you use this method, the meat could be cooked in 12 hours. If the meat is not required in a hurry, a little sugar and less salt very much improves the flavor. This applies to curing hams as well.

Fresh Ham
Pressure Canner

Slice ham about ½ inch thick. Trim away excess fat. Cut in pieces of desired size. Sear in hot fat until lightly browned. Pack in jars to within 1 inch of the top. Add 1 teaspoon salt to each quart jar if desired. Add 3 or 4 tablespoons of fat from frying pan (broth or hot water may be used). Put on cap, screw band firmly tight.

Process: Pints   75 minutes
                Quarts   90 minutes

                10 pounds pressure

Home Curing of Bacon
Two Methods

METHOD 1:
Cut up the pig, removing the spine and pelvis. Rub each piece well with salt and pack in a cask or crock   not a metal container. The next morning, take the meat out and drain off liquid. Pour in brine when meat is again packed in the container, placing a heavy weight on top, as meat must be kept covered.

BRINE: To each 100 lbs. of meat use 2 lbs. of brown sugar, 1 oz. salt peter and enough salt stirred into boiling water to float a potato the size of an egg.

It takes approximately 8 pounds of salt to make 4 gallons of water into brine. Pour over the meat when cold. Turn meat every few days. Leave bacon in the brine for 3 weeks; hams and shoulders for 4 weeks. Then dry well in the sun. Hang in a dry cool place until thoroughly dry.

Smoke the meat for up to 2 days or until the meat becomes the desired shade. Meat may be hung at room temperature for 30 days. This practice allows salt to equalize and improves the flavor. Finished meat may be rubbed lightly all over with vegetable oil to improve the appearance. Beef can be cured in the same way.

Rice or oat husks can be bought and are most suitable for keeping meat packed in either bag or boxes.

METHOD 2:
Cut up the pig, removing the spine and pelvis. Rub each piece well with salt; and pack in cask, or crock (not metal).

Next morning take the meat out and drain off liquid and discard the liquid. Pour on brine when meat is again packed in the container. Place a heavy weight on top, as meat must be kept covered.

BRINE: To each 100 lbs. of meat, use 2 lbs. of brown sugar, 1 oz. salt peter and enough salt stirred into boiling water to float a potato the size of an egg.

It takes about 8 lbs. of salt to make four gallons of water into brine.

Pour over meat when cold and turn meat every few days.

Leave bacon in the brine for three weeks; and hams and shoulders for four weeks.

Then dry well in the sun and hang in a dry cool place.

Roast Beef (any red meat)
Pressure Canner

Select meat suited for a roast. Trim, wipe with a damp cloth. Heat suet and other fat in roasting pan. Cut roast in convenient pieces to go into jar. Put meat into hot fat in roaster, set in oven. Roast at a moderate (350°) temperature until 1/3 done. Pack in jars to within 1 inch of the top. Add 1 teaspoon salt to each quart jar if desired. Add 3 or 4 tablespoons of liquid from roasting pan. Put on cap, screw band firmly tight.

Process: Pints   75 minutes
                Quarts   90 minutes

                10 pounds pressure

Pork Chops
Pressure Canner

Slice chops about ½ inch thick. Trim away excess fat leaving only a small amount to add flavor. Sear chops in hot fat until lightly browned. Pack into jars to within 1 inch of the top. Add 1 tsp. salt to each quart jar, if desired. Add 3 to 4 T of fat from frying pan or hot water may be added to fat in pan and 3 or 4 T of this added to each quart jar.

Process: Pints   75 minutes

                      Quarts   90 minutes

10 pounds pressure

Rabbit
Pressure Canner

Rabbit is processed identically to chicken. Prepare and process the same way.

Raw Pack Beef (any red meat)
Pressure Canner

Select meat suited for a roast. Trim, wipe with a damp cloth. Cut into convenient pieces to go into jar. Pack loosely to within one inch of the top of the jar. Add 1 teaspoon salt to each quart jar if desired. **Do not add liquid**. Put on cap, screwing band firmly tight.

Process: Pints   75 minutes

                      Quarts   90 minutes

                      10 pounds pressure

Venison Jerky

A friend of ours, who is also a lifelong hunter, passed this recipe along to us. It is the perfect combination of sweet and spicy – just right for that side of venison you have laying around.

1 C water
¾ C soy sauce
½ C honey
1 tsp. salt
1 T pepper
1 T garlic powder
¼ C Worcestershire sauce

Mix all ingredients of marinade together. Cut up strips of meat (about ¼ inch thick) and soak in marinade for 10 hours. Stir frequently. Dry at 150° for 10 to 12 hours. Cool jerky completely to test if done.

PICKLES

Bread and Butter Pickles
Water Bath

25 to 30 medium cucumbers
8 large white onions
2 large sweet peppers
½ C salt
5 C cider vinegar
5 C sugar (2 ½ pounds)
2 T mustard seed
1 tsp. turmeric
½ tsp. cloves

Wash cucumbers and slice as thin as possible. Chop onions and peppers; combine with cucumbers and salt; let stand 3 hours and drain. Combine vinegar, sugar and spices in large kettle, bring to boil. Add drained cucumbers; heat thoroughly but do not boil. Pack while hot into sterilized jars to within ½ inch of the top.

Process: Quarts   5 minutes

Dill Pickles
Water Bath

30 to 36 cucumbers (3 to 4 inches long)
3 C vinegar
3 C water
6 T salt
Fresh or dried dill
Garlic
Mustard Seed

Wash the cucumbers. Make a brine of the vinegar, water and salt. Bring it to a boil. Place a generous layer of dill, ½ to 1 clove of garlic (sliced) and ½ tablespoon of mustard seed in the bottom of each sterilized quart jar. Pack the cucumbers into the jars. When the jars are half filled with cucumbers, add more dill and complete the packing of the jars. Fill the jars to within ½ inch of the top with the boiling brine. Put caps on jars, screw the band firmly tight.

Process: Quarts   20 minutes

* The pickles will shrivel after processing. They will later plump in sealed jar.

Green Tomato Pickles
Water Bath

Green tomatoes
Stalk celery
Sweet green peppers
Garlic
2 quarts water
1 quart vinegar
1 C salt
Dill

Use small, firm green tomatoes. Pack into sterilized jars. Add to each quart jar a bud of garlic, 1 stalk of celery and 1 green pepper, cut into fourths. Make a brine of the water, vinegar and salt. Boil with the dill for 5 minutes. Pour the hot brine over the pickles to within ½ inch of the top of the jar. Put on cap, screw band firmly tight.

Process: Quart   15 minutes

*These will be ready for use in 4-6 weeks.

Sweet Pickles
Water Bath

Into a clean stone jar, put 2 gallons of cucumbers, washed and sliced lengthwise. Regardless of size, cucumbers must be sliced or they will shrivel. Dissolve 2 cups of salt in one gallon of boiling water and pour while hot over pickles. Then cover and weight down pickles and let stand for 1 week. Remove scum daily. On the eighth day, drain, then pour 1 gallon of boiling water over them and let stand 24 hours. On the ninth day, drain and pour 1 gallon of boiling water with 1 tablespoon of powdered alum over the pickles and let stand 24 hours. On the following day or tenth day, drain again, pour 1 gallon boiling water over them, let stand 24 hours, then drain.

For the pickling mixture, combine 5 pints of vinegar boiling hot, 6 cups of sugar, ½ ounce (1 tsp) celery seed, 1 ounce (3 T, broken) cinnamon sticks. Pour this over the pickles. Drain off liquid for three mornings, add 1 cup sugar with each morning, reheat and pour back over pickles. With third and last heating pack pickles into sterilized jars to within ½ inch of the top. Cover them with boiling syrup to within ½ inch of top of jar. Put on cap.

Process: Quarts   5 minutes

262

SAUCES

Tomato Catsup
Water Bath

1 peck (12 ½ pounds) ripe tomatoes
2 medium onions
¼ tsp. cayenne pepper
2 C cider vinegar
1 ½ T broken stick cinnamon
1 T whole cloves
3 cloves garlic (finely chopped)
1 T paprika
1 C sugar
2 ½ tsp. salt

Wash and slice tomatoes and boil until soft. Into another kettle slice the onions. Cover with a small quantity of water and cook until tender. Run the cooked onions and tomatoes through a sieve. Mix the onions and tomato pulp. Add the cayenne pepper. Boil this mixture rapidly until it has been reduced to about ½ original volume.

Place vinegar in an enamel pan; add a spice bag containing the cinnamon, cloves and garlic. Allow this to simmer for about 30 minutes, then bring to boil. Place cover on pan and remove from heat. Allow this to stand in covered pan until ready to use. When tomato mixture has cooked down to ½ original volume, add vinegar mixture, of which there should be 1 ¼ cups. Add the paprika, sugar and salt and boil rapidly until thick. This should require about 10 minutes. Pour while boiling into sterilized jars to within ½ an inch of the top.

Process: Pints   5 minutes

Barbecue Sauce
Water Bath

6 T brown sugar
3 T paprika
3 tsp. salt
3 tsp. dry mustard
¾ tsp. chili powder
1/8 tsp. cayenne pepper
6 T Worcestershire sauce
3 C tomato juice
¾ C chili sauce
¾ C vinegar
1 ½ C onions, chopped

Mix all ingredients thoroughly. Boil for 15 minutes. Pour into sterilized jars to within ½ inch of the top.

Process: Half-pints   10 minutes

Chili Sauce
Water Bath

1 gallon (or 6 ¼ pounds) ripe tomatoes (peel and core before measuring)
2/3 C white onions, chopped
1 ½ C sugar
1 tsp. nutmeg
¾ tsp. Tabasco sauce
½ tsp. curry powder
2 C vinegar
5 tsp. salt
2 tsp. ginger
1 tsp. cinnamon
1 tsp. mustard

Put tomatoes and onions through food chopper. Add all other ingredients and boil 2 hours or until thick, stirring frequently to prevent scorching. Pour into sterilized jars to within ½ inch of the top.

Process: Pints   5 minutes

Hot Sauce
Water Bath

72 hot red peppers
2 cloves garlic
2 T sugar
1 tsp. salt
4 tsp. grated horseradish
2 C water
2 C vinegar

Peel and mince garlic. Wash peppers and combine with garlic.
Place in saucepan with water. Cover pan. Cook until very
tender. Press through sieve. Add other ingredients to pureed
product. Cook until well blended and thickened. Pour into jars
to within ½ inch of the top.

Process: Half-pints   10 minutes

SOUPS/STOCKS

Chicken Soup Stock
Pressure Canner

Such bony pieces as back, neck, feet and wings may be used. Cover with cold water and allow to simmer for several hours. Seasoning such as a small amount of onion and celery and bouillon or soup base may be added. Simmer until meat can be removed from bones. Cook down until you've reached the desired flavor. Remove onions and celery and pour into jars to within 1 inch of the top. Meat removed from the bones may be added to the jars if desired. Add hot soup stock to within 1 inch of the top of the jar. Put on cap, screw band firmly tight.

Process: Pints   45 minutes
             Quarts   45 minutes/90 min. with meat
             10 pounds pressure

Pea Soup
Pressure Canner

Boil peas until soft in enough water to cover. Remove from the heat and press through sieve. If consistency is quite thick, add boiling water to make medium thick. Add 1 tsp. salt to each quart. Fill jars to within 1 inch of top.

Process: Pints   60 minutes
             Quarts   60 minutes
             10 pounds pressure

Soup Stock
Pressure Canner

Cover soup bones and trimmings of meat with water. Salt if desired, and cook about two hours. Remove meat and bones. Skim off excess fat and pour stock into jars to within 1 inch of the top. Meat removed from the bones may be added to jars if desired. Put on cap, screw band firmly tight.

Process: Pints   45 minutes
              Quarts   45 minutes/90 min. with meat
              10 pounds pressure

Tomato Soup
Pressure Canner

14 quarts ripe tomatoes
7 medium-sized onions
1 stalk celery
14 sprigs parsley
3 bay leaves
14 T flour
14 T butter
3 T salt
8 T sugar
2 tsp. pepper

Wash, cut up tomatoes. Chop onions, celery, parsley, bay leaves. Add to tomatoes; cook until celery is tender. Put though sieve. Rub flour and butter into smooth paste thinned with tomato juice. Add to boiling soup; stir to prevent scorching. Add salt, sugar and pepper. For smoother consistency put through sieve again. Fill clean jars to within 1 inch of the top.

Process: Pints   35 minutes
              Quarts   40 minutes
              10 pounds pressure

VEGETABLES

Asparagus
Pressure Canner

Remove scales and tough ends. Wash thoroughly. Cut into jar lengths or 1 inch pieces. When cutting asparagus into jar length pieces, be sure that the pieces will be ½ inch from the top of the jar.

Pack into jars to within ½ inch of the top. Add ½ tsp. salt to each pint (1 tsp. to each quart). Fill to within ½ inch of top of jar with boiling water.

Process: Pints   25 minutes
                  Quarts   30 minutes
                  10 pounds pressure

Beans (string, Wax)
Pressure Canner

Wash, string, trim or cut into 1 inch pieces.

Pack into jars to within ½ inch of the top of the jar. Add ½ tsp. salt to each pint (1 tsp. to each quart). Fill to within ½ inch of the top of the jar with boiling water.

Process: Pints   20 minutes
                  Quarts   25 minutes
                  10 pounds pressure

Cabbage
Pressure Canner

Wash, remove outside leaves. Cut into desired size pieces and boil for 5 minutes. Pack into jars to within ½ inch of the top of the jar. Add ½ tsp. salt to each pint (1 tsp. to each quart). Fill to within ½ inch of the top of the jar with precooking liquid or boiling water.

Process: Pints   45 minutes
       Quarts 55 minutes
       10 pounds pressure

Carrots
Pressure Canner

Wash and peel carrots. Slice, dice or leave whole.

Pack into jars to within ½ inch of the top of the jar. Add ½ tsp. salt to each pint (1 tsp. to each quart). Fill to within ½ inch of the top of the jar with boiling water.

Process: Pints   25 minutes
       Quarts 30 minutes
       10 pounds pressure

Corn
Pressure Canner

Use only fresh corn that is tender and juicy. Shuck and remove silks. Cut out any damaged spots. Wash the ears. Cut corn from cob.

Pack loosely into jars to within an ½ inch from the top. Add ½ tsp. salt to each pint jar (1 tsp. to each quart jar). Fill to within ½ inch of the top of the jar with boiling water.

Process: Pints   55 minutes
       Quarts   85 minutes
       10 pounds pressure

Mushrooms
Pressure Canner

Soak the mushrooms in cold water for 5 minutes. Trim stems. Wash in cold water. Leave small ones whole, cut large ones and boil for 3 minutes. Pack into jars to within ½ inch of the top. Add ½ tsp. salt to each pint (1 tsp. to each quart). Fill to within ½ inch of the top of the jar with the water used to boil the mushrooms or freshly boiled water.

Process: Pints   30 minutes
       Quarts   35 minutes
       10 pounds pressure

Onions
Pressure Canner

Wash and peel onions. Boil for 5 minutes. Pack into jars to within ½ inch of their top. Add ½ tsp. salt to each pint jar (1 tsp. to each quart). Fill to within ½ inch of the top of the jar with water in which onions were precooked or freshly boiled water.

Process: Pints   40 minutes
             Quarts   40 minutes
             10 pounds pressure

Peppers, Bell
Pressure Canner

Can the sweet bell peppers with the skin on. Remove the seed pod. Boil for 5 minutes and pack tightly into jars to within ½ inch of the top. Add ½ tsp. salt to each pint (1 tsp. to each quart). Fill to within ½ inch of the top of the jar with the water the peppers were boiled in or freshly boiled water.

Process: Pints   35 minutes
             Quarts   35 minutes
             10 pounds pressure

Pumpkin, for Pie Filling

(Also for Acorn squash, Buttercup squash, Butternut squash, Winter Crookneck, Golden Delicious, Hubbard or Banana squash)

Pressure Canner

*NOTE: ALTHOUGH THIS RECIPE ORGINATED IN A KERR CANNING PAMPHLET, RECIPES USING THICK SUBSTANCES ARE NO LONGER ADVISED FOR HOME CANNING. THIS RECIPE IS INCLUDED FOR EDUCATIONAL PURPOSES ONLY.

Cut in medium pieces. Remove peel. Steam, boil or bake until tender. To steam, add little or no water. To boil, add only enough water to cover. Put pumpkin and liquid from precooking through a food mill or strainer. Spices may be added. Simmer until heated through, stirring often to prevent sticking. Pack loosely while hot, into jars to within ½ inch of the top.

Process: Pints   60 minutes
              Quarts   80 minutes
              10 pounds pressure

Squash, summer
Pressure Canner

Wash, do not peel. Cut in inform pieces.

Pack into jars to within 1 inch of the top. Add ½ tsp. salt to each pint (1 tsp. to each quart). Fill to within ½ inch of the top of the jar with boiling water.

Process: Pints   25 minutes
              Quarts   30 minutes
              10 pounds pressure

Stewed Tomatoes
Pressure Canner

2 quarts tomatoes, cut in chunks
½ green pepper, chopped
½ medium onion, chopped
3 stalks celery, chopped
2 tsp. celery salt
2 tsp. sugar
¼ tsp. salt

Mix all ingredients and pack into jars (do not add water) to within ½ inch of the top. Put on cap, screw band firmly tight. Yield: 2 quarts.

Process: Pints   35 minutes
              Quarts   40 minutes
              10 pounds pressure

Tomatoes
Pressure Canner

Wash tomatoes. Scald in boiling water long enough to remove peel (1/4 minute). Plunge into cold water. Peel, core, quarter and firmly pack into jars to within ½ inch of the top. Add no liquid. Add ½ tsp. salt to each pint jar (1 tsp. salt to each quart).

Process: Pints   35 minutes
              Quarts   40 minutes
              10 pounds pressure

Water Glass
(Sodium Silicate)

Water Glass (also known as Sodium Silicate) is an age old, time-tested way to store eggs over the winter. Water Glass is a sealant, commonly used to seal cement, but also used to seal eggshells. Depriving the porous eggshells of oxygen slows the rate of spoilage, making water glass an effective method of egg preservation. It is found in most hardware stores and some drug stores.

Sodium Silicate
Water
Eggs
Glass jar or earthenware crock

Mix 1 part of water glass (sodium silicate) to 9 parts of water.

Put eggs in a gallon glass jar or an earthenware crock and pour water glass mixture over the top of the eggs and cover by 2 inches of water glass mixture. Store in a cool, dark place.

NOTE: *Eggs stored in water glass will remain fresh for about 6 months. Toward the end of their storage shelf life, the yolks break easily and are best for use in baked goods and scrambled eggs.*

Chapter VI

Wildcrafting

Wildcrafting has become on of my favorite pastimes. I am amazed with the bounty God provides for us in our own backyard. Roses, Elderberry and Honeysuckle yield their goodness in due season and herbs and berries abound.

Wildcrafting has become a cherished time spent with my children. It is truly a family affair. Regardless of the busyness that fills our lives, when the harvest is ready we must stop whatever we are doing and gather God's goodness unto ourselves. We spend days in the wood, clambering up hillsides and sliding back down, laughing as we go.

Once we are home, the real work begins, but as we see our efforts take shape, our work seems more like fun than labor. When completed and lining the shelves, the beauty of the sparkling jars in a multitude of colors, brings a satisfaction all its own.

Seasons come and go, and with them, ample opportunities to indulge in the art of wildcrafting. God's bounty is limitless – you just have to find it.

Apple Snacks

2 qts. Wild Apples

Peel, core and halve the apples. Shred apples coarsely and put on buttered cookie sheet. Bake at 225° until dry. Remove from the cookie sheet with a spatula, break into pieces. Store in an airtight container.

Elderberry Cordial

You must be very careful with cordial, as it is very "hot".

Elderberries
Vodka
Cinnamon sticks
Whole cloves
Sugar syrup (1 C. sugar to 2 C. water)

Fill a jar (quart or gallon) with elderberries. Add cinnamon sticks (2 for quart, more for gallon) and cloves (a pinch for quart, more for gallon) and cover with vodka. Allow to sit for 6 weeks (or more), shaking periodically. The berries will change color as the juice is extracted. After 6 weeks, strain the berries, cinnamon and cloves out of the liquid and add a simple syrup (water and sugar) to taste. If you prefer, you could make your syrup using honey instead of sugar.

Elderberry Wine

As I was contemplating the numerous health benefits of the Elderberry, I struck upon an idea that generations before me knew instinctively. Why not Elderberry wine? Think about it – the main ingredient in most flu and cough medicines on the market is alcohol. Why not combine the health benefits of Elderberry with the sleep inducing attributes of a glass of wine? If we can't get cough medications, or a flu remedy or a sleep aid, wouldn't it make sense to have something on hand to help care for your family when they have been laid low?

I sought a recipe that would use only what we had on hand – nothing fancy or exotic. I ended up with an old recipe that came from the Scottish Highlands. It uses nothing more than berries, sugar, lemon juice, raisins and yeast – all things that are easily stored.

11 pounds Elderberries
18 C sugar
¾ C lemon juice
3 ¼ pounds raisins
1 pkg. vintners yeast (Bordeaux)
3 ¼ gallons water

Remove the berries from the stalks using a fork.

Put berries in a sanitized bucket and pour in a gallon of boiling water. Mash the berries against the side of the bucket, then put in the raisins. Cover and leave for 3 to 4 days.

Strain the berries and raisins out of the liquid and tip the liquid back into the bucket. Add the sugar and stir until dissolved. Add the lemon juice. Sprinkle the yeast on the liquid. Cover for 3 days, strain again and pour wine into a demijohn (carboy).

Fix the airlock and leave until bubbling completely stops (about 5 months). Strain and bottle off. The wine could be ready to drink in about 4 months. This wine has a lovely red color.

Honeysuckle Jelly

Honeysuckle grows abundantly in the woods and vales where we live. During June, the children and I spend the lion's share of our time gathering the bounty of nature and transforming it into delectable preserves. This is one of our favorite wildcrafting recipes. It is dainty and delicate and just right with scones and biscuits.

8 C Honeysuckle liquid
2 tsp. lemon juice
3 boxes of pectin (or 1 C bulk - each package contains 1/3 C of pectin)
10 C sugar

To make the liquid: Pick blossoms that are opened, but not old. You'll need at least 2 to 3 quarts of flowers (I used 2 1/2 liters). Pick through the flowers, removing leaves and stems and rinse. In a large pot, place the flowers and enough water to cover well. Bring to a boil. Reduce heat and simmer, covered, for 20 minutes. Remove from the heat and cool. Pour the flowers and water into a gallon jar and refrigerate for at least 24 hours - two days is even better.

To make the jelly: Strain the flowers from the water (I used a colander). Rinse the gallon jar and strain the water through 4 layers of cheese cloth into the clean jar (this removes the impurities and results in a lovely, clear jelly).

Measure the honeysuckle liquid into a large pot, add the lemon juice and pectin. Stir well. Bring to a full, rolling boil, stirring constantly. Stir in the sugar. Continue to stir, return to a rolling boil and boil for 1 minute (timed from the beginning of the rolling boil).

Remove the pot from the heat. Skim foam from the top and ladle jelly into jars. Wipe threads and rims carefully, then top with prepared lids and rings. Process in a water bath for 10 minutes.

Rosehip Jam

Rosehips are an excellent source of Vitamin C. They can be dried and used as a tea or processed into jam. The jam they yield is very delicate in flavor – perfect with crumpets or toast.

Fill a pint measure with rosehips (fully ripe). Snip off the dead flower ends. Wash and drain the hips. Put into 2 pints of boiling water. Reduce heat and boil gently until hips can be crushed with a wooden spoon. Mash well and turn contents of the pan into a freshly scalded jelly bag. Leave to drip overnight. Great care must be taken to strain the hips carefully through the jelly bag and never to press or squeeze during the process. The tiny hairs on the hips, must be eliminated or they can cause irritation to the mucous membrane of the throat or stomach.

Measure juice the next day and make up to 1 ½ pints, with water. Meanwhile, wash, dry and chop up 1 lb. or less of cooking apples (green). Put in a saucepan with water just to cover. Stew (lid on pan) until apples are a soft, thick pulp. Rub through a sieve. Mix with rosehip juice. Bring nearly to boiling point. Stir in 2 lbs. sugar. When dissolved, boil until setting stage (test on a cold saucer). Bottle and seal at once. Can in a water bath for 10 minutes.

Rose Petal Jam

When wildcrafting, the bounty starts early. This jam is lightly sweet and oh, so delicate.

1 lb. rose but petals
1 pint water
Juice of 2 lemons
3 lbs. sugar

Cut petals into thin strips; arrange on plates and sprinkle with lemon juice. Stand overnight. Put in saucepan with the water. Bring to boiling point. Strain. Keep aside half of the petals. Return water to saucepan, add sugar and remaining lemon juice. Add reserved petals. Simmer gently for 30 minutes. Cool a little before bottling. Process in a water bath for 10 minutes.

Witchetty Grubs

So, I'll admit it – I've never actually eaten Witchetty Grubs. I am glad to know how to cook them, if ever the need arises.

Those fat, white grubs found in the damp rotting bark of old trees, are delicious cooked in honey. Wild honey can sometimes be found in the bush.

Chapter VII

Miscellaneous Recipes

In every cookbook there really ought to be a section with recipes that are useful, fun and have no other place to go. This is just such a chapter.

Although we always seem to have more to do than we can possibly accomplish, I try to make time to play with my children. I know that these days of small children, muddy boots and runny noses will end all too quickly. If I don't stop and play from time to time, I will miss the opportunity entirely. And that would be terrible.

I love butcher paper (meat wrapping paper) for all manner of childhood craft projects. It comes on a huge roll, is fairly inexpensive and serves multiple purposes. Before any major craft is undertaken, the butcher paper makes its appearance. I cover the kitchen table in butcher paper, making sure to tape the ends to the table (this really keeps the mess to a minimum) and then let the kids go wild. Butcher paper is the perfect medium for finger paints, just right as a drop cloth under a Paper-Mache project and, with the waxed side up, is marvelous for rolling out fresh play dough.

In a book full of useful recipes, don't overlook the fun recipes. Believe me, your children will thank you for it.

Finger Paint

All children, at some point, should experience the joy of dipping their fingers in colorful paint and spreading it across clean, white paper!

1/3 C. cornstarch
3 T. sugar
2 C. cold water
Food coloring

Mix cornstarch, sugar and water in saucepan. Cook and stir over medium heat for about 5 minutes or until thickened; remove from heat. Divide the mixture into separate cups or containers (a muffin tin works well). Tint mixture in each container with a different food color. Stir several times until cool. Store in an airtight container (yogurt containers are good). The paint works best if you use it the same day you make it.

Paper-Mache

Do you remember those messy hours spent in kindergarten with glue up to your elbows while pasting strips of newspaper onto balloons? Now you can re-create that experience in the comfort of your own kitchen. Have fun!

2 C. cold water
1 ½ to 1 ¾ C. flour
Newspaper, cut into strips that measure about 1x15 inches

Mix water and flour in a large bowl with a wire whisk until smooth. Mixture should be the consistency of heavy cream. Coat a mold (inflated balloon or cardboard shape, etc.) with one layer newspaper strips which have been dipped in water. Then dip strips in flour mixture and lay over first layer of strips until mold is well coated. Let stand until the strips on the mold are dry and hard. Paint over the strips, if you like.

Mrs. Gust's Paste that Sticks

Mrs. Gust was a dear, sweet elderly neighbor of ours when I was a little girl. I have fond memories of her meeting my brother and I early in the morning as we made our way past her house on our way to school. She would stand at the end of her driveway with a small paper bag in each hand anticipating our arrival. When we approached, she would motion us to her and deposit in each of our waiting hands a bag of warm, fresh caramel corn. Oh, what a sweet walk we would have! And this is an old time recipe that Mrs. Gust shared with my mother when she was a young mother.

1 C Sugar
1 C Flour
1 Tablespoon Alum
1 Quart Water
Clove oil

Mix and cook ingredients in a double boiler until you have a mixture that is clear - like cooked starch.

Remove the mixture from burner and add 30 drops of Oil of Cloves.

Makes a little over a quart of paste.

Play-Dough

My children have spent many a happy hour rolling colorful dough into shapes, forming it into creatures and pressing it against their cheeks. This is hands-down our favorite play-dough recipe.

1 C. flour
2 tsp. cream of tartar
½ tsp. salt
1 C. water
1 T. oil
1 tsp. vanilla (optional)
15 drops food coloring (optional)

Cook all ingredients in saucepan over medium heat, stirring constantly, about 4 minutes or until mixture forms a ball. Remove from saucepan and let stand on the counter or 5 minutes. Knead dough about 30 seconds or until it is smooth and blended. Cool completely. Store in an airtight container in the refrigerator.

Chapter VIII

Homestead Beauty, Hygiene & Cleaning

I am of the opinion that if you can buy something in the grocery store you should be able to make it at home. If you can't make it at home, perhaps you shouldn't be using it!

I have experimented with making a number of household items in the comfort of my kitchen. I find it to be a very satisfying pastime. Never one for craft projects, I have come to discover that I love making things that are useful. Making soap, lotion bars and lip balm allows me to be creative but also provides our family with healthy, cost effective, wholesome alternatives to mass produced products. These homestead crafts not only enhance our lives, but serve us in some useful way.

While somewhat uncommon today, these homestead crafts used to be a way of life. If you didn't make it, you didn't use it. I still like that philosophy and will continue my quest to revive the skills and knowledge lost in past generations.

Anti-Fungal Baby Wipes

Although washcloths work just fine, I like the idea of a wipe that is all-natural, good for the skin and ready to go. I really like both of these recipes. I found that thick paper towels worked best, although thin washcloths work also.

½ C water (boiled)
1 tsp. vinegar
¼ C aloe vera gel
1 T calendula oil
1 drop lavender essential oil
1 drop tea tree essential oil

Place your wipes (folded paper towels or bulk wash clothes) in a container and pour on enough solution to moisten them. Store extra solution in the fridge.

Baby Wipes

1/8 C olive oil
1/8 C baby shampoo
1 ½ - 2 C water
8 drops lavender oil
5 drops tea tree oil

Mix oils. Shake oils with water. Mix in baby shampoo. Pour over a half-length roll of paper towels with the cardboard removed, in some kind of plastic container. Dispense from the inside of the roll.

Bar Soap

I love making bars of soap and always having a large assortment of lovely scents. During particularly lean years, a couple of bars of our homemade soap, along with Russian tea and our hot cocoa mix filled baskets to give as Christmas gifts to our family. They were humble but made with love.

Makes 2 lbs. (about 6 – 7 standard sized bars)

¾ C coconut oil (159 gr.)
1 ½ C tallow (310 gr.)
¾ C olive oil
¼ C + 2 T lye (93.5 gr.)
¾ C distilled water
¼ C + 2T ground oatmeal
2 tsp. honey
1 – 2 tsp. cloves (for cinnamon soap)
¼ C goats milk
½ fl. oz. essential oil.

IMPORTANT
- Use only glass mixing containers
- Shake lye in can before opening
- Do not use molds, wood spoons, jars, thermometer for anything but soap making
- Label wooden spoons for each fragrance

STEPS
(Place layers of newspaper on worktable)
1. Melt 1st three ingredients in wide mouth jars (1 quart) in microwave (or in saucepan on stove – on low) 2 – 3 minutes *stir with wooden spoon 'til well mixed
2. Carefully measure and put lye and distilled water in a 1 quart jar labeled "lye" jar. *use a labeled "lye" wooden spoon to mix thoroughly (don't use for anything else) – (this step is best to do in a garage or in another well-ventilated area).

3. Wait for lye/water mixture to cool to 80° (about 1 hour at room temperature or 45 minutes when jars are outside placed on concrete). *Wait for oil mixture to also reach 80° **Use a metal thermometer labeled (for soap making only) to check temperature.

4. Carefully pour lye/water into oils very slowly and stir for 10 minutes (timed)....let rest; then stir for 10 minutes, rest, stir, rest, stir....until soap has "saponified"----the substance feels thicker.....***Keep Stirring*** (I like to use a stick blender for this part)

5. When mixture begins to TRACE (path of drops can be made & seen with a spoon) add: oatmeal, honey, goats milk & cloves (optional)   **Stir**Stir**Stir

6. Right before TRACKING (when drops lay on top don't fall back in) occurs, add essential oil

7. Mix well; pour immediately into "vaselined" plastic molds. (Smooth the soap by tapping mold on table).

8. Cover with lids and then towels in a cool place; remove from molds in a few days

9. VERY IMPORTANT – Place on wax-papered cookie sheets to cure for at least 3 weeks before use!

Laundry Soap

We used this laundry soap for years when we first moved into our "shouse" and were completely off-grid. I found that, over time, our clothes became dingy and grey, however, washing in hot water seemed to clear things right up.

1/3 bar Fels Naptha soap, grated
½ C Super Washing Soda (Arm & Hammer)
½ C Borax (20 Mule Team)
3 pints water (more water added later to make 2 gallons)

Put all ingredients in a large saucepan and heat until dissolved. Stir gently over medium heat until it thickens like honey. Sometimes the mixture won't thicken up like honey. Don't worry though, it will still work.

Remove from heat. In a two gallon bucket, put 1 quart of hot water, then add the soap mixture. Mix. Fill bucket with cold water. Mix until well blended.

Set aside for 24 hours. It will turn to gel and may look as though its separated – don't worry, it still works. Stir well before using if it is separated.

Use ½ C per load.

Lotion Bars

Lotion bars are best used after you wash your hands or when you first get out of the shower or bath. They are somewhat greasy until the lotion has been thoroughly rubbed in. They feel wonderful on work roughened hands! I add a little essential oil, usually Lavender or Tea Tree for the ladies and Fir Needle Balsam for the gents, but you can use whatever you want. If you leave them plain, they smell slightly of beeswax and cocoa. Yum!

Melt in a double boiler or in saucepan over low heat:
4 oz. beeswax (112 gr.)
4 oz. coconut oil (112 gr.)
4 oz. cocoa butter (112 gr.)

Remove from heat and stir constantly with a wooden spoon. When the mixture is starting to cool but still liquid, add:
1 tsp. essential oil (optional)

Stir and pour quickly into molds.

When solid and cooled, remove from molds. Package in baggies until ready for use.

Solid Deodorant

Homemade deodorant is very versatile. It is easy to add or subtract ingredients depending on the needs of your skin. I have found that a little beeswax goes a long way. If I use too much, the deodorant is so hard it hurts my underarms to apply.

4T beeswax, grated (or pellets)
2 T Shea butter
10 T Cocoa butter
¼ C cornstarch (or arrowroot powder)
¼ C baking soda (aluminum free)
10 drops tea tree oil (optional)
5 drops vitamin E oil (optional)
15 – 20 drops essential oil (optional – for fragrance)
2 – 3 new or used deodorant tubes (or empty toilet paper tubes)

Melt the beeswax. Add the Shea butter and Cocoa butter and heat just until the butters are melted, stirring occasionally. Remove from heat and add the cornstarch and baking soda. Stir until the lumps are gone and the texture is smooth. Add vitamin E oil and essential oils and stir until well mixed. Pour into prepared deodorant tubes and let sit for a few hours before adding the lids.
*You will want to fill the tubes to almost overflowing.

NOTES:
- Don't over-apply. 2 to 4 swipes is ideal.
- Only twist up as much as you need. It will be slightly softer than store-bought deodorant and it may fall off if you twist up too much.
- You will need to give the deodorant a good 2 – 3 weeks of use before deciding if it works for you.
- This deodorant will stay solid at room temperature. If you live in a very warm area, you may want to refrigerate it to harden it up a bit.
- This is deodorant – it will not keep you from sweating, but it will keep you from smelling bad.

Simply Wonderful Lip Balm

One evening, my lips were cracking and I was desperate. I had no lip balm and all of our local stores were closed so necessity required me to improvise. I only had basic ingredients on hand, but the results were nothing short of spectacular. I LOVE this lip balm .

½ oz. beeswax
1 tsp. honey
4 oz. olive oil (1/2 cup)
Peppermint oil or peppermint extract to taste (optional)

In a small saucepan (or double boiler) melt wax. Add honey and oil. Stir for two minutes. Add peppermint (or other flavor). Stir well. Pour into lip balm tubes or pots.

NOTE: *The honey will not really combine, but it is great for your lips and doesn't adversely affect the lip balm.*

Whitewash

Whitewash used to be commonplace. It not only kept buildings looking tidy it also had antiseptic properties, making it perfect for use in most any farm building.

For general use (inside and outside) on farm buildings, shed, fences, poles, on either wood, glass or metal surfaces:

Dissolve 2 lbs. of common salt in a 10 quart bucket, three-quarters filled with water. Stir well to hasten solution. When all of the salt has dissolved, add slowly 10 lbs. of Lime and stirring constantly, continue until the mixture has the consistency of a smooth cream.

Allow the mixture to stand overnight, or for a few days if possible, keeping the bucket well covered, and stir the contents occasionally. When needed again, stir thoroughly and add sufficient water to make a good workable wash.

Alum added to this mixture prevents it rubbing. Once ounce to a gallon of wash is sufficient.

FOR MASONRY SURFACES SUCH AS BRICKWORK, CONCRETE, STONE, CINDER BLOCKS, STUCCO, ETC.

Make a mixture in the proportion of 50 lbs. of Lime, 25 lbs. of grey or white cement, and 5 lbs. of common salt. Stir mixture in with water until it is of the required consistency and the salt is fully dissolved.

If two coats are to be applied, allow one full day for the first coat to dry. Do not make up more of this formula than can be used in one hour. Whitewash must be applied thin. Best results will be obtained if the application is so thin that the surface to which it is applied can be easily seen through the "film" when it is wet. When using a brush, do not attempt to brush out the coating as is done with oil paint. Spread it on as evenly as possible.

If possible, apply whitewash in clear, dry weather and take care in preparing the surface to be treated so that all dirt, grease, scale and other loose material is removed before the whitewash is applied.

Whitewash brushes, after use, should be washed thoroughly in clean water and hung in the air to dry with the brush part downwards. Do not allow the brush to come into contact with dry Lime. The makers of Lime say a gallon of whitewash should have the following cover capacity:

On wood, about 225 square feet (10 ft. x 22 ½ ft.)
On brick, about 180 square feet (10 ft. x 18 ft.)
On plaster, about 270 square feet (about 9 ft. x 30 ft.)

It is estimated that a man using a 4 inch brush should cover in an hour; on rough walls, 22 square yards; on smooth walls, 38 square yards; on flat surfaces, 40 square yards; on ceilings (using a step ladder), 25 square yards.

Chapter IX

Homestead Medicine

There are so many wonderful plants in God's creation that are perfectly suited for medicinal purposes. A few that we like to keep on hand are:

- St. John's Wart: Skin problems, burns
- Elderberry: Cold and flu symptoms
- Mullen: Breathing difficulties, ringworm, earaches, mumps
- Plantain: Antiseptic, antibiotic, pink eye, laxative (seeds) staph, thrush
- Shepherds Purse: Internal hemorrhages, cuts, wounds, earaches
- Yarrow: Respiratory problems, cold & flu, fever, cuts, wounds, tooth aches
- Clove oil: tooth aches
- Raspberry Leaf: Canker and mouth sores, dysentery, diarrhea, increases milk supply
- Nettle: Iron source, gout, urinary problems, hay fever
- Garlic: Infections, asthma, whooping cough, bronchitis, strep throat
- Peppermint: Colic, flatulence, dysentery, vomiting, headache, toothache

In addition to herbs, we keep a store of essential oils that we use frequently. Not only are these good for medicinal purposes, we use them to scent soaps, lotion bars, candles and lip balms. The ones we use the most frequently are:

- Eucalyptus essential oil
- Peppermint essential oil
- Fir Needle Balsam essential oil
- Lavender essential oil
- Clove essential oil
- Tea Tree essential oil

Medical supplies and pharmaceuticals are every bit as important in your preparedness stores, what follows is a basic list of things you may want to have on hand:

- **Fleet Saline Enemas**. As people age and become less active, a little help in the waste management department is indicated. Also, a change in diet, from a heavily laden fiber diet to a diet including mostly protein (as in a wild game driven TEOTWAWKI diet) will cause things to "stop up". If not dealt with quickly and efficiently, constipation could prove to be a life-threatening condition.

- **Stool Softeners**. Basically, they are indicated for the same condition mentioned above, however, they would be a preventative, taken before complete stoppage.

- **Cough Drops**. For soothing relief of itchy throats due to PND and bothersome colds. Something along the lines of Chloraseptic Throat Lozenges would be in order for sore throats.

- **Ibuprofen**. Fever relief and pain management. Ibuprofen is good three years past the expiration date (per doctor), then throw it away.

- **Quick Release Caps Ibuprofen**. For super fast acting pain relief or fever reduction. Gel caps are more expensive and the shelf life is shorter, but can be worth the extra price.

- **Tylenol**. Fever relief and pain management. Tylenol has no shelf life (per doctor), so it is an excellent long term storage option.

- **Aspirin**. Fever relief and pain management. It also works as a blood thinner. Aspirin lasts forever (per doctor), making it perfect for long term storage.

- **Children's Tylenol**. As indicated previously, but with children's dosage.

- **Children's Ibuprofen**. As indicated previously, but with children's dosage.

- **Tylenol PM**. Use as you would for Tylenol, but with the added benefit of a sleep aid. In cases of extreme illness or pain, sleeping can be a great healer.

- **Benadryl Allergy**. Benadryl is the first course of action for an anaphylactic reaction. It can be the difference between life and death. We keep quite a supply on hand.

- **Children's Benadryl Allergy**. Same as above, but with dosage for children.

- **Neosporin**. An antibiotic ointment to be used on minor scrapes and scratches to prevent infection. It can keep minor injuries minor.

- **Bag Balm**. Truthfully, we use bag balm in place of Neosporin regularly, with great success, although we do find that the Neosporin tubes are easier to transport in packs and bags.

- **Visine**. When allergies come calling or you get something in your eye, there is no better eye wash. It can bring immediate relief.

- **Hydrogen Peroxide**. The uses for hydrogen peroxide are too numerous to mention! We use it extensively to remove blood from clothing and linens. It is also a great gargle and antiseptic.

- **Betadine**. We use Betadine as a topical antiseptic. You can scrub for minor surgery (or major) with a Betadine solution by mixing 2oz. of dish soap to 1 gallon of Betadine. This is an excellent solution to wash with and sterilize wounds.

- **Isopropyl Alcohol**. Yet another topical antiseptic for use in wound care (ie. sterilization of instruments).

Personal Protection Equipment

- **Nitrile Exam Gloves** (S, M, XL). It is wise to have gloves on anytime you are dealing with blood products or bodily fluids. It is the first line of defense in infection control

- **Surgical Masks.** If you are dealing with a communicable disease a surgical mask offers a modicum of protection.

- **Fluid Shield Surgical Masks.** To protect you from contracting diseases due to small droplets.

Band Aids (aka boo boo strips)

- **Butterfly Closures.** For closing lacerations that don't quite require sutures.

- **Fabric Adhesive Bandages 1"x3"**

- **Fabric Fingertip Bandages**

- **Fabric Adhesive Bandages 2"x4"**
- **Fabric Knuckle Bandages** (we find that fabric band aids move better and wear better than plastic band aids)

Dressings and Bandages
- **Sponges 4"x4".** Use as a dressing for a wound, or to clean a wound.
- **Kling rolls.** To be used over a dressing - holds dressing in place.
- **Surgical tape.** Secures kling over wound.
- **Sponges.** Use as a dressing for wounds.
- **Gauze Pads.** Use as a dressing for wounds (sterile) 4"x4".
- **Vaseline Petroleum Gauze.** Use as a dressing for weeping wounds or sutured areas. We use these extensively. They will not stick to the wound.
- **CoFlex.** Cohesive flexible bandage. This can be used in place of Kling and tape. It sticks to itself, but not to skin. It is stretchy and applies nicely. We purchased our CoFlex through **KV Vet Supply** for half the price we could purchase it for at our medical supplier.
- **Sterile oval eye pads.** You never know when someone is going to get "pucker brush" in their eye and require first aid! We also like to use these as bandages in places that need a little extra padding.

Bumps, Bruises and Sprains
- **Triangle Bandages.** Stabilize dislocated shoulders and fractured arms and wrists. Also used for wrapping head wounds.
- **Elastic Bandage (Ace Bandage).** (2", 3", 4") Multiple uses. Used for supporting sprains and sore joints. Can be used as bleeding control (without cutting off circulation). For the price we pay for them, they can be used for bandaging any wound.

Burn Care
Burn Jel. Made by Water Jel, Burn Jel contains Lidocaine and offers almost instant relief for burns. The thick jel cools the burn and seals out air.

Clear Liquid Diet

If someone is suffering from excessive vomiting or diarrhea a clear liquid diet would be advised until they feel better. This is also recommended for people who have suffered an extended illness or malnourishment.

Step 1:
Oral Rehydration Solution, water fruit juice, Jell-O, Gatorade, Popsicles, PowerAide, ginger ale, cola, tea and bouillon

Step 2:
To step 1 add white toast (no butter or oils), white rice, cream of wheat, soda crackers and potatoes without the skin

Step 3:
To Step 2 add canned fruit and chicken noodle soup

Step 4:
To Step 3 add a source of protein like canned meat, fish or egg

Step 5:
To Step 4 add milk and other dairy products, vegetable oils, butter, raw fruit and vegetables and high fiber whole products

Elderberry Syrup

This syrup is wonderful if you are suffering from a common cold or the influenza. It is wonderfully handy to have on the shelf. This is a nice option to use during the day, saving the Elderberry wine for when you are ready for bed!

1 C. elderberries (fresh)
2 C. water
2 cinnamon sticks
6 whole cloves
3 T. fresh ginger
1 C. wildflower honey
2 T. lemon juice

Simmer the elderberries, water, cinnamon, cloves and ginger gently for 15 minutes. Strain this mixture through cheesecloth two times. Add the honey and lemon juice and mix well.

NOTE: You can make up a large batch of this when the elderberries are ripe and water bath can (for 10 minutes) for future use.

Electrolyte Replacer

Electrolyte Replacer is what is needed with extreme dysentery. Diseases like Cholera will be successfully treated with this recipe.

½ tsp. table salt
¼ tsp. salt substitute (or Potassium Chloride or other potassium source – banana, elderberry juice etc.)
½ tsp. baking soda
2 T. sugar

Mix everything together with 1 quart boiling water. Cool to serve.

You may add 1 packet of Emergen-C to the mixture for flavor and added vitamins.

Lemon-Honey Cough Syrup

Nearly every family has this recipe in one form or another. Make sure that you use good, non-pasteurized honey so that you are getting all of the wonderful benefits that honey has to offer.

1 ½ C. raw honey
½ C. virgin olive oil
¾ C. lemon juice (give or take, depending on taste)

Combine honey, olive oil and lemon juice in a saucepan and stir. Heat over medium heat just until steaming, stirring constantly. Remove from heat and cool. Pour into a jar, cover and refrigerate. Take 1 T as needed (preferably warmed).

Lemon-Honey Throat Lozenges

Sometimes, when the throat tickle is making you crazy, there is nothing like a cough drop. You really can make almost anything in the comfort of your own kitchen!

2 C. sugar
1 C. honey
½ C. water
8 tsp. lemon zest (or 2 tsp. dehydrated lemon zest)

Combine sugar, honey and water in a saucepan, mix together over high heat until boiling. While still boiling, cover for 4 minutes. Remove the cover and place a candy thermometer in the boiling mixture. When mixture reaches 295°, remove from heat and allow to cool for 5 minutes. The mixture should thicken. Mix in the lemon zest or powder.

Using ½ tsp. measuring spoon, drop onto parchment, making sure to leave some space in between dollops, as they will spread. Work quickly because the mixture thickens very fast.

Let cool for ½ hour and then store in an airtight container with layers separated by parchment or waxed paper. Store up to a week at room temperature, longer if refrigerated.

Lice Shampoo

Nobody wants to have to deal with the inconvenience of lice, but if is occurs, here is an all-natural way to handle it.

5 tsp. olive oil (or pure coconut oil)
5 drops tea tree essential oil
5 drops rosemary essential oil
5 drops lavender essential oil
5 drops peppermint essential oil
5 drops eucalyptus essential oil

Add a small amount of regular shampoo to the mixture and massage through hair. Leave on hair for an hour under a towel or tight-fitting shower cap to prevent drips. Rinse the hair and shampoo the hair.

(The olive oil or coconut oil kill lice by dissolving their exoskeletons – other oils will not have the same effect.)

NOTE: 1) The respiration of a baby or child under 5 can be slowed or even stopped if peppermint oil or eucalyptus oil is close enough for the baby to breathe. 2) High blood pressure may be elevated by peppermint essential oil. 3) Peppermint or rosemary may be harmful during pregnancy. In any of these cases, just use the recipe without the oil that may be harmful in your case.

Onion Poultice

Poultices used to be commonplace. They are an excellent drawing agent, good for numerous infections. Be careful, they are powerful and if left on too long, can burn sensitive skin.

1 onion, large (or more if necessary)
flour or cornmeal
cloth
hot water bottle

Cut up a large onion (or more) into rings.

Sauté the rings in a cast iron skillet, with a little olive oil, until the onions are transparent (not caramelized).

Add enough flour or cornmeal to make a thick paste.

Using a clean piece of cloth, cover your patients chest with two layers of cloth.

Spread moderately cooled (just cool enough not to burn) onions over the chest.

Cover with another layer of cloth.

Place warm (not hot enough to burn) hot water bottle over the poultice.

Let sit until the poultice cools.

Repeat of necessary.

Onion Syrup

When a friend gave me this recipe, I balked. Onion syrup? Are you kidding me? Well, after a lingering chest cold, I finally gave in and made a jar. The first thing I noticed was that it wasn't as bad tasting as I thought it would be. The next thing I noticed was that it worked. Really. Give it a try – you'll see.

1 C chopped onion (fresh)
¼ C lemon juice **(or apple cider vinegar)**
1 tsp. ginger root *(optional – fresh is best but can use powdered)*
5 cloves garlic *(optional)*
Enough honey to cover

Place onion, lemon juice and ginger and garlic in a quart jar. Cover with honey. Stir to remove the air bubbles and cover. Let sit overnight or 8 hours.

The honey will suck the juices of of the onion. After sitting overnight, strain out the onion solids (or you can munch on them if you prefer).

Dosage:

Child (7-11 years) 1 tsp. every 3 to 4 hours
Adult 1 Tablespoon every 3 to 4 hours

Teething Gel

Although gentle enough to use on baby, with a little extra clove oil, this is powerfully effective against adult tooth aches. The effectiveness of clove oil on tooth aches is not to be underestimated.

1 oz. pure vegetable glycerin
2 drops essential oil of clove

Add one drop of clove to your glycerin and shake it until it is well blended. Test it on yourself to make sure it is not too strong before adding another drop. For a young baby, I use 2 drops. You could use vegetable oil instead of glycerin if you want. Glycerin is very sweet, so it makes the remedy a bit more appealing to young children.

Chapter X

The Dairy

Many years ago, my husband and I had a baby girl that was stillborn. I was devastated. Although I had two other children at the time, I found it nearly impossible to get out of bed in the morning. I wanted nothing more than to be alone with my pain. Sleeping was the only thing that brought even a moment of relief.

Knowing that I was needed, not only by my children, but my husband as well, I decided to take action. I needed something to do that required me to get out of bed, and so, I bought a milk cow.

My husband and I knew little to nothing about milk cows, other than having milked one for a friend once, with disastrous results. Before taking the milk cow plunge, we invested in the definitive work on the subject – *The Family Milk Cow*.

After pouring over the book, buying milking pails, feed and bedding material, we bought our first milk cow. She was a beautiful, gentle Jersey named Ginger. We bought her from a family that was trying to become a successful small family farm. They purchased animals from other sources, gentled them and passed them along to the next owner. Our Ginger had been rescued from a Dairy. She was imperfect, having only two working "quarters" and was very narrowly saved from the butcher.

Ginger was a wonderfully patient creature that would stand for the better part of an hour while I fumbled around trying to milk her. She would finish up her grain, munch on her alfalfa and then turn to look at me with those huge, doe-like eyes as if to say "could we please hurry this along?".

Soon, my arms grew stronger, our milking sessions shorter and our kitchen overflowed with an abundance of dairy products. Although our friends helped us out by drinking some of our overflow, we still had an enormous overabundance.

Not wanting to waste a single drop of that liquid gold I got busy. Soon, cream was poured in every cup of coffee, whipped to accompany even the most humble of desserts and poured over fresh fruit. I learned how to make ice cream, yogurt and butter. Sour cream soon followed, along with cream cheese – and then I tackled the really intimidating dairy products – hard cheeses!

After reading everything I could get my hands on regarding cheesemaking, my dear husband took it upon himself to buy me the most beautiful cheese press ever made. It was made in England, using hardwood and stainless steel and was a piece of art in its own right.

My cheese press came with a few recipes which I immediately put into good use. I started out with "Farmhouse Cheddar" and moved on to Caerphilly, Gouda and eventually tried my hand at Parmesan. Oh, a whole new world opened up to me!

I came to find that cheesemaking was simple and straightforward, if not time consuming. I learned that there was nothing quite as wonderful as a well-made brick of cheese fresh from the cellar. What in indulgence home-made cheese is when coupled with fresh bread or crisp, home-made crackers. You will find, as I did, that the time and effort invested in cheesemaking is nothing compared with the glorious rewards of fresh cheese.

Caring for Milk and Milking Equipment

One of the first things we learned when we began our milking adventure was the importance of cleaning milking equipment and properly caring for the milk.

Our first purchase (even before we bought the cow) was a stainless steel milk bucket and strainer. Milk buckets are more than just stainless steel buckets, they are unique, in that they are seamless. The lack of a seam allows the entire surface of the bucket to be cleaned and sterilized. We not only sterilize our milk bucket, we also sterilize the stainless steel strainer, the cheesecloth (if we aren't using disposable filters) and the jars. Dairy products absorb bacteria very easily, rendering the milk putrid or even dangerous. Sterilizing your dairy equipment results in milk that stays fresh longer and tastes sweet. It is well worth any amount of time and effort.

To sterilize our milking equipment we first wash the bucket and strainer thoroughly with hot, soapy water, followed by a quick washing with Arm & Hammer Super Washing Soda. The Super Washing Soda is a miracle cleaner when it comes to banishing rotten dairy smells. Milking equipment washed in Super Washing Soda will smell sweet and fresh. After our initial washing, we fill our milking pail with water, submerge the strainer (along with all the parts) and the cheesecloth (if using) and boil for 15 minutes.

Another crucial element of properly caring for fresh milk is the straining and cooling process. During the milking process, small particles fall into the milking pail. Even with careful cleaning of the cow's udder, it is impossible to keep every hair or barn speck out of the milk. Straining the milk through a filter (available at most farm stores) or a sterilized double layer of cheesecloth, is essential.

After the milk has been strained, it must be cooled immediately. In the "old" days, farmers often plunged their milk cans in an ice cold creek. Now, we often don't have creeks at our disposal, but we do have ice. The method that we have used for years is filling a laundry tub with ice water and putting our jars in the tub up to their necks. Cooling the milk quickly ensures the sweetest, most wonderful milk.

During the cooling process, it is important not to cover the milk with a solid lid. If you cover your milk, any off flavors will condense on the lid and drip back into the milk, giving it a characteristic "barnyard" flavor. We cover our milk with cotton lids that I sewed out of old flour sacks and secured with elastic. As the milk cools, the cotton lids allow evaporation, expelling any potential "off" flavors.

Once the milk has cooled (about ½ hour), cover the mouth of the jar with plastic wrap, put the lid on and refrigerate. Including the date (with both date and a.m. or p.m.) is particularly nice when wanting to use the oldest milk first.

Our regular milking routine:

- Set sterilized 1 gallon jars on counter, awaiting fresh milk
- Fill wash bucket with hot, soapy water (for washing the udder)
- Go to the milking parlor with sterilized milking pail and wash bucket in hand
- Fill feed bin with grain ration and hay
- Add a handful of loose salt to the grain
- Bring cow into the milking parlor
- Wash udder with soapy water (sterilize with udder wash, if you prefer) and pat dry with clean towel
- Squirt first few streams of milk from each quarter onto the ground (this cleans any debris out of the teat)
- Milk cow, being careful to strip each quarter
- Wash udder again, Bag Balm the end of each teat
- Return cow to the pasture
- Bring milk and wash bucket into the kitchen (or milk processing area

- Weigh milk bucket with milk (is a good indication of your milk cows health) and record
- Strain milk through filters into sterilized gallon jars
- Put cotton cap on jars and put in ice water to cool
- Wash milk bucket and strainer with hot, soapy water
- Fill milk bucket with water, put in strainer and cheesecloth (if used) and boil for 15 minutes
- Steam sterilize glass jars for next milking
- Retrieve your milk, cover it, date it and refrigerate
- Sterilize (bleach) wash bucket

Equipment Needed for Cheese Making

- Dairy Thermometer
- Measuring jug for fluid ounces
- Stainless steel measuring spoons
- Long knife or palette knife for cutting curds
- Flat ladle or skimmer for stirring curds
- Stainless steel bucket or pot to contain the milk
- Cheese cloth
- Dairy bleach for sterilizing the equipment
- Good supply of hot water for bringing up the temperature of the milk by standing the container in a sink or wash boiler

IMPORTANT: All equipment must be very clean and be sterilized by scalding with boiling water, even after it has been immersed in a bleach solution!

STARTER: Cheese starter is a growth of special cultures in sterile milk to turn the milk sour for cheese making and to give the cheese a good flavor.

RENNET: Rennet is a liquid to coagulate the milk, but it must be cheese rennet – Junket rennet is unsuitable. The rennet should be bought in small quantities and kept cool and dark, preferably in a refrigerator.

Vegetable Rennet
(Thistle Flower)

Thistle Flowers

Pick the thistle flower head (the purple part) after it has turned brown but has not yet begun producing thistle down. After thistle down is evident the thistle flower is unusable. Make sure you dry enough thistle heads to last you until the next thistle harvest.

Dry the thistle heads well and store them in a clean, dry jar with a lid.

When you desire rennet, put a couple of dried thistle heads in a mortor and using a pestle, grind them into a fine powder. Continue with more thistle heads until you have 5 tsp. of powder.

In a bowl, cover the ground thistle with warm water (just enough to cover the grounds) and allow to soak for 5 to 10 minutes or until the water has turned a dark, concentrated brown color.

Pour the liquid (now thistle flower rennet) through a strainer to strain out the plant material.

To make cheese, add the liquid to 1 gallon of heated milk and wait for curdling to begin.

Animal Rennet
(suckling ruminant animal –
kid, calve, lamb)

1 Abomasum (the fourth stomach) of a sucking (not eating solid food) animal.

Trim off all of the stomach chambers and leave only the abomasum. Leave the folds (plica) in its inner wall intact. Do not wash it as it contains necessary enzymes.

Spread the abomasum out on a screen (preferably stainless steel) and sprinkle with salt to cover.

Rub the salt into the surface of the abomasum. Let it dry in a cool, dry place. Alternatively, you can rub the abomasum with salt, blow it up like a balloon and hang it in a cool, dark place.

Once the abomasum has dried, you can store it, sealed, in a cool, dry place.

To use: Cut off a square of abomasum about ¾" (about 1 gram). Cut the piece of abomasum into small pieces and stir into about 2 ½ T. of 86° water or cold acidified whey, overnight in the refrigerator (or other cold place).

Remove the pieces of soaked abomasum by pouring the liquid through a layer of cheesecloth or a sieve.

Stir the extract of abomasum into prepared (warmed) milk. 2 ½ T. of abomasum rennet will coagulate 8 gallons of milk. Cut that amount in half to coagulate 4 gallons and so on.

Clean break should be obtained in an hour.

Butter Making

When we got our first cow, we learned everything the hard way! Our first butter churn was a quart jar that we had the kids shake until butter started to form. From there we moved to an antique Daisy churn, which we used and loved for many years, even adding to our Daisy collection. One fateful day I moved a piece of furniture that the churns sat upon and sent them both crashing to the ground. In tears I cleaned up the pieces and vowed to find replacement jars. It was never to be. Apparently, it wasn't only I who had had the misfortune of breaking a Daisy jar. In desperation, I began using the mixer from my second-hand Bosch machine. What a stunning moment, as I churned cream into butter in less than 5 minutes. I was hooked!

Control of temperature, cleanliness at all stages and thorough working of the butter are the chief essentials for successful butter making.

Cream should never be allowed to stand near anything with a strong odor such as apples, soap, kerosene or onions as it will absorb any strong odors with which it comes in contact.

A traditional butter recipe states that to get the best of butter making, cream should be allowed to mature before churning – that is, kept for two or three days at a temperature of 60° - 65°. This allows lactic acid to ripen the cream. Butter made from fresh cream always has a flat, insipid taste, and usually contains too much moisture. Ripened cream is more easily churned.

Quit churning the butter when the butter separates from the buttermilk and is about the size of grains of rice. Drain the buttermilk (reserving it for baking). Rinse the butter with cold water until the water runs clear. Gather the butter up into a bowl and work the butter with a wooden spoon until you can press no more buttermilk from the butter. Working the buttermilk out will allow your butter to remain fresh and sweet much longer. Add salt to taste (about 1 tsp. to each 1 lb.

of butter), kneading this well into the butter. Measure into ½ C measuring cups or butter molds and store in refrigerator, cool room or freezer.

KEEPING BUTTER WITH NO REFRIGERATION
Using boiled water, make a brine with salt (until it will float an egg). Have butter in lots of 1 lb. or similar size, and wrapped separately in waxed paper.

Put the brine into a barrel, crockery or earthenware container, and when brine is quite cold, put the butter in with a weight on top to keep it under the liquid.

The butter must be kept under the brine. It will stay fresh for six months without absorbing salt.

More brine can be added to the container if necessary.

When you want to use some of the butter, take out 1 lb. without letting air into the rest.

Caerphilly Cheese

*This is our go-to cheese when we need a home-made cheese fix –
and we need it fast! Taking only 2 weeks from start to finish, it a
perfect, tasty, quick, hard cheese.*

Use 2 gallons of milk, ½ morning and ½ evening milk. For this
cheese, up to one third of the total quantity can be skim milk.
Heat to 90° (goat's milk 85°), add 4 oz. Starter, stir well, cover
and leave for 30 minutes. Add ½ tsp. of rennet, diluted with 2
tsp. cold water. Stir right down to the bottom of the bucket for
at least one minute, cover and leave for 45 minutes. Now cut
the curds as described in the Farmhouse Cheese recipe, then
stir the curds while heating rapidly to 92°, then continue to stir
for a further 40 minutes. Now allow the curds to settle in the
bottom of the pail, pour off all the whey, cut the curds into
slices, like a cake, turn them over and pile them up for more
whey to drain away. Do this 2 or 3 times more at 5 minute
intervals. Now break the curd into walnut sized pieces, add
salt at the rate of 1 oz to 4 lbs curd.

Have the press ready; line the mold with scalded cheese cloth,
fill in the curds, fold one layer of cloth neatly over the top, put
on the first follower, pile the rest of the cloth on top and put on
the second spacer. Now put under 20 lbs pressure for 10
minutes. Turn the mold upside down, replace follower and
spacer and increase pressure to 30 lbs. Do this twice more at
10 minute intervals, increasing the pressure by 10 lbs each
time and finally leave the cheese under the maximum pressure
for 14-16 hours.

Remove from mold and cloth. The traditional treatment of this
cheese is to dry it by sprinkling all over with rice and flour and
putting it to ripen at 50° for two weeks, turning it daily. You
can also air-dry and wax it, but it needs an extra week to ripen.

Cottage Cheese

This cottage cheese was one of the first recipes we tried when we began milking our own cow. It was simple, quick and produced the most divine cottage cheese ever! It actually tasted CHEESEY! We love this cheese with a little bit of heavy cream mixed in just before serving.

1 gallon skimmed milk (cow or goat)
4 drops liquid rennet
½ tsp. salt, plus more to taste
6 T heavy cream

Heat the milk, very slowly, to 85°. Turn off the heat and stir in the rennet, stirring deeply. Stir gently for 2 minutes. Cover the pot with a clean tea towel, followed by the pot lid and allow to stand at room temperature for 4 hours.

After 4 hours, the mixture will be softly set. Take a sharp knife and cut the cheese diagonally 5 to 6 times in one direction, then do the same in the opposite direction.

Sprinkle the salt over the curds and then set on extremely low heat and cook, stirring gently, until the curds separate from the whey. It will only take a few minutes. Do not overcook or your curds will be tough.

Line a colander with cheesecloth and pour the mixture through, draining the whey and saving the curds. (I like to save the whey and use the liquid in bread making – yumm!)

Fold the cheesecloth over the curds and chill in the colander, in the refrigerator for about 1 hour. The curds will continue to drain, so be sure to keep a bowl under the colander.

Spoon the curds into a bowl. When ready to serve, add a bit of cream and salt to taste. Enjoy the fruits of your labors!

Cream Cheese

Cream Cheese is perfect cheese with which to begin your cheese-making adventures. It is quick, simple and imminently satisfying. This is the perfect cheese to top scones and compliment lemon curd.

As much whole milk as you would like to use up
½ C buttermilk per gallon
Cream

Warm milk to 60-65°

Add rennet (1/4 tablet per gallon)

Custard forms after 12 hours (do not cut).

Drain in cheese-cloth lined colander then hang overnight.

Refrigerate in tightly covered container.

Farmhouse Cheese
(Cheddar)

1. Warm the milk. Pour 2 gallons of milk into a stainless steel or enameled pot, set in a sink of warm water, stir and warm the milk to 90° F.
2. Ripen the milk. Add 2 ounces of cheese starter culture and stir in well, yet gently. Cover pot and leave for 45 minutes to ripen at 90°.
3. Add cheese rennet. Dissolve completely one quarter of a cheese rennet tablet in a quarter cup of cooled, sterile water, breaking and crushing with back of spoon as you stir. Stabilize temperature of milk at 90° by regulating water temperature in sink outside cheese pot. Protect the pot from drafts. Add rennet solution and stir in thoroughly for one minute with a stainless steel spoon or ladle. Top-stir (if using cow's milk) ¼ inch with back of ladle for another minute to keep cream from rising.
4. Let set 'til curd "breaks clean". Let covered pot stand undisturbed until a firm curd forms (30 to 45 minutes). Test firmness with your finger. When it "breaks clean", it is ready to cut.
5. Cut curds 4 ways. Cut the curds into small (1/2 inch) cubes with a long-bladed knife or spatula. The blade must be long enough to reach all the way to the bottom of the pot without immersing the handle. Start at one side of the pot and cut vertical, parallel lines in the curd, ½ inch apart. Turn the pot 90° and cut again at right angles to the first cuts. Then, with the knife at a slant, using the original lines in the curd, cut at a 45° angle in both directions. Your aim is to cut the entire curd into ½ inch cubes. When the curd is all in cubes, gently stir them, turning them over, bottom to top, cutting any pieces of curd that are still too big.
6. Scalding the curd. Run some hotter water into the sink outside of the pot and raise the temperature of the curds slowly to 100°. The temperature must not rise more than 2° every 5 minutes. This should take 30 minutes, and you should stir gently as you cook. The

curd pieces will shrink in size as the heating continues. The whey will increase as the curds decrease in size.

7. Draining the whey. Cover the pot and let the curd settle for 5 minutes, then pour off the whey into another pot (save it for Ricotta). Pour the curds into a cheesecloth-lined colander.

8. Hang curds to drain. Knot one corner of the cloth around the other three corners and hang the bag of curds to drain for one hour at 70°.

9. Salting the curds. Pour the drained curds into a scalded bowl and break them up with your fingers (gently) into walnut sized pieces. Mix in thoroughly 2 tablespoons of cheese salt for each 4 pounds of curd.

10. Molding and pressing the curd. Scald and cool your mold and cheesecloth. Line mold with cheesecloth and put curds into the mold, folding cheesecloth neatly over the top when it is full. Put the follower on the top of the curds and place under 20 pounds pressure for 10 minutes. Then turn the mold upside down and replace the follower on top and increase pressure to 30 pounds for another 10 minutes. Repeat twice more at 10 minute intervals and increase pressure by 10 pounds each time you turn the cheese. The last time, leave cheese under 50 pounds pressure for 14 to 16 hours.

11. Finishing the cheese. Remove the cheese from the mold and carefully peel away the cheesecloth, taking care not to rip the surface of the cheese. Air dry the cheese at room temperature on a cheese mat until a rind has developed and surface is dry. Turn several times a day. After 3 to 5 days, it will be ready to wax.

12. Waxing and curing the cheese. Paint melted cheese wax (or paraffin) on a cool, dry cheese. Use a small, real-bristled paint brush kept just for this purpose. Wax must always be melted in a double boiler to reduce danger of fire. Cover cheese completely. Cure your Farmhouse Cheese at 50° for at least three months. It's flavor will be even better after six months. Turn the cheese daily for 2 weeks, and occasionally after that until it is eaten.

Cheese Starter

If you have a pressure cooker and a freezer, you can make your own starter. Get your first supply of starter and then make your own!

Have at the ready some pint canning jars. Scrub and brush the jars thoroughly with detergent, rinse several times. Half fill with skim milk, cap off the jars. Stand the jars on the perforated plate in the pressure cooker, add water to come 2" or 3" up the side of the jars, but not so much that the jars topple over.

Close the pressure cooker, bring to 15 lbs. pressure and hold it at that pressure for 20 minutes. Let is depressurize slowly, then let the jars get quite cool. Now, working very quickly, cleanly and diligently, take one jar at a time, removing the lids and adding ½ teaspoonful of your fresh starter. Immediately close the jar again. When all the jars have been inoculated, shake each one to mix well and then stand them in a sink or basin of water at 85° to 90° and gently shake the bottles from time to time. When they feel warm to your hand, set them in a warm place until the milk is thick. Give each jar a good shake to break up the curd. Have some small plastic bottles or other containers sterilized, pour into each either 2 or 4 oz. of the starter and at once cap it with a lid or foil. Store these containers in the freezer until ready to use for cheese making and use some when more starter is being made. Once thawed it must be used but as long as it is frozen it keeps for quite a long time. If there is the slightest suspicion of staleness it is advisable to get a fresh supply. When making butter add some starter to the cream and leave it in a warm place overnight. It makes lovely butter. The starter is, of course, also added to milk to make cottage or cream cheese (1 oz. to one gallon).

Gouda Cheese

For the most wonderful, creamy, incredible cheese, you must try this recipe. When done well, it is unparalleled! We love this cheese on crackers to enjoy the full flavor and texture.

Two gallons of milk, ½ morning and ½ evening. Heated quickly to 150° (stand pail in a wash boiler, stirring all the time) and then cool quickly to 90°. The milk is now pasteurized. Add 4 oz. starter, stir it well in and add 1 tsp. rennet diluted with 3 tsp. cold water, deep stir one minute, cover and leave for one hour. Cut curds and then take 30 minutes to heat to 100° stirring continuously. Continue to stir for a further 30 minutes and during this time take out 4 pints of whey at a time, replacing it with the same amount of water at the same temperature and do this 3 – 4 times. This gives the cheese the typical smooth texture. Now pour off all the whey and allow the curd to mat into one lump.

Have the mold ready: line with cheese cloth and pack the curd into it breaking it as little as possible, fold over the cloth, add the followers and put under 20 lbs. pressure for 20 minutes. Turn again, increase pressure to 40 lbs and leave for 3 hours. Prepare a 20% brine by mixing 1 ¼ lbs salt with ¼ gallons cold water and float the cheese in this for three hours. Take it out, mop it dry, ripen for three weeks at 50° and rub it daily with a dry cloth. Then wax it and ripen on for at least another two weeks.

Mozzarella Cheese

Mozzarella is a necessity if "Friday Night Pizza and a Movie" is an institution in your home like it is ours. This is an easy cheese to make and the flavor of homemade is unparalleled.

1 gallon milk
1 ¼ tsp. citric acid powder
¼ tsp. liquid rennet or 1/8 rennet tablet
½ C cool water (divided in half)

In a stainless or enamel pot, place the cool milk. Dissolve the citric acid powder into ½ cup cool water and add to the milk. Stir well. Bring the temperature of the milk to 88°. Mix the rennet with the other ¼ cup of cool water and stir into the milk, about 10 seconds.

Allow the milk to set at 88° for 15 minutes to coagulate. After setting for 15 minutes the curd should be firm and when you dip your finger into the curds, they will break cleanly over your finger and whey will fill the depression where your finger has been. Cut into 1 inch cubes and let rest for 10 minutes.

Then place the pot of curds into a sink of very hot water and slowly bring the temperature up to 108°. Curds will shrink during this process. Keep the curds at 108° for 35 minutes. Drain the curds into a colander for 15 minutes.

Save the whey if making ricotta or heat treating the curds in the whey rather than the microwave method. When curds have drained, they are ready to be heat treated to get their stretch.

Stove Top Method
For this method you can use either hot water or hot whey saved from draining the curds. Use a double boiler. You will need enough hot water or whey to cover the curds.

Heat the liquid to 150° to 155° and place in the curds, which have formed into a mass. Work quickly as it does not take long in the hot liquid before the curds melt together and become stretchy. This is an amazing process, which happens very quickly. Use a large slotted and a large regular spoon and bring the curds out of the liquid, pulling and stretching like you would taffy. Use your hands or the spoons to stretch the cheese.

Shape into balls and place into a brine solution for 10 – 30 minutes, depending on how salty you like your cheese. Remove from brine, pat dry or air dry. Refrigerate cheese for up to 2 weeks. Freeze for longer storage.

Microwave Method

Break up a cupful of curds onto a microwave safe plate or bowl. Add salt to taste. I like about 1 tsp of salt per pound of cheese, which is about ½ tsp. per cup. Place the curds into the microwave and heat on high for 50 seconds.

Take out and work the cheese with the back of a spoon, much like kneading the cheese. Place the cheese back into the microwave and heat on high, again for another 25 seconds.

Remove from microwave and again work with a spoon to stretch and shape the cheese. Work into a soft, ball shape with the hands and allow to cool. Cheese will become opaque and shiny.

Wrap in plastic wrap or freeze for later use. Cheese will keep for about 2 weeks in the refrigerator.

Old-Fashioned Vanilla Ice Cream

There is nothing like freshly churned ice cream on a hot summer's day! I learned early on to cool my custard mixture and beat the eggs well before adding them to the cooled custard – once when I added the eggs while the custard was hot, I ended up with something less than appetizing – scrambled egg ice cream! Now I am much more careful.

3 C milk
1 ½ T cornstarch
¼ tsp. salt
1 C sugar
3 eggs, slightly beaten
3 C heavy cream
2 T vanilla extract

In a saucepan, scald the milk. In the top of a double boiler, over hot water, mix the cornstarch, salt and sugar. Slowly add the scalded milk. Cook and stir for 8 minutes. Cool mixture slightly, add the eggs and cook for 2 more minutes. Chill well in the refrigerator (preferably overnight).

Add the cream and the vanilla and pour the mixture into the freezer can. Pack the freezer with cracked ice and salt and let everyone take a turn at cranking the handle. Remember to crank slowly for the first 5 minutes. Remove the dasher when the freezing is completed and pack the freezer with more ice and salt. Wrap it with blankets or newspaper and set in the shade for several hours until you are ready to serve the ice cream.

Parmesan Cheese

This recipe produces the most incredible Parmesan I have ever tasted! It does require months of aging, but, oh my goodness, it is sooo worth the wait!

4 gallons whole milk
1 tsp. liquid rennet
½ tsp. thermophilic culture
½ C cool water

Warm 4 gallons of whole milk to 86°. Add ½ tsp. Thermophilic DVI Culture to the milk. Stir well. Let set to ripen for 10 minutes. Mix 1 teaspoon liquid rennet into ½ cup of cool water. Stir rennet mixture into the milk. Mix well for about 30 seconds. Let milk set to coagulate for 45 minutes.

The curd is ready when it breaks cleanly over your finger and whey fills the spot where your finger was. Cut the curd into ½ inch cubes and let rest for 10 minutes.

Place the curd pot into a sink of hot water. Keep the curds at 90°. Stir gently for 40 minutes. You can maintain the temperature by adding more hot water to the sink as needed.

Slowly heat the curds to 120° over a 30 minute period, stirring often to keep the curds from matting together. Hold at 120° for 30 more minutes. Stir often.

Drain off the whey and put the curds into a cheese press that has been lined with cheesecloth. Press lightly for 1 hour at about 5 pounds pressure.

If you are unable to gauge the pressure on the cheese, you can turn the press handle down until you feel the cheese firmly in the press. Don't apply too much pressure on the first pressing stages.

Redress the cheese into fresh cheesecloth. Press for another hour at 10 pounds pressure. Remove the cheese from the press and put into another clean cheesecloth. Press for one hour at 15 pounds.

It is important to periodically redress the cheese in clean cloth to keep it from sticking to the damp cloth. This prevents your cheese from tearing when you try to remove it from the cheesecloth.

Finally, remove cheese from the press and redress in another cheesecloth and press at about 20 pounds for about 12 hours.

Tighten the press more firmly during the final stages of pressing. The pressure needs to be built up slowly allowing the cheese to expel as much whey as possible without becoming too dry and crumbly.

Remove the pressed cheese and place it into a brine solution. The cheese will float a little. Salt the top, then cover with a lid and place in the refrigerator. Allow the cheese to soak in the brine solution for 24 hours.

Remove cheese from brine and place on a clean plate. Air dry at room temperature for 1-2 weeks. Turn the cheese daily to allow all the surfaces to dry thoroughly.

The cheese will get very hard on the outside. To speed up the formation of the rind and to prevent the cheese from developing bad mold, rub the cheese with additional salt.

Once the cheese becomes dry and hard on the outside, dip into melted cheese wax to coat the outside. Dip carefully until you have built up several layers of wax.

Set the waxed cheese on butcher paper, shiny side up, to cool. Place the cheese on paper towels in a plastic bag and seal tightly. Use a straw to extract as much air from the bag as possible before sealing.

Age in a cool protected environment at 55° - 60°. You can store the cheese in your basement to maintain the proper temperature. Place the cheese in a freezer that is not running or an ice chest to protect it from unwanted guests such as mice or bugs.

As it ages the cheese will secrete oil. Replace the paper towel and plastic bag as needed. Turn the cheese daily for the first couple of weeks. Then turn weekly for another 4-8 weeks. As the aging progresses, turn it on a monthly basis.

Age for 6 to 8 months. The cheese will become very, very hard. The harder it becomes the better it will grate. It can age for a year or more.

Brine Solution
Mix two pounds of non-iodized kosher or canning salt to one gallon of cool water.

Yogurt

Yogurt was one of the first dairy products I learned to master when we were milking our first cow. I learned to add gelatin (I like really thick yogurt) and rarely make less than 1 gallon at a time (poured into 1 quart jars). A real treat is stirring a bit of homemade granola into a creamy bowl of homemade yogurt. Now that's living!

Milk, sweet
Yogurt starter (either powdered or container of plain yogurt with active cultures)
Honey (optional)
Vanilla (optional)
Gelatin (optional)

1. Scald all of your yogurt making utensils (in boiling water.

2. Prepare your milk. I generally make 1 gallon of yogurt at a time, however, you can begin with as little as 1 quart. You can use raw, pasteurized, powdered or even evaporated milk. If using fresh milk heat it to 180°. Use a candy thermometer and watch it closely so that it doesn't boil over. Cool milk to 110°.

3. Add the starter. Buy one container of plain commercial yogurt. Stir ¼ to 1/3 cup yogurt into 1 cup prepared milk. Add honey (for sweetening), vanilla (for flavor) at this point, along with gelatin that has been dissolved in a little bit of water (if you want thick, Greek-style yogurt). Pour the milk with starter into the warmed milk and stir vigorously. Pour milk into scalded jars and fasten lids loosely.

4. Incubate the mixture at 110° - 120°. There are a lot of different methods for yogurt incubation but I find that the simplest is the best. My preferred method is to heat towels (bath) in the wood cook stove, pack the yogurt in a cooler and pack the heated towels around the yogurt. I heat towels up periodically and pack new, warm towels around the jars until the incubation period is over.

5. Check consistency. Yogurt should not be moved while it is setting. Check it in 2 to 3 hours and every half hour after that. Usually 3 to 6 hours is needed for the yogurt to set. Generally, I incubate my yogurt for 6 hours. After 6 hours it is still a little "loose", however, after I refrigerate it, it becomes quite thick. When using whole milk there is a thick "scum" that forms on top of the yogurt. It is perfectly fine to eat, or if you are a little squeamish, feel free to feed it to the chickens.

Chapter XI

Off-Grid Living

For the past fourteen years, we have lived off the grid. When we began our adventure, we lived with no electricity, no running water and no indoor plumbing. Little by little we added a generator, inverter and batteries. We wired the shouse (shop/house) for electricity and added plumbing. We put up a wind turbine, added a couple of solar panels and invested in a second inverter. We upgraded from an antique propane refrigerator to an off-grid specific electric refrigerator. Then we went for broke and installed a large solar array in the hopes that it would provide us with more electricity than we could possibly need. But, regardless of the upgrades, improvements and advances we have made, we are still, unequivocally off the grid.

Being off-grid requires a complete and total change in lifestyle. Our family made the change cold-turkey. In a matter of days, we went from being a simple, suburban family, living the typical American Dream to modern day pioneers practicing the skills perfected by our great-grandparents. Our home became a living, working museum. Not a day went by when folks didn't drop by, just to see how we were living. Everyone had an opinion. Everyone had a suggestion. Everyone said we were "Living the Dream". But our guests didn't see our reality. They were filled with romantic notions of Little House on the Prairie while ensconced in their comfortable homes with hot running water and flushing toilets. They flipped a switch and the lights came on and they didn't give a thought to how much electricity they had generated that day.

The years have come and gone. We have gotten used to being off-grid. We hardly blink when we have to start the generator to take a bath or do the laundry. We check the Tri-metric as a matter of course, without consciously noticing. Even our youngest children can tell when the pressure tank is full and run out to shut off the gen-set. Living off-grid has become second nature. But, once in a while, we take stock, and then we realize how much work living off the grid truly requires.

Our new off-grid life brought more than a few changes. Back in the day, when I wanted to do laundry, I simply walked into the laundry room, tossed some clothes into the washer, pushed the button and let the washing machine do the rest. After the washing machine was done with it's magic, I would put the clothes into the dryer, let them spin and fold wonderfully soft, warm, clean laundry. Simple, yes? Not so much now that we are living the "simple" life. When I did laundry this morning, I had to go outside to start the generator. When I got to the shed, I realized that the generator was empty and I needed to fill it with fuel. Grabbing the funnel, I filled the generator, pulled the choke, switched the breakers off and pulled the cord. The generator hummed to life. I turned off the choke, flipped on the breakers and headed back into the shouse. Before I started the laundry, I took a few minutes to flush and plunge the toilet. Because we don't flush every time (limited water, you know), I have to flush and plunge every time the generator is on - every time - for fourteen years. The plunger and I are on a first name basis! After flushing, I started the laundry. I do have a washing machine (with hot water!), so washing clothes is really pretty simple. Once the clothes have been washed, I plop them into a laundry basket, cart it out to the kitchen and proceed to shake out each article and hang it on the clothes horse that hangs over the wood cookstove. After the clothes horse is full, I heft it up (on the pulley) to get it out of the way. Once the clothes have been hung, I take the towels and sheets and any other large items to the stairs and hang them to dry.

Continuing on with my day, I check our Tri-metric, which is a meter telling us how much electricity we are using or making. If we get low on power (22.5 volts or lower) I start the generator and charge our batteries. If the batteries are low, I turn off non-essential electronics and make sure the electric kettle and microwave are not used. If the batteries are particularly bad, I start the generator and plug in our industrial battery charger and really put the current to the battery bank.

Cooking and baking used to consist of turning on the electric oven, setting a timer and going about my other business. Now, my culinary skills have been honed by the heat of a wood cook stove. In order to get my oven ready for baking, I split kindling and small wood, open the drafts and put my arm in the oven to determine proper baking temperatures. Once in the oven, I rotate food regularly, put heat shields over the tops and sides of pans to keep things from burning and measure baking times with my nose.

I don't regret moving to a shouse in the middle of a prairie and leaving power lines far behind. I love the way that we live. But our lives are full of hard work and sacrifice. The romantic notions of oil lamps and cozy quilts have been tempered by the realities of noisy generators, heavy clothes horses and fussy wood cook stoves.

Had I known before going off-grid how much work it would be, I think I would have balked. I am so glad I didn't know - I would have missed so much. I would have missed learning what I couldn't live without - and what I could. I would have missed learning how to keep going when things got tough. I would have missed learning how to make do with little. I would have missed living the REAL dream.

Years of experience have taught us so much, here are some things we have learned:

Off-Grid Water

Obviously, water is an essential element for any homestead. In a perfect world, an off-grid homestead would have a water system that relied solely on a gravity-fed spring. When I was growing up, our property had an entire hill-side that bubbled with the sweetest water imaginable. My mom and dad chose what looked like a likely spot and started digging. They dug a hole about 4 feet x 4 feet square and 6 feet deep. They lined the hole with cedar boards (to keep the dirt from sloughing back into the hole) and filled it with drain rock. Then, they dug ditches, laid pipe and put a submersible pump in the spring and called it good. They did have grid power, so electricity was not a problem, but they were incredibly fortunate to have such a wonderful water source. That spring served our family (never running out of water) for over 20 years and required virtually no maintenance. Another benefit of our spring was the fact that because of the size of the hole, the water was easily accessible, even if the power went out, and, had the grid ever gone permanently down, the spring was uphill from our house, making a gravity fed water system highly likely.

Unfortunately, my husband and I don't have the option of a gravity fed spring system. Our well is deep (435 feet) and our pump requires 220 volts to run. We have run on two systems, neither of which is optimal for an extended grid-down situation. For most of the years that we have been off-grid, we have had to run our generator in order to pump water from our well into a pressure tank. The pressure tank holds about enough water to flush the toilet 3 times and fill the sink for dishes once or twice. If we conserve (ie. not flushing the toilet very often) we can make our pressure tank of water last all day. Doing laundry requires the generator to be on so that it can run the well pump. When we run a large generator (10kw) we can easily run the well pump and also charge our batteries (at about 70amps), however, when we are running a smaller generator (5kw) we can only run the well pump or charge batteries - not do both simultaneously. The other method we have used for pumping water (which is much more to my liking, not to mention much more tenable) is wiring both of our large inverters 180° out of phase so that they create 220 volts and run our well pump right off the batteries. I love this option because we are not wasting gas running the generator and we can flush the toilet every time we use it!!! And, of course, it is completely sustainable in a long-term off-grid scenario.

There are currently low voltage pumps that operate in deep wells that were not available when we put our system in. They run on either AC (alternating current) or DC (direct current). They are expensive, but definitely worth investigating Another viable option, if your topography supports it, is a buried cistern, uphill, that you can pump into by either a generator or solar pump, creating your own gravity fed water system. This is the best option for those of us without naturally occurring gravity fed water

Off-Grid Refrigeration

When we first moved into our shouse, we were lucky enough to have found and old Servel propane refrigerator at a yard sale and scooped it up. It was a 1950's model, and really pretty small, but after using a cooler filled with ice, we thought it was enormous. I loved that propane refrigerator. It was silent, used very little propane and kept things *very* cold. We used our Servel long before we had any electricity at all and it proved to be incredibly reliable. The "freezer" was tiny (it held about 6 ice cube trays) and wasn't capable of keeping ice cream frozen, but it did make ice and that was enough for us. Being as old as it was, it did ice up considerably, requiring thawing rather frequently, but, having refrigeration was well worth the effort.

After using our propane refrigerator for about 5 years, the burner began blowing out, forcing us to relight the fridge. Finally, we were no longer able to keep the burner going, so we contacted a propane appliance repair center to replace the burner. Our request was met with panic on the part of the repair man. Apparently, this particular fridge was prone to wearing out after nearly 60 years in service and a few of them had killed some folks with CO_2 poisoning. Servel would not sell the parts required to fix the refrigerator. Our beloved propane refrigerator now found its way into the scrap pile.

After our Servel, we found a used Sunfrost, 19cf refrigerator freezer. It was an older model and looked like it had been built in someones garage. It was, however, built specifically for off-grid use. Our refrigerator is AC rather than DC, which would have been much preferable for our off-grid system. It is the largest user in our entire house, cycling off and on with unending regularity. Because of the design, the refrigerator portion of the fridge was right on the floor and the freezer was at eye level. My husband built a stand for it, so that the refrigerator portion was easier to get to, which made it so much more user friendly. The freezer does not freeze particularly well, but it too makes ice, and does keep food exceptionally cold, so it serves its purpose.

If we had it to do over again, we would build a refrigerator out of a 24 volt DC **Nova Kool** refrigerator kit. We would build it using a highly insulated refrigerator body and even go so far as to cut holes in the back of the refrigerator (facing an outside wall), covering the holes with hardware cloth and make a sliding door that could be opened in the winter when the weather was cold, effectively cooling the refrigerator with outside air, possibly even using muffin fans on a thermostat.

Realizing the amount of power, either battery power or propane, required to keep refrigeration up and running, the most viable grid-down cooling option is an old fashioned root cellar. Properly constructed, a root cellar easily keeps perishable foods at an appropriately cool temperature year round with a minimum of effort or maintenance. Root cellars require no electricity, no battery bank and no propane. They are truly an off-grid marvel.

Off-Grid Power: *Wind Turbines*

Our family is not the definitive authority on wind power, however we do have experience with wind turbines. Our very first source of alternative energy (other than a generator) was a wind turbine. Living in a very windy location, we were positive that wind was the perfect alternative energy source. We bought an Air X wind turbine, built a tower, hoisted it into place and fastened 4 guy wires to secure the tower. We dug a trench, pulled the wires through and hooked them into our charge controller. We were so excited when we flipped the breaker, we ran to the kitchen to watch the Tri-metric (meter), expecting to see massive amounts of power coursing through our controller into our battery bank. Nothing! To be fair, there really wasn't much of a breeze, so our disappointment was tempered by the realization that there wasn't enough wind to make power - Just yet anyway. Later that evening, the wind kicked up and we knew we must be raking in the power, yet the Tri-metric only registered 17 amps. Not bad, we thought - it was better than nothing. Just then, the wind really began beating the shouse. Outside, a noise, something akin to a wounded, screaming animal, began emanating from the wind turbine. It got louder and louder until we thought the turbine might fly off the tower and rip through our house! In reality, the turbine was secure and the noise we were hearing were the wind turbine brakes coming on due to the high wind. What we came to learn was that although we had a lot of wind, it wasn't the right kind of wind. Either we had a gentle breeze, producing no power or we had gail force winds causing the turbine to put on the brakes, also producing no power. At the very most, in exactly the right conditions, we would produce 20 to 25 amps of power, resulting in little more than a trickle charge to our batteries.

After using our wind turbine for about 2 years, we had an electrical storm and the composite blades built up an excess of static electricity and fried our inverter. Literally. I mean we had flames and everything! After spending a whole lot of money to buy a new inverter, we were more than a little leery of connecting the wind turbine back up to our system. That turned out not to be an issue. One day during a particularly breezy spell, I looked out the window just in time to see the tower begin to list to port. Running outside, the kids and I arrived just in time to catch the tower and gently lower it to the ground. The guy wires had broken under the stress of the high winds and the weight of the tower and turbine. We laid the wind turbine to rest, never again to flutter in the breeze.

Our experience with wind power is not unique. Our local power company put up a testing facility near the airport (a very windy area). They installed a 2500 watt wind turbine and also put up a 2500 watt solar array in order to determine what alternative energy source was the most reliable. Completely confident in the fact that the turbine would noticeably outpace the solar array, they were stunned when the numbers were crunched and the results indicated that the solar system made more energy *by far*! They, too, found that although they had a lot of wind, they didn't have the right kind of wind. It was either too windy or not windy enough. And they also noticed that the turbine required regular maintenance and repair (adding to the cost and reducing the efficiency) while the solar array required none.

We can say with certainty, that for us, wind turbines are not an effective alternative energy option.

Off-Grid Power: *Solar*

We love our solar panels. They are the only part of our off-grid system that never require maintenance, other than occasionally wiping snow off of them, and work no matter what (well, as long as it is bright outside, that is). Solar panels require a system, complete with batteries, a charge controller and power inverters to work to their full potential. The solar panels are wired into a charge controller. The charge controller controls the amount of current that goes into the batteries so that the batteries do not overcharge. The inverter changes the power that comes out of the batteries from DC (direct current) to 120 volt AC (alternating current), which is normal household electricity, thus allowing you to use household appliances, computers, televisions and lights. Alternative energy systems utilizing a battery bank have limitations. They are great for using lights, small appliances, computers and televisions, however, they cannot power anything with resistive heating, such as electric stoves, electric hot water tanks or electric furnace systems. Solar systems can be very effective long term for household lighting and other small electrical users. But, as with any mechanic system, things will wear out and things will fail.

Off-Grid Power: *Failures*

In the 14 years that we have been off the grid, we have had two inverters fail. The first inverter we bought used, so we can hardly count that one. The second inverter failed after about 10 years of use, which we have since learned, is about the life expectancy of a power inverter. Batteries are another weak link. They require care and maintenance. They must be watered, kept from freezing and even have their acid adjusted from time to time. You have to run them low and then charge them up or they will develop a "memory" resulting in the loss of a significant amount of storage capacity. Charge controllers and power inverters both have electronic components that can fail.

I believe that solar is the best, long-term grid down option, however, it is not infallible. You have to know how your system works and how to keep it running. You have to maintain it and, realistically, you have to prepare for it to fail.

Although we have a great solar system, we also have back-up plans. We have a number of kerosene lamps and a stock of kerosene. We have wind-up radios and rechargeable batteries (which can be recharged with just the solar panels, bypassing the inverters) and we have books (just in case there are no movies and no computer access).

All in all, there are many ways to plan for survival. Have a back-up plan for your back-up plan. We have tried a number of things and have found what works best for us. You may want to explore what options are available to you and make plans accordingly. There are all kinds of methods of off-grid living, you just need to find the one that is most viable to you.

My Love/Hate Relationship with Generators

I love our generator. I hate our generator. No, I am not bi-polar, I just have a love/hate relationship with these mechanical beasts.

Years ago, when we jumped off the cliff and went off-grid, we had a 5kw generator that we had bought at Costco prior to Y2K. It didn't even live through the construction of our shouse. Luckily, it was still under warranty so we took it back and were refunded our money. We decided to buy what we thought would be a workhorse - literally. It was a Workhorse China Diesel 10kw. Our thoughts were that it was big enough to run our whole house plus charge our forklift batteries. It was an interesting adventure right off the bat. It didn't come with much of a manual and the booklet that did come with it had been translated (poorly) from Chinese - word for word. After my husband and my Dad filled all of the fluids, checked the belts and hoses and fired it up, it ran great - until they decided to shut it down. Nowhere were there directions on shutting it off! Nothing! Both my husband and my father are mechanically inclined and neither one of them could figure it out. Finally, after exhausting all other avenues, they unhooked the fuel lines and let it run out of diesel. That, of course, wasn't the best option, because diesels don't like to be run dry, but, it was the only option at the time.

Eventually, after much fiddling, we had the china diesel up and running. It had a Murphy Switch that was supposed to shut the generator down in case of low oil or high temperature, but it didn't work, so we just kept a close eye on the gages.

The china diesel kept us running for about two years. It ran our well pump, our washing machine, our few lights and charged our batteries. It leaked like a sieve and was fussy, at best, but it kept us chugging along. After two years, it developed an oil leak in the main seal. China diesels are designed to be worked on, but apparently not by Americans. The access points are inaccessible, the components nearly impossible to find and if you do find a part and replace it, it will NEVER work correctly again. The electrical panel shook so hard that it broke all of the soldered wires. My husband removed it, rewired it and mounted it to a wall. He was never able to completely fix the leak in the main seal so for six months we put oil in it every time we started it. Finally, one oil leak too many, and it threw a rod. I think I was actually thankful. No more putting up with that leaky, noisy, fussy contraption!

Our next generator adventure came in the form of a 1969 10kw Hercules Military Diesel. It was military - it should hold up to anything, right? We bought it from a dealer in Montana, and right away, Sir Knight had his suspicions. He changed the oil before we cranked it up and noticed little silver specs. We called the dealer that we had bought it from and he said to run it and see how it did. It lasted about 3 months. The silver specs in oil meant that the engine was shot. It threw a rod. I was doing laundry and heard it go. I thought "no woman should know what an engine sounds like when it throws a rod", but I did. When my husband got home that evening, I delivered the cheery news. We called the dealer and he arranged to send us another one and pick the dead one up.

On a cold, rainy, swampy day in late fall, our second 10kw Hercules generator rolled up our driveway on a delivery truck. I was so excited. We had been without power for almost two months and I had been hauling water and doing laundry by hand. We had reverted back to Coleman lanterns and I was feeling positively pioneerish. As the delivery driver was loading the new generator on his pallet jack we were chatting about how wonderful the new generator was going to be. He slid the pallet with the generator onto the jack, mentioned that he hated that jack because it didn't have any brakes, and proceeded to drop the generator, jack and all, off the back of his truck. I almost cried. My beautiful new generator, was in a million pieces on the cold, wet ground.

Another call to the dealer yielded yet one more machine (he must have bought a lot of them at an auction). This one was delivered with no mishaps and at least didn't have metal in the oil. Sir Knight got it up and running and we were in business. This generator even had a cold weather kit, so it started much easier when it was below zero. The generator ran well, most of the time, but like any mechanical tool, it had its moments. It was with this third military generator that I became a diesel mechanic. Not really, of course, but I learned to trouble shoot a diesel engine or an alternator with the best of them! Finally, this generator too, succumbed to the fate of all generators that call this place home. It died. I was a little gleeful at its funeral. In fact, I even asked my husband if I could put a couple of rounds through it with my shotgun. He wouldn't let me.

We were once again generator-less, which meant power-less. This time, my folks came to our rescue. They loaned us their little Honda 5kw generator. I loved that generator. No, really. It always ran. Always. It wasn't enough to power everything, but it worked it's little heart out. I couldn't do laundry and run the industrial power charger at the same time, but I didn't care. At least it ran.

We ran it to death. Literally. It lost its muffler. We bolted it back on. It fell off again. We propped it up. Finally we used a come-along to hold the muffler onto the engine. Poor thing looked like a redneck generator. Well, I guess it was, but, it was the little generator that could. I think I can, I think I can, I think I can. It always did. And then, it gave up the ghost. It was quiet about dying - no loud moaning or throwing rods through its engine. One day, it just wouldn't start. I know I can't, I know I can't, I know I can't. Mom and Dad didn't want it back. Go figure.

An Onan Emerald caught our eye. By this time, we had 2150 watts of solar, so we weren't quite so dependent on our generator. The little Onan was a 5kw, but it had a huge generator head. We thought we would give it a try. It started right up, after not having been run in over two years, but it had a few pops and hiccups here and there. We ran it for a while, loved the power that it generated and decided this might be the one. Then it died. Not really, it was just old and needed a little TLC. In the meantime, our dear friends let us use their Honda 5kw. I know, probably not a good idea, since they know what happened to the one my folks "loaned" us. But they love us, and let us use it anyway. It has been a good little beast, a little fussy, but dependable.

My husband repaired the Onan. He adjusted the points (they were way out of wack) and cleaned the carburetor until it was purring like a kitten.

We now have two more 5kw generators. They are all in working order and we rotate them frequently. We have learned, once again, that 2 is 1 and 1 in none.

I have a love/hate relationship with generators. I love them when they work. I hate them when it is 10 below zero with a 15 mile an hour wind and I am trying to beat the starter into the right spot so it will start. I love them when the whole area is out of power and we don't even know it. I hate them when they force me to be a diesel mechanic just so I can have a glass of water or flush the toilet. I love them when they purr.

Ah, it's just livin' the dream!

Off-Grid Simplicity

Hind-sight is always 20/20, and knowing what we know now, we would have done things a little differently. We have found truth in the adage "The simpler, the better". For true off-grid sustainability, simple trumps complicated every time. We have spent a lot of time trying to come up with the best off-grid ways to do just about everything. These are a few thoughts we have had on the subject.

Water: Gravity fed is always optimal, of course, but when that is unavailable, low tech options are best. Hand pumps for your well, water filters for ground water and water catchment systems are low tech, practical options. When you rely on two inverters (like we do), if one fails, you are out of luck. If you rely on your generator (like we do), running out of fuel or having your generator break down will really ruin your day.

Food Storage: Root cellars are great! They are practical, time tested, reliable methods of storing food for the long term. Keeping canned goods in a root cellar will increase their shelf life and your root crops will last all winter in their most nutritious state. You can keep many foods fresh longer in a root cellar. They require no power and very little maintenance. Everyone should have one!

Food Storage II: An ice house would be an incredible, wonderful luxury. With a little pre-planning, it is very attainable. Milk, butter and other dairy products will keep well, even in the heat of summer, in a well insulated ice house. Your lemonade and iced tea would actually have ice in it. Ice cream wouldn't be an unheard of treat.

Food Storage III: Creating a "winter refrigerator" is a convenient, do-able idea. We plan on cutting holes in the back

354

of our well insulated refrigerator and plumbing it to the outside, so that, when it is cool in the winter, we have the ability to open the holes in the back of the refrigerator and let the outside air cool our food. Low tech and non-electric, it is a wonderful food storage option for the cooler winter months.

Hot Water: Plumbing a hot water tank into your wood cookstove provides free domestic hot water. It too, is low tech, using only plumbing, not gas or electricity, just natural convection.

Waste Management: Everyone, and I mean everyone, should have an outhouse! Very few folks will be able to keep up with a water supply capable of running a toilet. An outhouse is a very sanitary method for dealing with the call of nature. It would be by far less expense to build the Taj Mahal of outhouses than it would be to have an alternative energy system capable of running basic plumbing.

Lighting: Having a number of high quality kerosene lanterns and a supply of fuel, having candles and knowing how to make them, or utilizing a very simple 12 volt solar system (not requiring inverters) are preferable to a solar system like ours, which requires inverters, huge battery banks and charge controllers.

All said and done, we have learned a huge amount in our off-grid adventure. One of the most valuable lessons has been "the simpler, the better". We will keep our off-grid system, however, we will make a concerted effort to simplify. My husband is collecting all of the cables necessary to rewire our system to bypass the charge controller and inverters, if need be. We are planning our root cellar and ice house. An outhouse is on the books. We have been stocking up on wicking, fuel and spare parts for our kerosene lamps and lanterns. Redundancy is good, but simple is better.

More on Off-Grid Lighting

After living for a year and a half with no electricity we learned a few things about non-electric lighting.

Kerosene lamps. Kerosene lamps work tremendously well, but only for mood lighting (you will hurt your eyes trying to read by these lamps). Real lamp oil is paraffin based and has an excellent shelf life, however, it is expensive. The paraffin can get waxy, so don't store it in your lamps. If you buy crystal clear kerosene, you can use it in your oil lamps. Shelf life is about the same as gasoline. It will discolor over time. It will still work, but will have more of a kerosene smell.

Aladdin lamps. Lehman's sells these, among other folks. They are the prettiest lamps on the market and put off the best reading light, however, if left unattended, for just a few minutes, the mantles will turn black and flames will shoot out of the top of the lamp. Some friends of ours almost burned their house down with an Aladdin lamp. We used to have three. We sold them all. The mantles are very expensive to replace, and quite fragile. They are not conducive to a household full of children.

Coleman lanterns. These aren't recommended for inside use, but if your house isn't airtight or if you crack a window, you shouldn't have a problem. We used these for over a year and found they were the BEST gas powered lamp. They were inexpensive, easy to use, easy to fill and the fuel (white gas) will last until the can rusts out. We put one in our kitchen and one in our living room (hanging - better light and the kids can't knock them over) and were able to read, work and function very well with them. We even liked the humming sound - very comforting.

Petromax (multi-fuel pressurized lantern). Without a doubt the best light was produced by this lamp (200 watts). Without a doubt, it was the fussiest lamp we ever owned. The learning curve on this lamp was steep. After one of the fittings blew off the main pressure tank (it was soldered on) and set our kitchen table on fire (again), I took it outside (on fire - with three foot flames shooting from the top) and swore I would never allow it back into the house. My husband finally fixed it permanently. He rewired it for electricity. It is one of my favorite lamps now - and has given us no problems since!

Candles. I have a thing for candles anyway - so I love them. My theory is "buy them cheap, stack them deep". Of course, with children, you do have to be careful because of the open flame. They are not good to read by and really are strictly mood lighting.

Flashlights. LED are the best. There is no end to flashlights. We try to standardize our battery size. All of our flashlight take AA or D size batteries. They are much less expensive than AAA or C size. One word of caution with LED flashlights - the LED's draw so little current and the batteries last so long that I have had two mini maglites (AA) and one Streamlite (two D batteries) ruined because the batteries lasted long enough that they leaked all over the flashlight and ruined them. You might want to keep the batteries separate for storage. Only buy good batteries (Duracell, Energizer) for your battery supply. They can last up to 10 years in a controlled environment. Store them in plastic bags, 3 to 4 to a bag. That way, if one battery leaks it doesn't destroy the whole pack.

Rechargeable Batteries. There are two basic rechargeable batteries. NiCad and NiMH (nickel metal hydride). The NiCad batteries have memory problems. If you charge them all of the time they will not hold a charge. They need to be discharged fully and then recharged (or they get a short memory). NiMH batteries do not have the same memory problems, however, they discharge themselves in 30-60 days, making them difficult for emergency use. If you can get a solar powered battery charger you could be way ahead of the game (if you have sun).

Off-Grid Things to Think About

The other morning, I awakened to the sound of incessant beeping. Groggy from a good nights sleep, it took me a bit to focus on the sound and determine its origin. Finally, it came to me. The beeping was coming from our bathroom, or more specifically, our inverter mounted on the bathroom wall. It was an alarm warning us our battery voltage was low and complete power shutdown was imminent.

I stumbled into the bathroom in time to shut the inverter down and was immediately plunged into quiet darkness. As I made my way to the kitchen I mentally took note of which oil lamps were full and accessible. I fumbled around in the dark locating my lighter and finally managed to light an oil lamp and place it on the wood cookstove so that I could go about heating water for a pot of tea. While the water was heating, I cozied up in the love seat in the kitchen, grabbed my phone and checked my email.

As I sat in my kitchen, listening to the gentle hiss of a propane flame, illuminated only by a single oil lamp, I marveled at the marriage of modern technology and primitive living. Here I was, in the 21st Century, checking email on my smart phone while bathed in the muted light of a kerosene lamp.

The first two years of off-grid living were primitive to say the least, but the last 12 years have been a hybrid of alternative energy. Having lived with grid power, been completely non-electric and currently in an alternative energy powered home, I have come to a number of conclusions.

1. Grid power is easy. When we lived in a "normal" house, I never thought twice about flushing the toilet, tossing a load of laundry into the washing machine or drawing a bath. I would grumble when the power bill showed up in the mail, mumble something about "someday having the freedom to live off the grid" under my breath and go grab an ice cold drink out of the fridge. On the few occasions the power would go out, I would light an oil lamp, build a fire in the wood stove and wax poetic about how wonderful it would be to live "the simple life" - and then the power would come back on and I would go make sure the electric stock tank heater was plugged in so that I wouldn't have to chop ice for the critters.

2. Being completely non-electric is a lot of work. Hauling water may sound romantic but I gotta tell you - it isn't. The reality of how much water we require for our everyday activities is phenomenal! And oil lamps are romantic, beautiful and provide a warm, soft glow, but did you know they stink? Oil smells less than kerosene, but when you have a house full of lamps just so you can have a modicum of illumination, you will have a definite odor. They require constant filling (which can be a messy job) and the light they give is never as good as a simple 60 watt electric light bulb. Even basic hygiene isn't easy. Because water is carefully guarded, flushing the toilet becomes optional rather than compulsory. When you begin calling your bathroom "the indoor outhouse", you know you are truly non-electric.

3. Hybrids are always high maintenance. If you choose to graduate from "non-electric" to "alternative energy" prepare for a whole new way of life. Now, rather than worrying about filling your oil lamps once a week, you will become obsessed with "ghost loads" and what appliances are actually viable on your system. You will judge the weather not by how nice it is, but whether or not you made any power. The longer you run your system, the more you realize that the price of running a hybrid system is constant maintenance. When we were non-electric, we got by with little. Now that we have alternative energy, we can't seem to settle for less. We must keep it running. And alternative energy is a hard taskmaster. When you make your own power you essentially run your own, miniature power substation. You make the power (generator, solar panels, wind turbine), control where it goes (charge controllers), convert it (inverters) from DC (direct current) to AC (alternating current) making it compatible for standard household use and store it (battery bank). Keep in mind that power companies employ full-time electricians to keep their plants up and running. Although your plant is smaller in scale, it is still a full-fledged power plant. YOU will become the full-time electrician.

So, where does that leave us? If it were up to me, I would choose either grid power (it is easy) or a completely non-electric system (supplemented only by 12 volt DC electric (solar) lights). Here's the deal - an alternative energy system is challenging. It is not a matter of IF something goes wrong, it's a matter of WHEN. If any portion of your system fails (generator, charge controller, inverter, battery) then your whole system fails. Alternative energy systems get old and wear out. The batteries need maintenance and the electronics are fallible. Essentially, I love having an alternative energy system, but only as a non-essential supplement to a completely non-electric system. Only non-electric systems are truly sustainable. An outhouse never fails. It doesn't freeze in the winter, require 5 gallons of water to flush or become a bastion of bacteria when the power goes out. A flushing toilet is nice but an outhouse is practical. I love my refrigerator, but it is a power hog. A root cellar is by far a better option. It is huge, can hold an entire harvest and isn't subject to power outages.

If you are in search of honest-to-goodness, long-term, off-grid sustainability, consider becoming completely non-electric. All it takes is a little pre-planning and a lot of ingenuity, but the benefits will be incalculable.

The Evolution of our Off-Grid Life

We live a pretty posh and comfortable life now (most of the time), but it hasn't always been that way! I thought I would take a minute and tell you how we got from "there" to "here".

When we first moved into our shouse, almost 14 years ago, we had no electricity, no running water, no drains - nothing that would resemble "normal". We had an 11 year old, a 4 year old and a 1 year old. We built our shouse as a shop, and with no foresight at all and neglected to put windows in it - mostly. We did have two windows... one in our "bedroom" and one in the "bathroom". I use the words bedroom and bathroom loosely because we had just one big room, with areas divided by group of furniture. We had no sheet rock on the walls, just insulation. No electrical wiring, no plumbing. It was pretty rustic! We hauled water from the neighbors (even though we had drilled a well - we still had to put in a pump and a pressure tank and get a generator to pump the water). We had a milk cow, so we went through about 35 gallons of water a day just for her! That didn't include drinking water for us or water for laundry, cooking, dishes and cleaning. We used a bucket with bags (located in our shed) for a bathroom. I did laundry on the wood cookstove and hung it in front of the stove to dry. In the beginning, we used Aladin lamps for light, but found they required CONSTANT attention! They provided good light, but I couldn't leave them unattended for a minute, or they would catch fire and a $7.00 mantle would go up in flames! We also had a Petromax multi-fuel lantern that was made in Germany, and was supposed to be the best. It was fussy to say the least. I would light it when I was schooling the children, because it was the only light we could see by and not get headaches. It was complicated and dodgy and it leaked like a sieve. One day it caught my kitchen table on fire and I threatened to take it outside and shoot it with the shotgun! Finally, my folks brought us two Coleman lamps. Joy!!! We could see and didn't have to battle the Aladins or the Petromax.

After hauling water for about 3 months, we put a pump in our well, got a generator, plumbed the house (after a fashion) and had cold running water. I was in heaven! I even got a sink and **drains**!!! I still had to heat water on the stove, but that was nothing! We could take baths in our bathtub, wash dishes in the sink and I didn't have to haul water for laundry or for watering the animals. We did have to start the generator any time the pressure tank was out of water, but that was a pleasure after the months of hauling water.

The first Thanksgiving in our shouse we were thankful indeed! My folks spent they day with us, helping my husband install a window in the living room and another one in the kids' room upstairs. We had a turkey dinner, cooked in our wood cookstove, fellowship by lantern light and hearts overflowing with thankfulness. It was truly a Thanksgiving to remember.

After about a year and a half, my husband wired our house for electricity and we bought a used Trace inverter. My husband arranged for his buddy (with a boom on his truck) to deliver our first battery bank - two HUGE forklift batteries. Our lanterns were on their last legs, it was getting dark, and the guys were in the shed fiddling with the batteries. Confident that we were ready to go, my husband came in, flipped on the inverter and.....nothing. He went to the bathroom, adjusted the inverter and suddenly light, electric light, flooded the room! I looked around in horror - my house was filthy! By the light of the Coleman lanterns it had looked romantically cluttered, but by the light of harsh fluorescent shop lights, it was hideous! I caught myself before I cried "hurry, turn off the lights". Instead I started cleaning and if you were to ask my kids, they would say I haven't stopped!

We have learned a few things about being off the grid and about being prepared in general. Some of the biggest lessons we have learned are:

1. Redundancy. We like to have 3 ways to do everything! Solar panels, wind turbine, generator. When trouble strikes, it is essential to have more than one way to deal with it.

2. Use your back-up plan. A lot of the things we used when we were first off the grid, we bought in anticipation of Y2K. Some worked. Some didn't. The Aladin lamps and the Petromax are a case in point. If we had depended on these, they would have let us down.

3. Change your expectations. I had it in my head that certain things would happen by a certain time. They didn't. My first reaction was to become discontent and mad at my husband. I learned that I just had to change my expectations. I had to live were I was, not were I

362

thought I should be.

4. These are the "Good ol' days". I learned to enjoy our hardship, because that is were memories are made and thankfulness is generated. Our first winter, we read the entire "Little House on the Prairie" series, "Swiss Family Robinson" and "Heidi" together as a family. Every evening we would snuggle under blankets, sip hot cocoa and I would read out loud. Those are the memories of a lifetime. With every improvement in our circumstances we had an opportunity to be truly grateful for things that most people take for granted. A toilet that flushed, a light switch that worked or a hot bath were true causes for celebration.

5. Life isn't supposed to be easy. It isn't in the good times that God molds and shapes us into the likeness of His Son. It is when the generator breaks, again. It is when you are 8 1/2 months pregnant and the water pipes break and your husband is at work and you have to get on your hands and knees and do a temporary repair. It is when you don't think you can take one more crisis, and your milk cow sinks in mud bog when it is 28 degrees and sleeting and you have to lay on your stomach in the mud to get a rope around her belly to haul her out with the tractor. That is when God is doing His work. And that is exactly where I want to be!

Recipe Index

Appetizers, Beverages & Tea Time Indulgences

Quick Breads

Yeast Breads

Breakfast Fare

Soup

Main Dishes

Cookies & Bars

Pies & Cakes

Candy & Confections

Salads, Sides & Sauces

Canning & Food Preservation

Wildcrafting

Miscellaneous Recipes

Homestead Beauty, Hygiene and Cleaning

Homestead Medicine

The Dairy

21963543R00201